MY WAR CRIMINAL

ALSO BY JESSICA STERN

ISIS: The State of Terror, with J. M. Berger (2015)

Denial: A Memoir of Terror (2010)

Terror in the Name of God: Why Religious Militants Kill (2004)

The Ultimate Terrorists (2001)

MY WAR CRIMINAL

Personal Encounters
with an Architect of Genocide

JESSICA STERN

ecco

An Imprint of HarperCollins*Publishers*

MY WAR CRIMINAL. Copyright © 2020 by Jessica Stern. All rights reserved. Printed in the United States of America. No part of this book may be used or reproduced in any manner whatsoever without written permission except in the case of brief quotations embodied in critical articles and reviews. For information, address HarperCollins Publishers, 195 Broadway, New York, NY 10007.

HarperCollins books may be purchased for educational, business, or sales promotional use. For information, please email the Special Markets Department at SPsales@harpercollins.com.

FIRST EDITION

Library of Congress Cataloging-in-Publication Data has been applied for.

ISBN 978-0-06-088955-5

20 21 22 23 24   LSC   10 9 8 7 6 5 4 3 2 1

For Chet and Evan

European nationalisms are yet to flame up. They think that the time for nationalism has passed.

—Radovan Karadžić to Dobrica Ćosić

As a psychiatrist I can tell you that a great part of what goes on in our mind has nothing to do with real events. The whole of psychiatry revolves around irrealities, around illusions and deceit.

—Radovan Karadžić

Contents

Abbreviations

BIA   *Bezbednosno-informativna agencija* (Security Intelligence Agency). Serbia's national intelligence agency. Analogous to the CIA.

BiH   *Bosna i Hercegovina* (Bosnia and Herzegovina).

CIA   Central Intelligence Agency. The United States' civilian foreign intelligence service.

DGSE   *Direction générale de la sécurité extérieure* (Directorate-General for External Security). France's intelligence agency. Analogous to the CIA.

EEC   European Economic Community. A precursor to the EU. Renamed European Community in 1993.

EU   European Union.

FRY   Federal Republic of Yugoslavia, or the State Union of Serbia and Montenegro (1992–2006). Comprised of Serbia and Montenegro, the two remaining federal republics of Yugoslavia after Yugoslavia's breakup in 1992. Claimed to be the sole legal successor to Yugoslavia.

GCHQ   Government Communications Headquarters. The United Kingdom's intelligence and security organization that provides signals intelligence to the government and armed forces of the United Kingdom. British equivalent of the United States' National Security Agency.

ICJ   The International Court of Justice. Based in The Hague. The principal judicial organ of the United Nations. Settles disputes between member states. Not to be confused with the International Criminal Court, which tries individuals for international crimes.

ICTR   International Criminal Tribunal for Rwanda. Based in The Hague. Established in 1994 in order to judge people deemed responsible for the Rwandan genocide and other violations of international law in Rwanda. Dissolved on December 31, 2015, with residual functions under the jurisdiction of the successor body, the International Residual Mechanism for Criminal Tribunals.

ICTY   International Criminal Tribunal for the former Yugoslavia. Based in The Hague. Established in 1993 as an ad hoc court to prosecute serious crimes committed during the Yugoslav Wars. Dissolved on December 31, 2017, with residual functions under the jurisdiction of the successor body, the International Residual Mechanism for Criminal Tribunals.

IFOR   NATO Implementation Force (December 1995–December 1996). Multinational peace effort in Bosnia and Herzegovina under a one-year mandate to enforce the peace under the Dayton Agreement. *See also SFOR.*

IMF   International Monetary Fund. Established in 1945 as an international financial institution. Manages balance of payment difficulties for member states, and manages international financial crises.

IRMCT   The International Residual Mechanism for Criminal Tribunals. Formed by the United Nations Security Council to take over the functions of the ICTY and the ICTR upon the completion of those tribunals' respective mandates.

JNA   *Jugoslovenska narodna armija* (Yugoslav People's Army). Former military of the Socialist Federal Republic of Yugoslavia.

MBO   *Muslimanska bosnjačka organizacija* (Muslim Bosniak Organization). Established by Adil Zulfikarpašić and Muhamed Filipović, who were formerly part of the Party of Democratic Action (SDA). They viewed the SDA as Islamist and wanted to establish a secular Muslim party.

MI6   Secret Intelligence Service (SIS, but more commonly known as MI6). Foreign intelligence service of the United Kingdom.

NATO   North Atlantic Treaty Organization.

NDH   *Nezavisna Država Hrvatska* (Independent State of Croatia). Established in 1941 as a Nazi puppet state on the territory of most of Croatia and Bosnia and some of Serbia and Slovenia. The NDH was governed by the fascist Ustasha organization, led by Ante Pavelić.

NSA   U.S. National Security Agency. Specializes in signals intelligence.

PIFWC   Persons Indicted for War Crimes by the ICTY.

RS   *Republika Srpska* (Serb Republic). One of the two constitutional and legal entities of Bosnia and Herzegovina along with the Federation of Bosnia and Herzegovina. RS was proclaimed on January 9, 1992, as a breakaway Bosnian Serb entity within Bosnia.

RSK   *Republika Srpska Krajina* (1991–1995). Self-proclaimed Serb proto-state within newly independent Croatia until it was overrun by Croatian forces in 1995.

SDA   *Stranka demokratske akcije* (Party of Democratic Action). Conservative Bosniak nationalist political party. Established in 1990 by Alija Izetbegović. The SDA continues to be a major party in Bosnia and Herzegovina today.

SDS   *Srpska demokratska stranka* (Serbian Democratic Party). Serb nationalist political party in Bosnia and Herzegovina. Prior to the Bosnian SDS, an analogous party in Croatia was established by Jovan Rašković (1990–1995/1996). The Bosnian SDS was founded by Radovan Karadžić in July 1990, encouraged by Rašković.

SFOR   NATO Stabilization Force (December 1996–December 2004). Multinational peacekeeping force in Bosnia and Herzegovina. Deployed to deter hostilities under the Dayton Agreement. *See also IFOR.*

SFRY   Socialist Federal Republic of Yugoslavia (or SFR Yugoslavia). Founded in 1942, with six socialist constituent republics: Bosnia and Herzegovina, Croatia, North Macedonia, Montenegro, Serbia, and Slovenia. In 1991, both Croatia and Slovenia declared independence from the SFRY, thus beginning the dissolution of the SFRY.

TWRA   Third World Relief Agency. A charity that was a front for funneling weapons and funds into Bosnia during the Bosnian War.

VOPP   Vance-Owen Peace Plan (1993). Proposed by United Nations special envoy Cyrus Vance and European Community envoy Lord David Owen. Would have divided Bosnia into ten semi-autonomous regions. Rejected by the RS.

VRS   *Vojska Republike Srpske* (the Army of the Republika Srpska, also known as the BSA or Bosnian Serb Army). Military of Republika Srpska. Led by General Ratko Mladić.

Dramatis Personae

Andrić, Ivo (October 10, 1892–March 13, 1975) Yugoslav novelist, poet, and short story writer. Won the Nobel Prize in Literature in 1961.

Angel, Dr. Croatian psychiatrist based in Zagreb. A pseudonym.

Bildt, Carl Former prime minister (1991–1994) and minister for foreign affairs (2006–2014) of Sweden. Bildt was appointed as the European Union's special envoy to the former Yugoslavia in June 1995. Cochaired the Dayton Peace Conference in November 1995. Former high representative for Bosnia and Herzegovina (1995–1997).

Buha, Aleksa Bosnian Serb philosopher and politician. During the war, Buha was the minister of foreign affairs of the Republika Srpska. Former leader of Bosnia's Serb Democratic Party (1996–1998). Presently member of the Senate of Republika Srpska.

Cerić, Dr. Ismet (1935–2017) Psychiatrist at a Sarajevo hospital clinic. Supervised Radovan Karadžić.

Ćosić, Dobrica (December 29, 1921–May 18, 2014) Serbian politician, writer, and political theorist. Former president of the Federal Republic of Yugoslavia (1992–1993). Helped Radovan Karadžić become the leader of Bosnia's Serb Democratic Party.

Dabić, Dragan David Radovan Karadžić's alter ego while he was on the lam as a fugitive from the ICTY. "Dabić" was an energy healer who gave public lectures on spirituality, until he was caught and revealed to be Karadžić on July 21, 2008.

Donia, Robert Professor of history at the University of Michigan. He served as an expert witness for the prosecution at the ICTY, and has testified in several cases, including the cases against Radovan Karadžić and Slobodan Milošević.

Filipović, Muhamed Bosniak politician, writer, and historian. Filipović founded the Muslim Bosniak Organization with Adil Zulfikarpašić. During the war, Filipović was the Bosnian ambassador to the United Kingdom.

Holbrooke, Richard (April 24, 1941–December 13, 2010) American diplomat. Former assistant secretary of state for Asia (1977–1981) and Europe (1994–1996); United States ambassador to the United Nations (1999–2001). Cochairman of the Dayton Peace Conference of November 1995. At the time of his death, Holbrooke was the U.S. special envoy for Afghanistan and Pakistan (2009–2010).

Hrebeljanović, Lazar (1329–1389) Also known as Prince or Tsar Lazar. Medieval Serbian ruler who created Moravian Serbia, hoping to resurrect the Serbian Empire. Killed at the Battle of Kosovo in June 1389, while leading a pan-Christian army against the invading Ottoman forces. Venerated in the Orthodox Church as a martyr and saint, and plays a central role in Serbian epic poetry.

Izetbegović, Alija (August 8, 1925–October 19, 2003) Former and first president of the Republic of Bosnia and Herzegovina (1990–1996); chairman of the Presidency of Bosnia and Herzegovina (1996–1998; 2000); Bosniak member of the Presidency of Bosnia and Herzegovina (1990–2000). Izetbegović established the Bosniak Party of Democratic Action (SDA) in 1990. Izetbegović led the Bosniaks through the Bosnian civil war.

Karadžić, Aleksander (Sasa) Radovan Karadžić's son.

Karadžić, Ljiljana Zelen Radovan Karadžić's wife. Trained psychiatrist and former head of the Red Cross in Republika Srpska (1993–2002).

Karadžić, Luka Radovan Karadžić's younger brother.

Karadžić, Jovanka (1922–2005) Radovan Karadžić's mother.

Karadžić, Radovan Leader of the Bosnian Serbs during the Bosnian civil war. Karadžić was the first president of the Republika Srpska (1992–1996), a role that also gave him command of the Bosnian Serb Army. He was the co-founder and leader of the Serbian Democratic Party (SDS) of Bosnia. Karadžić was indicted for war crimes by the ICTY, and spent 11 years as a fugitive. He spent much of his time as a fugitive disguised as an energy healer in Belgrade. Karadžić was caught in July 2008. On March 24, 2016, he was found guilty of genocide in Srebrenica, war crimes, and crimes against humanity. His appeal was rejected on March 20, 2019. *See also Dabić, Dragan David.*

Karadžić, Simeon Radovan Karadžić's cousin.

Karadžić-Jovičević, Sonja Radovan Karadžić's daughter.

Karadžić, Vuk (November 7, 1787–February 7, 1864) Serb philologist and linguist, considered to be the major reformer of the Serbian language, and the pioneer of the study of Serbian folklore. He was well-known outside Serbia, and was especially influential on Jacob Grimm and Johann Wolfgang von Goethe. Radovan Karadžić's ancestor.

Karadžić, Vuko (1912–1987) Radovan Karadžić's father. "Vuko" is a nickname for "Vuk."

Krajišnik, Momčilo Cofounded the Serb Democratic Party (SDS) with Radovan Karadžić. Speaker of the People's Assembly of Republika Srpska (1990–1992); after the war, he was the Serb member of the Presidency of Bosnia and Herzegovina (1996–1998). In 2006, he was found guilty of committing crimes against humanity during the Bosnian War by the ICTY. He was released in 2013.

Limonov, Eduard Russian writer, poet, and political dissident. He founded the banned National Bolshevik Party in Russia in 1993 and led it until it was banned in 2007.

Mehmedinović, Semezdin A Bosniak writer, poet, filmmaker, and editor. Former friend of Radovan Karadžić. Mehmedinović is one of Bosnia's most prominent poets, whose work *Sarajevo Blues* was translated into multiple languages. Mehmedinović and Radovan Karadžić were in the same literary circle in Sarajevo.

Milošević, Slobodan (August 20, 1941–March 11, 2006) Former president of the Federal Republic of Yugoslavia (1997–2000); first president of the Republic of Serbia (1991–1997); former president of the Presidency of the Socialist Republic of Serbia (1989–1991). Milošević threw his support behind the Bosnian Serbs during the war, and was indicted by the ICTY for war crimes in connection to the wars in Bosnia, Croatia, and Kosovo. He conducted his own defense for five years at the ICTY until his death on March 11, 2006.

Minić, Mina A Russian alternative therapy practitioner who became Dragan Dabić's mentor in 2005.

Mladić, Ratko Former chief of the Bosnian Serb Army's General Staff (1992–1996). Mladić led the Bosnian Serb Army as a general during the Bosnian war. He was found guilty of committing genocide in Srebrenica, war crimes, and crimes against humanity by the ICTY in 2017.

Plavšić, Biljana Former president of Republika Srpska (1996–1998) and first Serb member of the Presidency of Bosnia and Herzegovina (1990–1992). Plavšić was indicted by the ICTY in 2001 for war crimes committed during the Bosnian War. She was sentenced to 11 years in prison, but was released in 2009.

Princip, Gavrilo (July 25, 1894–April 28, 1918) Bosnian Serb member of Young Bosnia, a Yugoslavist organization with the goal of ending Austro-Hungarian rule in Bosnia and Herzegovina. Assassinated Franz Ferdinand and his wife, Sophie, on June 28, 1914. It is widely agreed that this event precipitated the outbreak of World War I.

Rašković, Jovan (July 5, 1929–July 28, 1992) Serb psychiatrist, academic, and politician. Rašković founded the Serbian Democratic Party (SDS) in Croatia, and later encouraged Radovan Karadžić to form an analogous party in Bosnia and Herzegovina.

Robinson, Peter American lawyer whose clients have included Radovan Karadžić and Liberian president Charles Taylor.

Tito, Josip Broz (May 7, 1892–May 4, 1980) Yugoslav communist revolutionary and president of the Socialist Federal Republic of Yugoslavia (1953–1980). Under Tito, Yugoslavia broke with Soviet hegemony and was a key player in the nonaligned movement during the Cold War.

Tudjman, Franjo (May 14, 1922–December 10, 1999) Former president of Croatia (1990–1999); president of the Presidency of the Republic of Croatia (1990). Tudjman founded the Croatian Democratic Union (HDZ) in 1989 and led Croatia through the Yugoslav Wars.

Tudjman, Miroslav Franjo Tudjman's son. Croatian scientist, academic, and politician. Member of the Croatian Parliament (2011–).

Vešović, Marko Writer, poet, and former friend of Radovan Karadžić. Vešović was in the same literary circle as Radovan Karadžić in Sarajevo.

Zelenović, Dragan Bosnian Serb soldier and de facto military policeman in the town of Foča, Bosnia and Herzegovina, in 1992. Zelenović was charged with the rape and torture of 25 Muslim women and girls. He was sentenced to 15 years' imprisonment in 2007.

Zulfikarpašić, Adil (December 23, 1921–July 21, 2008) Bosniak intellectual and politician. Vice president of Bosnia and Herzegovina during the Bosnian War (1990–1996), under Alija Izetbegović. Founded the Muslim Bosniak Organization with Muhamed Filipović.

Timeline

This timeline is based on information provided by Radovan Karadžić and four additional sources: the CIA's chronology of the Balkan Crisis, the International Criminal Tribunal for the former Yugoslavia's timeline for the case against Radovan Karadžić, Ivo Daalder's *Getting to Dayton: The Making of America's Bosnia Policy*, and Robert Donia's *Radovan* Karadžić: *Architect of the Bosnian Genocide.*

1940s

June 19, 1945	Karadžić is born in Petnjica, Montenegro, Yugoslavia. Parents Vuko and Jovanka.
November 29, 1945	Yugoslavia is proclaimed as a Communist federal state.

1950s

September 27, 1950	Vuko Karadžić is released after serving nearly five years in prison.

1960s

1960	Karadžić leaves Montenegro to study medicine at the University of Sarajevo.
1963	The Federal People's Republic of Yugoslavia is renamed the Socialist Federal Republic of Yugoslavia.
1967	Karadžić marries Ljiljana Zelen, a fellow medical student.
June 4, 1968	Karadžić gives a speech at the University of Sarajevo, protesting the Communist regime and the Vietnam War.

1970s

July 19, 1971	Karadžić graduates from the University of Sarajevo Medical School.
February 21, 1974	New constitutions adopted for Federal Yugoslavia and each of its six constituent republics and two autonomous regions. The new constitution empowers the eight constituent units at the expense of the federal government's own powers.
1974–1975	Karadžić studies at Columbia University on a U.S. government-funded grant (IREX scholarship).
1977–1992	Karadžić works as a staff psychiatrist at the Koševo clinic and in private practice.

1980s

Early 1980s	Karadžić takes a part-time position as a team psychologist to the "Sarajevo" soccer team.
1983–1984	Karadžić works as team psychologist to the "Red Star" soccer team.
Nov 1984–Oct 1985	Karadžić is imprisoned for fraud.

1990

February 17	The Serbian Democratic Party (SDS) of Croatia is established by Jovan Rašković.
April	Citizens in Slovenia and Croatia vote in favor of greater autonomy or independence from Yugoslavia.
May 26	The Bosniak Party of Democratic Action (SDA) is established. Alija Izetbegović is the party's first president.
May 30	The SDS in Croatia breaks off all ties with the Croatian Parliament.
July 12	The Serbian Democratic Party (SDS) of Bosnia is established. Karadžić is elected as the party's first president.
August 18	The Croatian Democratic Union of Bosnia and Herzegovina (HDZ) is established.
November 18	Elections in Bosnia produce wins for the SDS, the Bosniak Party of Democratic Action (SDA), and the HDZ, the three main nationalist parties of Bosnia. Social democratic parties are defeated.

1991

March 28	The presidents of Yugoslavia's six republics open talks in Croatia on the country's future.
June 25	Slovenia and Croatia declare independence. Fighting breaks out when the Yugoslav Federal Army attempts to maintain control over Slovene border stations.
July 5	European Community (EC) foreign ministers impose arms embargo on the former Yugoslavia until the situation normalizes.
July 18	The Yugoslav Federal Presidency de facto recognizes Slovenian independence, and orders the Yugoslav Army to withdraw from Slovenia within three months. Conflict in Croatia intensifies.
September 7	EC conference on peace negotiations opens in The Hague under the chairmanship of Lord Carrington.
September 18	North Macedonia declares independence.
September 25	The UN Security Council imposes an arms embargo on the former Yugoslavia (under Resolution 713).
October 3	Serbia and Montenegro seize control of Yugoslavia's Federal Presidency.
October 15	Karadžić gives his infamous "highway to hell" speech to Bosnian multiethnic Assembly.
October 24	Serb nationalists establish a separate Assembly of the Serb People of Bosnia and Herzegovina.
November 9–10	A referendum on independence is held among Bosnian Serbs. The majority vote to remain inside Yugoslavia.
December 19	The Republika Srpska Krajina, a breakaway Serb state in Croatia, is declared.
December 23	Germany recognizes Slovenia and Croatia.
December 24	North Macedonia, Slovenia, Croatia, and Bosnia-Herzegovina apply to the EC for recognition as sovereign states.

1992

January 9	Republika Srpska is established.
January 15	EEC member states and 15 other countries, including the U.S., recognize Croatia and Slovenia as independent states.

February 21	The UN passes Resolution 743 establishing a peace-keeping force in Croatia.
February 27–March 1	Bosnia holds a referendum on independence from Yugoslavia. Most Croats and Bosniaks vote yes, while most Serbs boycott the referendum. Bosnian Serbs react violently to the vote in favor of independence.
March 18	During EEC-sponsored talks in Sarajevo, Croat, Muslim, and Serb leaders agree to the Cutileiro Plan (or Lisbon Agreement), a framework for establishing ethnic cantons.
March 28	After a meeting with U.S. ambassador to Yugoslavia Warren Zimmermann, Alija Izetbegović withdraws his signature from the Cutileiro Plan and declares his opposition to any division of Bosnia.
April 6	The EEC agrees to recognize Bosnia and Herzegovina. The Serbs move almost immediately to partition the republic.
April 27	Serbia and Montenegro proclaim a new Federal Republic of Yugoslavia and declare it the successor state to Yugoslavia.
May 30	The UN Security Council passes Resolution 757, imposing economic sanctions on Serbia and Montenegro.
August 26–27	The International Conference on the Former Yugoslavia is established to lead negotiations to end the Bosnian war.
October 6	The UN Security Council adopts Resolution 780, which establishes a commission of experts to examine evidence of war crimes in former Yugoslavia.
October 9	The UN Security Council adopts Resolution 781, which establishes a no-fly zone over Bosnia.

1993

January 2	The Vance-Owen Peace Plan (VOPP) is presented, which includes a constitution and a military accord, in addition to dividing Bosnia into 10 semi-autonomous regions. Bosnian Croats accept the whole plan, Bosnian Serbs accept the constitutional principles and the military accord, and the Bosnian government accepts only the constitution.

February 22	The UN Security Council adopts Resolution 808 initiating the formation of an international war crimes tribunal.
March 5	The U.S. begins the airdrop of humanitarian aid over eastern Bosnia.
March 25	Bosnian president Alija Izetbegović signs the VOPP, isolating the Bosnian Serbs as the only warring party not to sign it.
May 1–2	In return for concessions, Bosnian Serb leader Karadžić accepts the VOPP, conditional upon ratification by the Bosnian Serb Assembly.
May 6	The Bosnian Serb Assembly overwhelmingly rejects the Vance-Owen Peace Plan. UNSC Resolution 824 declares Sarajevo and five other Muslim enclaves in Bosnia (Tuzla, Žepa, Goražde, Bihać, and Srebrenica) "safe areas" under UN protection.
May 15–16	A Bosnian Serb referendum confirms the Bosnian Serb Assembly rejection of the VOPP, despite support for it from Serbian president Slobodan Milošević.
May 25	UNSC Resolution 827 establishes an international tribunal to prosecute those responsible for war crimes in the former Yugoslavia.
June 16–17	Croatian president Franjo Tudjman, Milošević, and Izetbegović meet in Geneva with UN and EC envoys Thorvald Stoltenberg and Lord David Owen to discuss reworking the VOPP into an ethnic partition of Bosnia-Herzegovina.
June 18	Izetbegović walks out of the Geneva talks after objecting to proposals to partition Bosnia-Herzegovina.
June 19	Milošević presents his plan to partition Bosnia into three ethnic republics at negotiations in Geneva.
August 18	UN officials announce that NATO is ready to carry out air strikes to support UNPROFOR in Bosnia if the secretary-general asks for them.
August 20	Owen and Stoltenberg adjourn the Geneva talks for ten days after presenting a draft settlement package, including a proposed map for a confederal partition of Bosnia-Herzegovina.

August 28	The Bosnian Serb Assembly unconditionally accepts the proposed peace accord. The Bosnian Croat Assembly endorses the plan but stipulates that the Croats will have to be given more territory. The Bosnian Croat Assembly declares a Bosnian Croat republic.
August 29	The Bosnian government rejects the Owen-Stoltenberg Peace Plan, which was a combination of the Vance-Owen Peace Plan and Serbian plans for a tripartite ethnic confederation.
November 30	The UN war crimes tribunal—the International Criminal Tribunal for the former Yugoslavia—announces it will begin trials in April 1994.

1994

February 5	First Markale massacre. The VRS carries out a mortar attack on the Markale marketplace in Sarajevo. 68 people die and 144 are wounded.
February 23	The Bosnian government and Bosnian Croat forces sign a cease-fire agreement to be implemented on February 25.
February 28	In NATO's first-ever combat mission, U.S. planes shoot down four Bosnian Serb aircraft violating the no-fly zone.
March 18	Izetbegović, Tudjman, and Bosnian Croat leader Krešimir Zubak sign the Croat-Muslim Federation accord in Washington.
April 10	In NATO's first-ever air strike against a ground target, U.S. planes bomb Serb positions attacking Goražde. NATO conducts a second air strike on April 11 in light of continued Serb attacks against the town.
April 26	The Contact Group—comprised of representatives of Russia, the European Union, the UN, and the U.S.—meets for the first time in Sarajevo in an effort to bring the warring parties back to negotiations and work toward a cease-fire in Bosnia. The Contact Group supersedes the International Conference on the Former Yugoslavia as the principal convener of peace talks.

July 6	The Contact Group presents its peace plan to the warring parties in Geneva and gives them two weeks to respond to the proposal. The Contact Group plan would give 49 percent of Bosnia to the Serbs and 51 percent to the Bosnian-Croat Federation.
July 18	The Bosnian Assembly approves the Contact Group peace plan.
July 20	The Bosnian Serbs conditionally accept the Contact Group peace plan, which the Contact Group interprets as a rejection.
August 4	Milošević announces an immediate political and economic blockade against the Bosnian Serbs.

1995

March 8	Karadžić signes Directive 7, which instructs the VRS to "create an unbearable situation with no hope of further survival or life for the inhabitants of Srebrenica and Žepa."
May 10	UN commander general Rupert Smith requests air strikes on Bosnian Serb gunners in retaliation for the May 7 shelling of Sarajevo. He is overruled by UN special envoy Yasushi Akashi, who fears air strikes will upset the recently brokered cease-fire in Croatia. This frustrates UN officials in Sarajevo.
June 24	The U.S. National Security Council meets to develop an endgame strategy for the Balkan crisis.
July 9	Bosnian Serb tanks push very close to the town limits of Srebrenica. Bosnian Serbs detain seven Dutch UN peacekeepers during the incursion and take them to the town of Bratunac in Serb-held territory.
July 11–22	NATO jets bomb Bosnian Serb tanks attacking Srebrenica after UN troops come under Serb fire.
	Bosnian Serb troops break through Dutch defenses and overrun Srebrenica, forcing thousands of Muslims to flee north to a UN base at Potočari.
	The Bosnian Serb assault on Srebrenica kills 8,000 men and boys.
July 12	The UN Security Council demands Bosnian Serb forces withdraw from Srebrenica. The EU and

	NATO issue similar statements and NATO demands the immediate and unconditional release of Dutch peacekeepers held by Bosnian Serbs.
July 14	The Bosnian government refuses to cooperate with either Akashi or special UN envoy to Bosnia Thorvald Stoltenberg, blaming the fall of Srebrenica on UN inaction.
	Bosnian Serb forces launch a major attack on the UN-declared safe area of Žepa.
July 24	The ICTY issues an initial indictment against Radovan Karadžić and Ratko Mladić, with charges of genocide, war crimes, and crimes against humanity.
August 4–7	Operation Storm, the last major battle of the Croatian War of Independence, takes place, marking a decisive victory for the Croatian Army against the breakaway republic of Serbian Krajina.
August 4	Bosnian Serb president Radovan Karadžić replaces General Ratko Mladić as commander of the Bosnian Serb Army.
August 11	Karadžić reinstates General Mladić as top military leader.
August 14	The U.S. steps up diplomatic efforts by sending a delegation headed by U.S. assistant secretary of state Richard Holbrooke on a tour of Balkan capitals.
August 17	U.S. envoy Holbrooke meets with Serbian president Milošević to present the U.S. peace initiative. Milošević supports the plan.
August 19	U.S. special envoy Ambassador Bob Frasure, Deputy Assistant Defense Secretary Joseph Kruzel, and Air Force Colonel Samuel Drew are killed when their armored personnel carrier vehicle slides off the Mount Igman road outside Sarajevo and crashes into a ravine.
August 28	A Bosnian Serb artillery round impacts near the Markale market in Sarajevo and kills 37 civilians and wounds 85 others. This later becomes known as the second Markale massacre.
August 29	The Bosnian Serb Assembly welcome the U.S. initiative for the political resolution of the Balkan conflict. Radovan Karadžić agrees to subordinating nego-

tiations on behalf of the Bosnian Serbs to Slobodan Milošević.

NATO forces begin massive air strikes against Bosnian Serb targets near Sarajevo, Mostar, Tuzla, Pale, and Goražde.

August 30	NATO begins Operation Deliberate Force.
October 10	Cease-fire goes into effect.
October 11	NATO approves Implementation Force (IFOR) operation plan.
November 1	Dayton proximity talks begin.
November 15	Further initial indictment issued by the ICTY against Karadžić and Mladić, including charges of genocide and other crimes perpetrated in Srebrenica.
November 21	Dayton Accords initialed.
December 14	Dayton Accords signed.
December 29–30	IFOR enters Bosnia.

1996

July 11	The ICTY issues international arrest warrants against Radovan Karadžić and Ratko Mladić.
July 18	Radovan Karadžić resigns as president of both the SDS and the Republika Srpska. He additionally pledges to step back from public life. He is succeeded as RS president by Biljana Plavšić, and as SDS leader by Aleksa Buha.
December 29–30	IFOR is succeeded by the Stabilization Force in Bosnia and Herzegovina (SFOR).

2000s

July 21, 2008	Karadžić is arrested in Belgrade, Serbia, after evading arrest for 13 years.
July 30, 2008	Karadžić is transferred to ICTY custody.
July 31, 2008	Karadžić's first initial appearance before the ICTY.
Oct 27–Nov 2, 2009	Prosecution opening statement in the trial of Karadžić.

2010s

March 1–2, 2010	Defense opening statement in the trial of Karadžić.
July 22, 2011	Anders Breivik, a Norwegian white supremacist, carries out two terrorist attacks in Norway—killing

	eight people by detonating a car bomb in Oslo, then shooting sixty-nine people at a summer camp on the island of Utoya.
Sept 29–Oct 7, 2013	Closing arguments in the trial of Karadžić.
March 24, 2016	Trial judgment of Karadžić. He is found guilty of the majority of counts in the indictment. Karadžić is convicted of genocide in the area of Srebrenica in 1995, as well as persecution, extermination, murder, deportation, and inhumane acts, among other counts. He is acquitted of the charge of genocide in the other municipalities in his indictment. Karadžić is sentenced to 40 years in prison.
June 23, 2016	The United Kingdom holds a referendum on whether or not the United Kingdom should remain part of the European Union—also known as Brexit. 51.9 percent of those voting vote in favor of Brexit.
November 8, 2016	Donald Trump is elected president of the United States
December 5, 2016	Karadžić files his appeal brief with the International Residual Mechanism for Criminal Tribunals.
April 23–24, 2018	Appeal hearing for Radovan Karadžić's case takes place.
March 15, 2019	Brenton Tarrant, a white supremacist terrorist, kills fifty-one Muslim worshippers during Friday prayers at two mosques in Christchurch, New Zealand.
March 20, 2019	Karadžić's appeal is dismissed. Karadžić's sentence of forty years in jail is set aside in favor of life imprisonment, in a major victory for the relatives of the victims of Srebrenica.

Maps

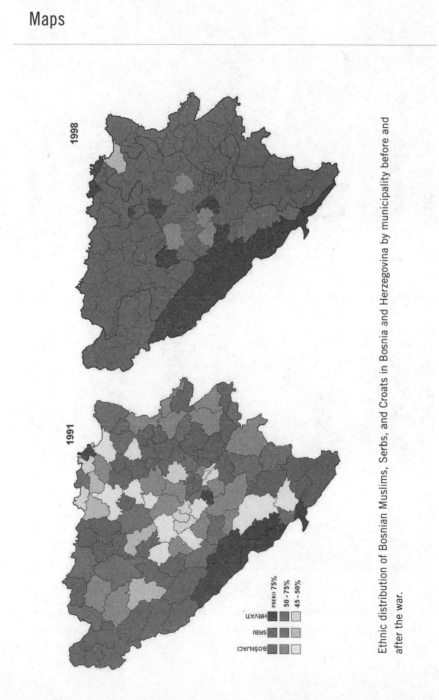

Ethnic distribution of Bosnian Muslims, Serbs, and Croats in Bosnia and Herzegovina by municipality before and after the war.

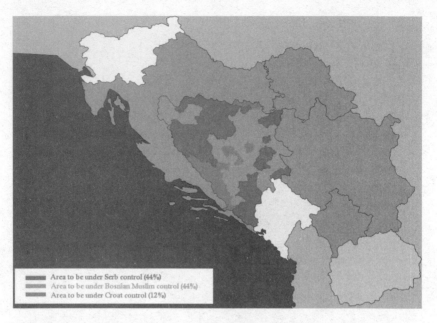

Cutileiro Peace Plan, also known as the Lisbon Agreement (Source: Data from the ICTY Geographic Information Systems Unit).

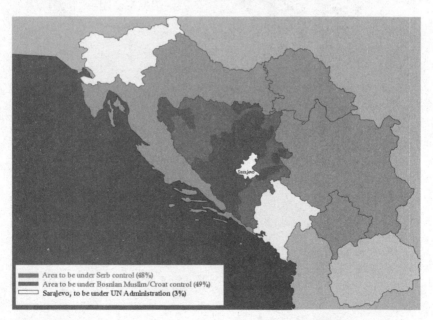

Contact Group Peace Plan (Source: Data from the ICTY Geographic Information Systems Unit).

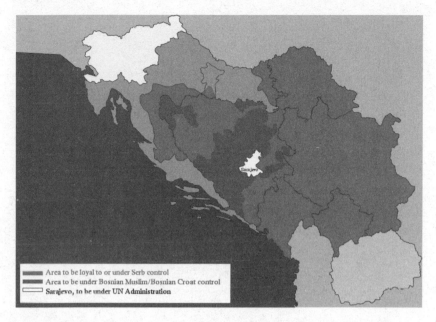

De facto Serb control under the Contact Group Peace Plan, and location of the eastern enclaves (Source: Data from the ICTY Geographic Information Systems Unit).

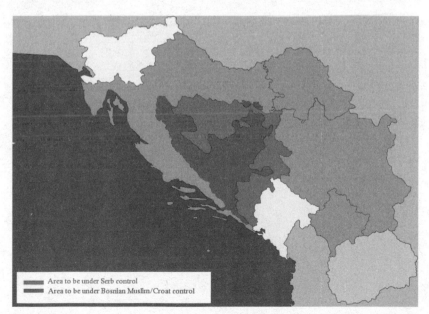

Dayton Agreement plan (Source: Data from the ICTY Geographic Information Systems Unit).

Preface

Fear lies at the center of my story.

I used to interview terrorists in the field. And there were times, for the sake of deepening my understanding of their hidden motivations, that I'd let them take me into their homes or camps. For me, in retrospect, the really strange thing was that whenever I happened to see a group of men with Kalashnikovs slung over their shoulders, I was unaware of the sensation of fear. Nothing seemed out of the ordinary. That's just the way things are when men are at war. During my interviews, it was almost as if I were one of them. An odd phenomenon. Absolutely true in the moment of experiencing, while in hindsight utterly incomprehensible.

It's not that I didn't feel fear; I just felt it, as a child might, in reaction to certain relatively harmless things that I did my best to avoid: boisterous crowds, leaving the house at night, swimming, certain smells, certain kinds of light. Meanwhile, and perhaps ironically, terror became a central preoccupation, the primary concern of my professional life. Eventually I learned that I was making creative use of the sequelae of childhood trauma.

It was only after my son was born that it came to me how dangerous my work had actually been. I vowed to never again take those kinds of risks—for his sake first, but also for my own. I am no longer burdened by the need, or the foolishness, or the recklessness that led me to expose myself to danger. But I have been left with a deep curiosity about the causes of evil. And I seem to have an aptitude, cultivated over many years, for uncovering people's underlying motivations for violence.

Some years ago, I decided that the best way to deploy this skill was to focus on imprisoned perpetrators—both terrorists and war criminals. It would be safer than interviewing terrorists in the field. There was continuity with my lifelong work: what terrorists and war criminals have in common is that both deliberately target noncombatants, in violation of ethical norms as well as international law. When nonstate actors target civilians, we call their actions terrorism. When state actors target civilians, we call their actions war crimes. Thus, the only difference between the two—war crimes and terrorism—is the identity of the perpetrator. In some cases, even this distinction isn't clear, such as when new states are forming; when warlords assume political office; or when the purpose of war crimes is not primarily to harm victims, but to terrify or influence those who observe.[1]

There is a large literature that proposes to explain the utility of mass atrocities in wartime, as well as the economic and political determinants of genocidal wars.[2] But I was curious about the individuals involved. How do leaders persuade ordinary people to kill their neighbors? What is the "ecosystem" that creates and nurtures such genocidal leaders? Could anything about their personal histories, personalities, or exposure to historical trauma shed light on the formation of their identities in opposition to a targeted Other?

Just before the Nuremberg trials, a diverse group of psychiatrists, professional societies, professors, and intelligence officers lobbied to have the Nazi leaders held in the Nuremberg jail examined.[3] Several psychiatrists and psychologists spent time with the Nazi leaders, ostensibly ensuring they were psychologically fit for trial, but also with the aim of trying to understand the nature of their evil. Their work resulted in a number of books, which sparked a long-running debate about whether these leaders were "demonic psychopaths" or "morally flawed individuals influenced by the society they lived in."[4] Since Nuremberg, there have been a number of international war crimes trials, but no researchers have been allowed into the detention units controlled by the international tribunals to write about the leaders tried for serious war crimes.[5] In the words of a psychiatrist who studied the evaluation of the Nazi leaders held at Nuremberg before their trials, "It is regrettable that in contemporary War Crimes trials we see no continuation of the efforts at scientifically studying the perpetrators."[6] Political scientist Janine Natalya Clark proposes that the reasons for scholars' "neglect of perpetrators" are both moral and practical. The moral reason, which she sees as misplaced, is that scholars imagine that understanding might lead to forgiveness, in essence conflating empathy and sympathy. The practical reason is that the tribunals have resisted allowing such studies.[7]

When I first approached the International Criminal Tribunal for the former Yugoslavia (ICTY) in 2011, hoping to interview the Bosnian leaders indicted for war crimes held in the UN prison at The Hague, I did not realize what I was up against, or that no such studies had been done since Nuremberg. Not surprisingly, I was repeatedly rebuffed. To begin with, the rules of detention state that the registrar, who is in charge of all court procedures at both the ICTY and the United Nations Detention Unit, where indictees are held, "may refuse to allow a person to visit a detainee if he has reason to believe that the purpose of the visit is to obtain information which may be subsequently reported in the media."[8] I'm a professor, not exactly a member of the media, but this stricture would seem to apply equally to me, as my sole purpose was to obtain information that would subsequently appear in a book.

Many times, I considered giving up on this project. But something would push me on—an image in a dream, a colleague's enthusiasm, a surprisingly friendly, if noncommittal, response from the prison authorities. I reapplied, asking to meet only one indictee, a more manageable request for the ICTY bureaucracy. I chose Radovan Karadžić, the former president of Republika Srpska (the Serb entity inside Bosnia), indicted for genocide and other war crimes. (Conforming with common practice, throughout this book, I use the term "Bosnia" to refer to Bosnia-Herzegovina.) Karadžić was a psychiatrist and a poet who had spent twelve years on the lam, disguising himself as an energy healer. He was known by the monikers the "Bin Laden of Bosnia," the "Butcher of Bosnia," and the "Heinrich Himmler of the Balkans."[9] He was reputed to be smart. Maybe even brilliant.

Finally, I received permission to interview Karadžić. Nearly four years into the project, I met Radovan Karadžić for the first time.

This book is based on my conversations with Karadžić, which took place in Scheveningen Prison between October 8, 2014, and November 11, 2016.

NOTES

1. See John A. Lynn, *Another Kind of War: The Nature and History of Terrorism* (New Haven: Yale Universtiy Press, 2019).
2. Political scientists have found that genocide is a rational strategy, used by leaders whose aim is to win a civil war.

    Ben Valentino argues that mass killing is a brutal, instrumental strategy "designed to accomplish leaders' most important ideological or political objectives and counter what they see as their most dangerous threats." Benjamin A. Valentino, *Final Solutions: Mass Killing and Genocide in the Twentieth Century* (Ithaca, NY: Cornell University Press, 2004), p. 3. Similarly, in a study of the mass killing in the Balkans, V. P. Gagnon found that ethnic hatred was deliberately provoked by politically conservative elites determined to defend their position in society as well as the status quo. V. P. Gagnon Jr., "Ethnic Nationalism and

International Conflict: The Case of Serbia," *International Security*, Vol. 19, No. 3 (1994–1995), p. 132. John Mueller highlights the role of thugs and gangs in the former Yugoslavia. The mass killings were carried out, he says, not by a disciplined army, but by small bands of "opportunistic marauders" whose actual goals were thievery and, in some cases, satisfying sadistic urges. John Mueller, "The Banality of 'Ethnic War,'" *International Security*, Vol. 25, No. 1 (2000), p. 43. There are several studies of lower-level war criminals, convicted of war crimes by Rwandan courts for their involvement in the genocide there. Lee Ann Fujii, *Killing Neighbors: Webs of Violence in Rwanda* (Ithaca, NY: Cornell University Press, 2009); Jean Hatzfeld, *Machete Season: The Killers in Rwanda Speak* (New York: Farrar, Straus & Giroux, 2005); Scott Straus, *The Order of Genocide: Race, Power, and War in Rwanda* (Ithaca, NY: Cornell University Press, 2006). There are also a few excellent studies of the perpetrators in the Balkans, but thus far they are not based on in-person interviews while the perpetrator was held by an international tribunal. See, e.g., Slavenka Drakulić, *They Would Never Hurt a Fly: War Criminals on Trial in The Hague* (London: Penguin, 2004). Janine Natalya Clark interviewed "a very small number of perpetrators," as she put it to me by email, convicted by lower-level courts in Bosnia, but gave up on the ICTY because of the practical difficulties. Janine Natalya Clark, "Genocide, War Crimes and the Conflict in Bosnia: Understanding the Perpetrators," *Journal of Genocide Research*, Vol. 11, No. 4 (2009), pp. 421–445. Olivera Simić conducted several phone and face-to-face interviews of Biljana Plavšić, a Bosnian Serb convicted of crimes against humanity by the Yugoslav Tribunal, in 2017, after she was released from prison. Olivera Simić, "'I Would Do the Same Again': In Conversation With Biljana Plavšić," *International Criminal Justice Review*, Vol. 28, No. 4 (2018). Plavšić was the only woman and one of the highest-ranking politicians—alongside Radovan Karadžić and Momčilo Krajišnik—indicted by the ICTY. Mina Rauschenbach and Damien Scalia conducted interviews of eighteen individuals convicted by the Yugoslav Tribunal. These interviews were conducted after their trials were complete, once the interviewees had been transferred to prisons across Europe, or had been released. Mina Rauschenbach, "Individuals Accused of International Crimes as Delegitimized Agents of Truth," *International Criminal Justice Review*, Vol. 28, No. 4 (2018).

There is a vast literature that assesses the causes of Yugoslavia's

breakup and the wars that accompanied it. Some attribute the dissolution to internal centripetal factors, some to forces external to Yu-
goslavia. For an excellent overview of the literature on the breakup
of Yugoslavia, see Jasna Dragović-Soso, "Why Did Yugoslavia Disintegrate? An Overview of Contending Explanations," in Lenard J.
Cohen and Jasna Dragović-Soso, eds., *State Collapse in South-Eastern
Europe* (West Lafayette, IN: Purdue University Press, 2008). See also:
Dejan Jovic, "The Disintegration of Yugoslavia: A Critical Review of
Explanatory Approaches," *European Journal of Social Theory*, Vol. 4,
No. 1 (2001), pp. 101–120. In the West, the dominant views changed
over time, affected by, and affecting, the policy debate, in a simultaneous relationship. When policy makers wanted to avoid intervening in
the increasingly obvious humanitarian crisis, they attributed the wars
to "ancient hatreds" that could not be influenced by outside intervention. Later, when there was greater support for intervention, the
West identified villains who had to be stopped. Jon Western, "Sources
of Humanitarian Intervention: Beliefs, Information, and Advocacy
in the U.S. Decisions on Somalia and Bosnia," *International Security*,
Vol. 26, No. 4 (Spring 2002), pp. 112–142.

3. They proposed even to have the Nazi leaders' brains studied postmor-
    tem. Joel E. Dimsdale, *Anatomy of Malice: The Enigma of the Nazi War
    Criminals* (New Haven: Yale University Press, 2016).

4. Douglas Kelley, *22 Cells in Nuremberg: A Psychiatrist Examines the Nazi
    Criminals* (London: W. H. Allen, 1947). American psychiatrist Doug
    Kelley concluded that the Nazi leaders were morally flawed individu-
    als who were not mentally ill. American psychologist Gustave Gilbert
    viewed the Nazi leaders as "demonic psychopaths." Gustave Gilbert
    as quoted in Florence R. Miale and Michael Selzer, *The Nuremberg
    Mind: The Psychology of the Nazi Leaders* (New York: Quadrangle/New
    York Times Book, 1975). Cited in Joel E. Dimsdale, "Use of Rorschach
    Tests at the Nuremberg War Crimes Trial: A Forgotten Chapter in
    History of Medicine," *Journal of Psychosomatic Research*, Vol. 78, No. 6
    (2015). Dimsdale provides an overview of the conflict between these
    two clinicians, and others who got involved in their debate. He also
    summarizes the many experiments that followed, including Stanley
    Milgram's 1963 experiment, which showed that most subjects were
    willing to follow orders, even if it meant "harming" others; and Philip
    Zimbardo's 1971 prison experiment, which showed that subjects play-
    ing the role of prison guards were willing to hurt those playing the

role of prisoners. Joel E. Dimsdale, *Anatomy of Malice: The Enigma of the Nazi War Criminals* (New Haven: Yale University Press, 2016). There are of course thousands of studies of the Nazi leaders, not based on prison-based interviews. See, for example, Hannah Arendt, *Eichmann in Jerusalem: A Report on the Banality of Evil* (New York: Penguin Books, 2006); Christopher Browning, *Ordinary Men: Reserve Police Battalion 101 and the Final Solution in Poland* (London: Penguin, 2001); Dan Bar-On, "The Use of a Limited Personal Morality to Rationalize Horrendous Evil: Interviews with an Auschwitz Doctor and His Son," *Journal of Traumatic Stress*, Vol. 3, No. 3 (1990), pp. 415–427; H. V. Dicks, *Licensed Mass Murder: A Socio-Psychological Study of Some SS Killers* (New York: Basic Books, 1972); D. J. Goldhagen, *Hitler's Willing Executioners: Ordinary Germans and the Holocaust* (New York: Vintage, 1997); Raul Hilberg, *Perpetrators, Victims, Bystanders: The Jewish Catastrophe 1933–1945* (New York: HarperPerennial, 1992); Ervin Staub, *The Roots of Evil: The Origins of Genocide and Other Group Violence* (New York: Cambridge University Press, 2007). For an excellent review of the literature on perpetrators, see J. Waller, *Becoming Evil: How Ordinary People Commit Genocide and Mass Killing* (New York: Oxford University Press. 2002).

5. Helinä Häkkänen Nyholm and Jan-Olof Nyholm, "Psychopathy in Economical Crime, Organized Crime, and War Crimes," in Helinä Häkkänen-Nyholm and Jan-Olof Nyholm, eds., *Psychopathy and Law* (Chichester, UK: John Wiley & Sons, 2012), pp. 177–200, cited in Joel E. Dimsdale, *Anatomy of Malice: The Enigma of the Nazi War Criminals* (New Haven: Yale University Press, 2016), p. 201.

6. Joel E. Dimsdale, "Use of Rorschach Tests at the Nuremberg War Crimes Trial: A Forgotten Chapter in History of Medicine," *Journal of Psychosomatic Research*, Vol. 78, No. 6 (2015), p. 518.

7. Janine Natalya Clark, "Genocide, War Crimes and the Conflict in Bosnia: Understanding the Perpetrators," *Journal of Genocide Research*, Vol. 11, No. 4 (2009), pp. 421–445.

8. "Detention—FAQs," International Criminal Tribunal for the former Yugoslavia, http://www.icty.org/en/about/detention/faq#4.

9. This is how the last U.S. ambassador to Yugoslavia, Warren Zimmerman, referred to Karadžić. Warren Zimmerman, "Impressions of Karadzic," The World's Most Wanted Man, *Frontline*, PBS, http://www.pbs.org/wgbh/pages/frontline/shows/karadzic/radovan/impressions.html.

Author's Note

One of my research assistants was born in Bosnia. She was annoyed every time she saw the words, "my war criminal" in the text. "Why do you, an American, have the right to call him yours?" she asked. "Why on earth would you want to claim him?"

Here is how I would answer her, and other readers confused or annoyed by those words. Most of the time, when I interview a perpetrator, when the interview is going well, I enter an altered state in which my subject's feelings become more central to my experience than my own. I try to sense his every move, his every expression.

I follow his moral logic so closely that it becomes my own, at least when I'm with him. This process—of embracing the perpetrator's subjectivity—feels necessary to me, in order to come fully to know how he thinks, but it's exhausting. It's exhausting to alter my wavelength to match his, even though, in the moment that I join him, I'm not aware of the effort. Afterward, I'm disgusted. I dread returning to my notes, to the person I was when I embraced his subjectivity, when I became a fellow perpetrator.

It doesn't always work this way, but it did with Karadžić.

Later, I return to my notes, and the person I became when I was with him. A fellow war criminal. This is a painful process. I have to beat back the urge to leave my notes in their hastily written, handwritten form, locked up in a drawer forever. While I was writing up our conversations, and trying, for the first time, to feel my own reactions to the material that Karadžić and I discussed, the words "my war criminal" kept coming to my mind, and I dutifully wrote them down, even though they might seem odd. Even though they might seem to say something surprising or unflattering about me.

This didn't really happen the first time I met with a perpetrator. When I first started doing this work some thirty years ago, a psychologist named Steve Kull gave me some advice. I was interviewing a white supremacist at the time, trying to understand the convoluted logic that led this man to believe that killing blacks and Jews was a way to worship God. In order to explain terrorism to others, the psychologist told me, you need to picture yourself joining the group. You need to sustain that feeling, go into it completely, but at the same time trust that you will recover yourself at the end of the conversation. It can't be a superficial feeling, he said. You need to become the terrorist.

When I first heard this advice, it sounded patently absurd. How could I, the daughter of a Holocaust survivor, empathize with a white supremacist? But after a few interviews, I came to understand what he meant on a visceral level. This "becoming the terrorist" was, and remains, something that I am able to do. Not every time, and not every perpetrator.

It worked with Karadžić. The conversations I had with Karadžić were unusually intense and unusually prolonged. He took up residence in my mind. I became a fellow prisoner, and he became "my war criminal."

MY WAR CRIMINAL

Chapter One

THE MESMERIST

There were several times, during our discussions, that Radovan Karadžić wanted to demonstrate his skill at bioenergetic healing. The first time was January 23, 2015, the third of twelve four-hour conversations we had between October 2014 and November 2016. We were sitting in our little chairs at our little wooden table in the small room allocated to us by the prison. Karadžić had gone into hiding following his indictment for genocide and crimes against humanity, including for his role in the murder of some eight thousand men and boys in Srebrenica during the Bosnian War. I wanted to understand why he had disguised himself as an energy healer when he was on the lam, a fugitive from international justice.

During the twelve-year period he was a fugitive, Karadžić took on a new identity. He lost thirty-two kilograms (around seventy pounds), and grew out his famously styled hair, wearing it in a hippie-style topknot tied with a black ribbon. In lieu of tailored suits, he took to wearing ratty, unwashed clothes. He grew a very long beard, the beard of a mystic, and took on a new name and a new profession. He became Dragan David Dabić, an energy healer offering spiritual cures for infertility and disease. Karadžić was the subject of the largest manhunt in modern history, prior to the hunt for Osama bin Laden. NATO forces had tried to capture him, more or less energetically, for twelve years, reportedly spending billions of dollars.[1] He was finally apprehended by Serbian intelligence operatives in Belgrade in 2008. On March 24, 2016, the Tribunal found him guilty of genocide and crimes against humanity and sentenced him to forty years' imprisonment. On March 20, 2019, the Appeals Chamber increased Karadžić's sentence to life in prison.

Source: https://www.kurir.rs/vesti/politika/2812717/karadzic-otkrio-tajnu-dugu-20-godina-ovako-sam-ziveo-kao-david-dabic-detalji-prvi-put-u-javnosti.

"Why did you decide to become a naturopath when you were in hiding?" I asked him. "Is it really true that no one recognized you when you were in disguise?"

He laughed. Big grin. "I always say that those who knew me had no idea where I was, and those who knew where I was had no idea *who* I was." He smiled, like a prideful, naughty child.

So he thinks he was Houdini, able to disappear.

For a moment I could see what he must have looked like as a boy.

It wasn't really a disguise, he said. He was truly interested in bioenergetic healing. He had experienced folk medicine as a child and had experimented with it as an adult. It wasn't something he had to make up.

"When I was a small child I fell ill," he told me. "I cried a lot. I wasn't eating. I couldn't stand. My mother took me to see an old lady. The old lady measured me from my right shoulder to my left knee, again and again; touching me on my shoulder and knee each time. I stopped crying. I stood up. I started eating again."

I noticed his features relaxing. He was more himself. Up until this point, in the ten hours we had already spent together, we had stuck mostly to "safe" issues—history and literature. But this subject—the period he'd spent as a doctor of alternative medicine—seemed to revitalize him.

"When I was very, very young and not wise, and I heard this story from my mother, and other stories like it, I laughed, knowing it couldn't possibly be true. But later I understood that there are things we don't understand that are still true."

He explained that chiropractors sometimes heal children by lifting up the soft palate. "Sometimes one of the cervical bones is a very tiny amount shorter, it's not straight, and even the slightest movement can correct the problem. Maybe that is what the old lady was doing," he mused. "Maybe just by measuring me, she was adjusting the vertebrac." I wondered if he was trying to come up with a rational explanation in order to persuade me of the truth of the story.

"I've seen some very strange things," he said. "A relative of my mother used to whisper to animals to heal them. I saw her do it. One of our sheep got bitten by a snake. The sheep was dying. She grabbed the sheep's ear and whispered something into it. Then the sheep stood up, shook itself off, and walked away." The memory of this marvel gave him obvious pleasure. I noticed that his prison-pale face had grown flushed, that he looked younger than his seventy years.

Imagining this scene, I relaxed my guard somewhat. In my mind's eye, I saw the sheep stand up, shake itself, and walk free.

"We had a lot of land, some cultivated, some quite wild," he continued. "We children were very curious about the wild land, but also scared. There were many snakes. We had a cat. The cat liked to run out in the uncultivated part of our property, just as we did. One day I saw the cat staring at a snake. The two of them just staring at each other." He paused. I tried to imagine the scene. I don't like snakes.

"Finally the snake bit the cat," he said. "Then I saw the cat start to eat some leaves. Many leaves. Who ever heard of a cat eating leaves? After two hours she threw up. Then she was fine."

Was he talking about the two of us? Did I need to learn which leaves would heal me from this encounter?

"When we were young psychiatrists, my wife and I became interested in bioenergy," he said. "I saw it myself, on my own. I put my hands together, I felt something like magnets." He put one palm above the other to show me what he meant. "I tried it on my wife. I put my hand above her arm, and I realized I could actually move her arm! Then I noticed I could cure people's headaches." He was getting more excited now, speaking faster, with better English diction. "We did this research but we kept it secret. I put my hand in ice water. Very, very cold. My wife could feel that my hand was freezing. But if I put my hand near her, she would feel intense heat. That is when I realized the heat wasn't coming from me. It was the Holy Spirit."

Now I go back to my professional self. "Why would you keep this research secret?" I asked. "I thought this kind of folk healing was very common in Eastern Europe."

"Yes, but not for medical doctors or scientists. Now there is a lot of interest in complementary medicine. But I'm talking about forty years ago."

Karadžić looked straight at me. "Would you like me to show you how it works?"

I was startled. Unsure how to respond. I thought: If I say no, he will have won. He would see that I was afraid of him and of his claim to mystical power. But saying yes meant exposing myself to his touch. Not just his touch, but his "healing" energy. He was still looking at me, indicting me with his gaze. It came to me that he wanted me to sense his power, maybe to frighten me.

I reminded myself that Karadžić, although convicted of genocide, has never been suspected of committing violent acts himself. I did not think he would strangle me. No, he would not strangle me. But I knew that the guard on duty, who was supposed to be monitoring us and keeping me safe, was sitting at a desk, idly flipping through the pages of a magazine—not watching us through the window in the door, as he normally did. I had seen him when Karadžić went to fetch the teakettle, as he always did when I first arrived.

By then I already knew, having spent many days watching him in court and some ten hours speaking with him one-on-one, that whatever this man was, whatever evil he might have committed or supervised, he was also a believer in the divine. I told myself that I would be more or less safe with him, even if he came physically closer to me. And yet . . .

"Yes," I said.

He stands up in a courtly manner, all six feet of him. A gentleman at all times, at least with me. He has a slight stoop now and an old man's paunch, but he can still exude power.

He walks around the table and stands directly behind me. I am sitting in the prison chair, low to the ground. I can sense him behind me. I hoped he couldn't feel the tension in my back.

He directs me to put my hands out flat, palms up, parallel to the table.

Now he walks around to the side of me and actually touches

the center of my palms. He'd been born into a family of peasants, though he'd trained as a psychiatrist and never worked the
fields. He has the soft, clean hands of a doctor or a gentleman,
with scrubbed, unevenly clipped, too-long nails, the kind of nails
that nauseate me. He directs me to think of God, or of someone
I really love.

"Say a prayer again and again without stopping," he com-
mands me.

He stands behind me again and puts his clean hands above
my head.

I could sense him moving his hands back and forth, but I
wasn't sure exactly where his hands were. I felt a kind of electricity heating up my head, making me slightly dizzy. But soon I began to calm down, at least a little.

"What do you feel in your palms?" he asked.

"Nothing," I said.

He didn't respond right away.

I turned to look at him. I saw that "nothing" was the wrong
answer. I had failed the test.

"You have to concentrate," he said, admonishing me, but gen-
tly, very much in control of himself. "Concentrate harder."

A shame-inducing thought floated into my mind: I wanted an
A from this man. I had just received the first F of my life, and it
stung. It's been many years since I've been graded; usually I'm the
teacher, not the student. Under his gaze, I regressed.

I did as I was told. Like an obedient child, or a star student, I focused my thoughts on the center of my palms as hard as I was able.

Once again he asked me, "Did you feel anything at all?" His
tone was a little supercilious now, but still polite.

This time, I told him I'd had the sensation of cypress trees
growing out of the center of my palms. Why and how this image
came to me, I do not know. The trees were tall, growing higher
than my own head. Then I told him about the heat in my head.

"Interesting," he said.

He walked back around to his side of the little table and sat down. A bemused smile was visible in his eyes. Even if I wasn't sensitive enough to perceive all his powers, at least I could sense the energy he was calling down into my head.

He had wanted me to see him as a person with a special kind of power. But the truth is, I understood what he was doing. I, too, have studied Reiki. I don't know how this energy works; all I know is that it does. It came to me that if I didn't tell him that, he might sense I was trying to manipulate him by allowing him to think I was in awe of him.

As I write this, I realize that I had a childish hope that if I came clean with him, he would be honest with me. I told him about my having studied Reiki.

"Then you understand," he said, all smiles. "Reiki is the Holy Spirit! It's the same with prana, the Sanskrit word for the same thing."

"Yes, I understand," I said, though I didn't. Not really. I was embarrassed by what had transpired. Maybe even shamed. In spite of my initial sense of discomfort, the energy in the room was now much lighter. His face was brighter, and I, too, felt more relaxed.

———

I had known, when I'd persuaded the Court to let me interview Karadžić, that I would have to surrender to his idea of himself—as a powerful mystic, a great poet, and a respected psychiatrist. Even so, I was shocked to find myself, in that moment, wanting an A from a war criminal. I wondered if he could detect the longing in me.

This is dangerous work, the work I do, studying violent men or men who incite violence. I have to listen without judgment. I have to yield, if only temporarily, to their image of themselves. I can often hover above myself in my imagination, monitoring my reactions. But that doesn't mean I'm never afraid of falling in or losing myself.

I indulged in some anxious worry. What had he done to me? Perhaps I was worrying as a way to titrate the atmosphere in the room. There was, for me, a disconcertingly lovely feeling, as if we'd been praying together. This was not what I wanted.

That's enough, I thought to myself. No more energy work from an indicted war criminal, even if he could present himself as charming and genteel. I felt deeply embarrassed. Still, I could see that something about making myself vulnerable to him had worked to establish rapport between us, even if it was a wary rapport.

In that moment, and in the days afterward, I vowed never to tell anyone about this incident. But later, it seemed to me that so much of our relationship is captured in this story. Cat and mouse. Or maybe cat and snake.

—

Already, by this time, I had come to think of Radovan Karadžić, psychiatrist, poet, and former leader of the Bosnian Serbs, as "my war criminal." I had interviewed many others, but I had chosen to focus on him. Something about the challenge, something about him, compelled me. Not a strangler. Not a professional military man. Not a soldier who shot people, but both a killer and a healer. After so many years of studying violent men, it felt that I had met my match.

When you see Karadžić in the Court, he is always impeccably dressed in a suit and tie, his famous hair perfectly in place. But during our interviews, he tended to look rumpled. On the day he demonstrated his bioenergetic healing, he was wearing a wrinkled lavender shirt and a faded gray cardigan that made him look very much like the old man he now is.

I have a snapshot taken of him in his late twenties. He doesn't know that I have it. During our second meeting, he'd given me the name of a psychiatrist he'd met during his psychoanalytic training in Croatia. I will call her Dr. Angel.[2] He was certain she was dead, as she was significantly older than he. I searched for her and found her in Zagreb, still practicing psychiatry. I have visited her several times, and it was she who gave me the picture of Karadžić. In the photo, Karadžić is wearing hip-huggers and a slightly open shirt, his impatient doctor's fingers pulled into loose fists. It is 1974. He stares haughtily at the viewer: tall and handsome, with flowing brown hair. A Byronic figure.[3]

—

During our second conversation, he told me, "I can control a mob with my eyes." Over the next couple of years, I would ask him many times to explain what he'd meant by that statement. I had assumed he would be careful with his every word, and that the image he would want to project would not be that of charismatic crowd manipulator. But I discovered that he was eager to talk about his skill as a public speaker.

He told me that he never wrote his speeches beforehand. "I would come into the hall, sense the atmosphere. I would try to achieve rapport with the crowd. I used metacommunication." I dutifully wrote down that word: "metacommunication," though

I had no idea what it meant. I learned later that the term had become fashionable in the 1970s and meant forms of nonverbal communication that can either amplify the meaning of what we say or be at odds with it. When words and meaning don't match, listeners can become confused.

Another time, he said, "I tried to make my speeches interactive. I would wait to see who was in the room. I would try to please them, to meet their expectations and desires. Many mobs have been transformed before my eyes." Then he added, "It's not controlling people with the eyes—it's an interactive form of address. You have to continually monitor their reactions and adjust your approach accordingly."

Was this what he was trying to do with me?

What he sensed in the crowds he spoke with before and during the Bosnian War, he said, was fear. "Serbs were frightened. The Muslims wanted to control Bosnia." This was a theme in our discussions, his insistence that the Bosnian Muslims—now known as Bosniaks—wanted not only to control all of Bosnia, but wanted to turn it into a state run according to sharia law.[4] "With the vote for Bosnia's independence, things were changing rapidly, in a chaotic and cruel way," he said. He felt it was his sacred duty to defend his people from harm. He referred to this sacred duty again and again. But he also said, many times over the two years we spoke, in what I came to see as a kind of leitmotif for him, that we always have to figure out whether the snake we believe we see is real or imaginary. "If it's not real, you're neurotic. If it's real, you have to do something about it."

Having met with him repeatedly, I now believe that part of what he did with his "metacommunication" was conjure a cobra out of a Balkan whip snake.[5]

I'm not going to pretend that the Serbs didn't perceive a real threat. Indeed, although I started this project subscribing to the common narrative—that the Serbs were evil perpetrators and the

Bosniaks guileless victims—I have come to see that the situation was somewhat more complicated. From the Serbs' perspective, Bosnia's secession from Yugoslavia was not only a provocation, but also illegal. There is no question that Serbs were responsible for the vast majority of atrocities, but Bosnia's wartime president, Alija Izetbegović, was also being investigated for war crimes at the time that he died. It is now clear, based on declassified documents and the work of terrorism researchers, that the "jihad" in Bosnia was a very important chapter in the development of the al Qaeda movement.[6] But it still was not a cobra. Contrary to Karadžić's claims, the Bosniaks were never going to create a sharia-based state in the middle of Europe.

When I asked him how it had happened that neighbors killed neighbors, people who had lived together in peace for many years, he said it was easy to explain, and again he spoke of fear.[7] "Even inside families, people will turn against each other when they fear being overpowered or overshadowed. But it is much easier for this to happen when people are of different nationalities. Different cultures. There were economic resentments, too. But fear was the main ingredient."[8]

—

After spending so much time with Karadžić in our little room, with the little desk and little chairs and the fluorescent lights flickering overhead, I feel I've learned how an ethnic war can start, maybe even a genocide. First, there is the fear of an Other, a fear of being eclipsed, based on a kernel of truth. Someone's social status is improving at someone else's expense; someone's demographic advantage may be at risk. A particular kind of leader may arise at such moments: a populist who understands the pain of those whose luck is running out, who claims to know how to protect those who are feeling victimized. He will profess to have no desire for political power. He may be a poet or an artist or a billionaire "drafted" into the position by the will of the people. He will simultaneously stir up people's fear—of globalization, or demographic shifts, or multiculturalism—and claim to be the only one able to redress it. The binding ingredient is fear. Fear knits the leader to his followers. Fear becomes a rallying cry and a weapon. Over time, the victims, in thrall to their savior, become perpetrators.[9]

NOTES

1. Julian Borger, *The Butcher's Trail: How the Search for Balkan War Criminals Became the World's Most Successful Manhunt* (New York: Other Press, 2016), p. 145.
2. Karadžić mentioned Dr. Angel on January 22, 2015. My first meeting with her was March 6, 2015. At her request, I have disguised her identity, due to her fear that she could be targeted by Serb nationalists.
3. My research assistant thought he looked a lot like Pierce Brosnan at that age.
4. At the time Karadžić said this to me, I assumed it was a wild exaggeration. Later, I would learn that Izetbegović was, in fact, a self-avowed Islamist. However, I found no evidence that he intended to turn Bosnia into a state run by sharia law. Adil Zulfikarpašić, who cofounded the Party of Democratic Action (SDA), the Muslim party in Bosnia, with Izetbegović, explains that it would not be possible to impose sharia law in Bosnia. "The situation in an Islamic country is quite different from that in Bosnia. From its very beginning Bosnia has lived as a multinational and multi-faith environment, in which tolerance was always the foundation of a harmonious society." Adil Zulfikarpašić, Milovan Djilas, and Nadežda Gaće, *The Bosniak* (London: Hurst, 1998), p. 163.
5. A whip snake will bite mammals if threatened, but it's not venomous.
6. A great deal of information about Saudi funding of al Qaeda was collected by attorneys for family members of the 9/11 victims, in preparation for court cases against the Saudi government. The attorneys for

the families and their insurance companies have collected hundreds of thousands of pages of financial records, declassified Treasury Department reports, court testimony, and other documents. The Saudi government denies that it financed al Qaeda, although it has admitted that it supported charities that we now know were supporting al Qaeda members in Bosnia. Many of the documents collected by the attorneys, a large cache of which were shared with me, reference Bosnia. When I asked an attorney involved in one of the cases why so many of the documents reference Bosnia, he said that in the early 1990s, communications were rarely (or imperfectly) encrypted, and since al Qaeda happened to have been involved in Bosnia at that time, those documents show up.

Some of the documents were published in the *New York Times*. For example, lawyers in one of the cases against Saudi Arabia interviewed a Bahraini national named Ali Ahmad Ali Hamad, who was a member of al Qaeda. He said that he fought in both Afghanistan and Bosnia, and renounced his membership in al Qaeda after the 9/11 attacks. In the interview, he said that foreign fighters traveled to Bosnia shortly after the outbreak of the war, under the command of the al Qaeda leadership together with a Bosnian military unit. The ostensible goal was to help the Bosnian Muslims, but the more important aim was to "establish a base of operations in Bosnia to support al Qaeda's future operations in Europe and the West." When he arrived in the Balkans, he was met by the leader of a charity called the Third World Relief Agency (TWRA). His commander in Bosnia was someone he knew from Afghanistan as a senior leader of al Qaeda. He said that the TWRA and the Saudi High Commission for Aid to Bosnia delivered food to his unit, as well as money, shelter, and Toyota Land Cruisers with Office of the UN High Commissioner for Refugees license plates or Saudi diplomatic insignia. "I realized," he said, "that Bosnia-Herzegovina was very, very important for al Qaeda because Bosnia-Herzegovina would enable al Qaeda to spread its soldiers and its strikes to all the countries of Europe in the future," especially Italy and Spain. Eric Lichtblau, "Documents Back Saudi Link to Extremists," *New York Times*, June 23, 2009, https://www.nytimes.com/2009/06/24/world/middleeast/24saudi.html; Exhibit 224, "Evidence of Financial Links Between Saudi Royal Family and Al Qaeda," *New York Times*, https://www.nytimes.com/interactive/projects/documents/evidence-of-financial-links-between-saudi-royal-family-and-al-qaeda.

For more on the role of international jihadis in Bosnia, see John R. Schindler, *Unholy Terror: Bosnia, Al-Qa'ida, and the Rise of Global Jihad* (St. Paul, MN: Zenith Press, 2007); J. M. Berger, *Jihad Joe: Americans Who Go to War in the Name of Islam* (Washington, DC: Potomac Books, 2011); Lorenzo Vidino, "Islamism and the West: Europe as a Battle-field," *Totalitarian Movements and Political Religions*, Vol. 10, No. 2 (2009), pp. 165–176.

7. As discussed in subsequent chapters, Bosnia's secession from Yugoslavia was much more fraught (and violent) than Slovenia's or even Croatia's due to the fact that it was a multiethnic republic.

8. Ottoman-style feudalism in Bosnia, which economically favored Muslims, ended in 1911. In 1910, Bosnian Muslims comprised 91.15 percent of landowners with tenants, 70.62 percent of landowners without tenants, and 56.65 percent of free peasants in Bosnia. The majority of tenants, at 73.92 percent, were Orthodox; 21.49 percent were Catholic. Aydın Babuna, "The Bosnian Muslims and Albanians: Islam and Nationalism," *Nationalities Papers*, Vol. 32, No. 2 (June 2004), p. 292.

9. As discussed in subsequent chapters, both sides—Bosnian Muslims and Bosnian Serbs—wanted to use their status as victims as a weapon of war. In the 1990s war, the Serbs had significantly more weaponry and personnel at the start of the war, but the Muslims used their status as victims to manipulate international attention.

   In an award-winning book, historian Max Bergholz explains how fear and mutual distrust in a small Bosnian town led not only to ethnic violence during World War II, but that the violence itself hardened ethnic group boundaries, triggering "a rapid categorization of the 'ethnic other' as the enemy." Intercommunal violence, he argues, "fuels simultaneous processes of ethnicization." Max Bergholz, *Violence as a Generative Force: Identity, Nationalism, and Memory in a Balkan Community* (Ithaca: Cornell University Press, 2016), p. 15.

Chapter Two

VISITING THE POET IN PRISON

The International Criminal Tribunal for the former Yugoslavia (ICTY) was created by the United Nations in 1993. Located in The Hague, it was the first international war crimes court established since the Nuremberg and Tokyo tribunals were set up by the Allies at the end of World War II.[1] The ICTY generally did not permit researchers and journalists to interview detainees in person.

There were several reasons that the Registrar, John Hocking, eventually decided to support my proposal to interview Karadžić, as long as Karadžić agreed to be interviewed.[2] Hocking recognized the importance of Hannah Arendt's study of the Nazi war criminal Adolf Eichmann.[3] The psychologists' interviews of the Nazi detainees at Nuremberg had revealed some useful information, and Hocking hoped that my research might also prove valuable. I had no vested interest in affecting the outcome of the trial. And he knew that I specialized in this kind of work—talking to alleged perpetrators, trying to understand their motives, and writing books about them.[4]

While their cases are under way, ICTY indictees are held in the UN Detention Unit, which is located within a high-security Dutch prison complex. If they are convicted, they will complete their sentences in UN-approved prisons in other European countries.[5]

Early on in this project, before the ICTY bureaucracy had given me permission to speak with Karadžić (or anyone else held in the UN Detention Unit), my research assistants and I wrote to more than fifty ICTY-convicted prisoners and their attorneys. Both the prisoner and the prison had to agree to allow me to visit. Often, permission from the state's Ministry of Justice or Prison Authority was also required. Fewer than ten of the convicted prisoners consented to be interviewed: I went to see five of them in Austria, Belgium, Germany, and Denmark. I learned quite a bit from interviewing these subjects, as background for my study of Karadžić. I also thought of these conversations as practice for interviewing him.

Two of the prisoners I interviewed had been convicted of crimes against humanity in the form of systematic rape or sexual enslavement. Rape is a common practice in war. But the Yugoslav and Rwanda Tribunals were the first courts to have convicted persons of using rape as a weapon of war.[6] Although all sides in the Bosnian War—Croats, Muslims, and Serbs—used rape as a weapon, the vast majority of reported rapes were perpetrated by Bosnian Serb military or paramilitary personnel as part of their ethnic-cleansing campaign.[7] The number of victims is contested, ranging from 12,000 to 50,000.[8]

One of the rapists I interviewed was Dragan Zelenović. He was convicted of torture, rape, aiding and abetting rape by others, and of participating in gang rape. In one case the rapes were so violent that the victim lost consciousness. In another, Zelenović held a gun to the victim's head while she was being raped. One of his victims was fifteen years old. At the time I spoke with him, in September 2013, he was serving the remainder of his fifteen-year sentence in the Prison de Lantin in Liege, Belgium.[9]

Because Zelenović's rapes took place in a "special sociopolitical context" and within a "specific framework of various military and paramilitary functions," the Belgian Ministry of Justice did not consider him to be of particular risk to society outside the context of the Bosnian War.[10] He was a certain kind of perpetrator: a man who raped vulnerable young women but only during wartime.

I did not carry out this interview alone, but with a translator who accompanied me to several European prisons. When we arrived, there was a general sense of chaos, very different from prisons I'd visited in other Western countries. Although we had a specified appointment time, it was in the middle of visiting hours, and a long line was waiting to get in: mostly young, harried-looking women in hijabs. There was an uncomfortable commotion, and a loud din echoing in the hallway. After my translator and I showed our passports to a guard, we were taken directly inside and immediately led to an administrative area, where it was quieter.

Zelenović was brought in to meet us. My first observation: coarse looking. Burly. But maybe my perceptions were influenced by what I knew he'd been convicted of.

The guard unlocked a door and ushered the three of us into a room. To my surprise, we were informed that the room would be locked from the outside. The room was usually used for prisoners meeting with their attorneys. The door was locked to prevent prisoners from escaping, but this security measure placed the same constraint on my translator and me: we could not escape either.

I started the interview in a state of annoyance. I suppose fear was in the room, too, but it wasn't a fear I felt.

Let me try again: I know that I was afraid, but at the time I didn't feel the fear. And there were protections in place. There was a button to push in case we needed a guard to let us out for any reason. And my translator was a solidly built young man, with recent military training. He towered over Zelenović. He could have—and I believe would have—knocked Zelenović down if Zelenović had made a move to attack me. However, for reasons I don't fully understand, I remember being locked in that room *alone* with the rapist. It was only when I checked my notes that

I realized that my translator had been with me. I must have felt more vulnerable than I acknowledged to myself at the time. (I see in my notes that at one point the translator left to go to the bathroom, leaving me truly alone with Zelenović. I don't want to think about that.)

We sat at a kind of desk—Zelenović and I across from each other, and my translator next to him. Zelenović told us that he had been severely wounded in the war. "I was wounded twice," he said. "I don't want to show you," he said, though I had not asked, and had no desire to see his wounds.

He grabbed his shirt abruptly and lifted it up to display the ropy scars that disfigured his stomach.[11] What was this? Was I supposed to feel sorry for him? He explained that he'd been judged to be 80 percent invalid, though he didn't explain by whom or why that was important. He also had high blood pressure and told me he'd gotten tuberculosis in the Russian prison system when he was incarcerated there. (After the war, he had gone into hiding in western Siberia.) "I was very ill," he said. "Sick and wounded."

I *did* feel sorry for him after seeing what was left of his stomach. But only a little. It's not so easy for me to regard rapists as human.

I turn away, suddenly fascinated by the quality of light coming in the windows. Part of me was talking to Zelenović, and part of me was floating to the windows. Maybe I was afraid to look at him. I must have been. A loud racket was coming in from the courtyard. The prisoners in the next building—a cement structure with a corrugated metal roof—were shouting at each other through the windows. It was a Stalinist-looking building. The courtyard below us was overflowing with garbage that the prisoners had tossed out through the windows. It looked as though the garbage had been accumulating for months, maybe years. I wondered if the prison was understaffed. The building, the Stalinist building, was surrounded by barbed wire. But the windows looking out over the garbage sea did not appear to be barred. The prisoners shouted at each other incessantly. I noticed a system of strings and pulleys running between the windows of the prisoners' cells, with mysterious plastic bags attached to the strings.

"They are trading drugs," Zelenović explained, adding that it was the guards who brought the drugs into the prison. Marijuana, I asked? "Heroin, cocaine," he said. He told me that the guards were happy with the prisoners on drugs, as they were calmer. They didn't seem calm to me, and I wondered whether or not to believe him.

"Ninety percent of the prisoners are Arab," Zelenović told us. "Moroccan or Algerian or Tunisian." He was afraid of them, he said. Because he was a Serb known to have been convicted of raping Muslim girls, Muslim prisoners had beaten him up in the last prison he was housed in, and he had only recently been moved to Liege. It wasn't clear how long he'd be able to remain. A guard had told Zelenović he'd heard the prisoners talking about him.

The memory of this ill-managed prison would come back to me when the stories of jihadi recruitment in Belgian prisons first came to light.

—

Zelenović had received a reduced sentence, due to his professed remorse.[12] I have watched a film of his confession, and I saw the way he lowered his eyes, in what seemed to me a pantomime of shame. Maybe he really was ashamed. But not in our conversation. He told me that he had had sex with twenty-five Muslim girls during the war, and of these he'd been accused of raping only five. Furthermore, if he had really raped any of them, he said, he would have killed them afterward to prevent them from testifying against him. He insisted that it was physically impossible for a man to rape a woman because she could always force her legs closed. While he was speaking, he held his right hand above the table, palm up, thick fingers jammed tightly together. In a sudden unexpected movement, he seized an empty Coke bottle and began smashing it repeatedly into his tightly closed fingers. "A woman can force her legs closed just as tightly as I can keep my fingers closed," he argued.

This was his proof that a woman can stop a rapist. I wanted to slap him across the face but I refrained. He apparently felt that I had passed a test.

At the end of our conversation, he astonished me with a parting gift, a novel by Frederick Forsyth that Slobodan Milošević, the wartime president of Serbia, had given him while they were both imprisoned at the UN Detention Unit. I wished I had worn gloves. A crazy thought came into my mind. Was there some invisible toxic substance hidden inside the book? Was he trying to poison me? I took the book. I hoped he couldn't sense or smell my fear. I brought the book back with me from the Belgian prison to Cambridge, where I live. I kept it on a shelf in the basement for a while. But I couldn't force myself to look at it, to try to figure out if it contained some kind of message. Eventually, I threw the noxious thing out.

That book by Frederick Forsyth had been carried to Belgium by the rapist from the UN Detention Unit in The Hague: it was my first exposure to the UN prison, where a few years later I would finally meet with Karadžić.

—

The UN Detention Unit is located in a residential part of The Hague called Scheveningen, very close to the beach and the North Sea. To get there, you drive along leafy boulevards, passing by some of The Hague's most stately mansions. From the outside, the prison looks like a medieval citadel, but inside it's modern and clean. The Unit has unusually high security. However, the Court's rules of detention specify that the "physical and emotional welfare of detainees is of paramount importance," and inside, the

Unit is more like a dormitory than a prison.[13] There is no violence, and "no smells and sounds typical of 'normal' prisons," in
the words of the Commanding Officer, who identified such smells
as smoke, sweat, and bleach.[14] (I have a sensitive nose, however,
and I often smelled disinfectant as well as sweat.)

Detainees have their own cells, equipped with their own
showers. They have access to an open-air exercise yard for at least
an hour a day, and to indoor exercise equipment as well. They are
provided with satellite television and news reporting from their
home countries. If detainees desire to read something not held by
the prison library, they are allowed to order in reading material
from outside. (All of this made me wonder exactly what Radovan Karadžić would learn about me, but he never shared what
he learned, or even whether he'd tried.) Classes are offered to the
prisoners in English, computer skills, yoga, and arts and crafts.
Detainees are allowed to order special foods, such as Serbian-style
cheeses. Milošević is said to have spent his free time in the prison
reading thrillers, gossiping with his former enemies, and listening to Celine Dion CDs. He died in the UN Detention Unit on
March 11, 2006, a few months before the verdict in his trial for
genocide was to be announced by the Court. Because of all the
privileges afforded to the detainees, the Unit is often sardonically
referred to as "The Hague Hilton."[15]

—

The Detention Unit is patrolled by UN guards, but to get there,
you first have to pass through the high-security Dutch prison in
which the Unit is housed. There are a series of steps to go through,
the same steps I've gone through every time I've entered the UN
prison. I exchange my passport for a prison ID card, which I'm
required to wear around my neck. I lock up everything I have
brought with me—purse, coat, writing implements—so that I am
stripped of money, telephone, and ID. A sense of lightness floats

down. I am shorn of history and identity, and there is no way to communicate with the outside world or the people who knew me before I entered the prison. I'm a very fast typist. Left to my own devices, I would have typed while Karadžić was speaking to me and recorded his words as well. But in the Detention Unit, I was allowed no recording devices. No computer. No camera. No pen. No paper.

I have been to high-security prisons all over the world: Graz-Karlau Prison in Graz, Austria; Prison de Lantin in Liege, Belgium; the State Prison in Nyborg, Denmark; JVA Bochum in Bochum, Germany; Ayalon Prison in Ramla, Israel; Swaqa Prison and Juweideh Prison in Jordan; al-Ha'ir prison just south of Riyadh, Saudi Arabia; Florida State Prison in Bradford County, Florida; Sussex 1 State Prison in Waverly, Virginia. Scheveningen has the most sensitive metal detector I've ever encountered.

While my shoes go through an X-ray machine, I walk through the metal detector, hoping against hope that it won't sound. I have learned to walk sideways like a crab, having been told by a guard that the small amount of metal in my bra will then be less likely to sound the alarm. I try not to be a woman in these situations, but some things can't be helped.

Walking sideways in my stocking feet feels like a walk of shame. I become painfully aware of how much my identity is created, how much it depends on other people confirming that I'm the person I claim to be. How long could I hang on to the picture I hold of myself if the guards started treating me like a prisoner?

A Dutch guard unlocks a door that opens to a waiting room, where he leaves me to wait alone for a UN guard to retrieve me. There is a smell of disinfectant here, and the kind of old fluorescent lights that flicker, the kind we're supposed to have replaced with LEDs. Whenever I am under fluorescents like these, whenever I am halfway to hell, the walls close in on me.

Sometimes, when I come to visit my war criminal, I find myself sitting alone in this halfway house, trying to count my breaths to keep myself calm. But I don't feel the apprehension. What is there to be anxious about?

Outsiders, as I've said, are not usually allowed into the UN prison. No journalists. No writers. No scholars. Perhaps that is why, on my first visit, the UN guard who met me in the waiting room seemed excited to see me. He knew I was going to meet with Karadžić. He was chatty.

We walked past the "regular" Dutch Ministry of Justice prison. "Over there is where the worst of the worst are housed," he said, pointing to a big building on our right. He told me that one of the guys who kidnapped Freddy Heineken spent time in there.[16] (Heineken was the richest man in the Netherlands. He was kidnapped for almost $22 million in ransom in 1983.)

The men in there are violent, he said, and sometimes attack the guards. "Not like the old men in the UN detention facility." We walked past the playground where the violent prisoners play with their children. I took note of the incongruously diminutive chairs in the shape of a duck and a dog.

Next we approached the inner sanctum, where the "old men," the former national leaders and generals, are housed while they await the outcomes of their trials. There is a second metal detector to pass through, a second X-ray machine. We go through the same procedures, this time under the eyes of three UN guards rather than the gruff Dutch Ministry of Justice personnel. The removal of any jewelry, the sideways, stocking-footed walk of shame through the metal detector. There are six locked doors that I need to go through to get to the room where I will meet with my war criminal. Yes, by now, he is mine, and I, uncomfortably, am his. His what? I don't know what I am to him, but it is something I may learn.

—

The first time we met, we weren't anything to each other. Or anyway, not really. I had researched him thoroughly and knew a lot about what other people thought of him. My students had assembled a hundred-page dossier for me to read. I had read quite a bit of what had been written about the war at the time, but not the recently declassified materials. Not about him. Not about his enemies. Those declassified documents and research that was based on them, I was later to learn, make all sides involved in the war look even worse than we believed them to be at the time, including Western governments.[17]

That first time I came to see him, Karadžić was not in the room. The guard had brought me to an empty room to wait. He gave me a pen and a pad of paper, plus a printout of the questions I had sent two weeks earlier, which had to be approved by the Court. The Court had not provided many ground rules. I was instructed not to interfere with the administration of justice or the security of the prison. And I understood that the identity of protected witnesses had to be safeguarded. But when I'd included a question about General Ratko Mladić, the former general who had led the Bosnian Serb Army (VRS), they informed me that I was not allowed to ask questions about any other detainees.

I still have the notes I scribbled down while waiting for Karadžić that first time. I took note of the radiator under the window, the two fluorescent lights flickering overhead, the little table with the two little chairs. I wrote the words, "stay present," and "discipline your mind."

The date was October 8, 2014, six days after the completion of the closing arguments in his case. He was representing himself with the assistance of a legal team that included Peter Robinson, a former American prosecutor, now a prominent defense attorney. Robinson had also defended Charles Taylor, the former president of Liberia who was convicted of crimes against humanity. I had watched Karadžić through a window in the courtroom where he was tried; the glass was there to protect the accused from the audience and the audience from the accused. He delivered his arguments without stumbling, composed despite the presence of international media. He had played many roles in his life—poet, psychiatrist, warlord, fugitive—and now he was playing a new one: celebrated expert on the person the West called the "Butcher of Bosnia," often referring to himself in the third person. He was ostentatiously polite, calling Alan Tieger, the prosecutor who was trying to put him behind bars for life, the "distinguished prosecution lawyer." Obviously accustomed to being in the spotlight, he read through his prepared documents, repeatedly licking his finger as he turned to a new page, occasionally switching into charmingly accented English with the confident air of a senior professor of law rather than the hounded aura of a war crimes suspect. He insisted he was innocent of masterminding the massacre of an estimated eight thousand men and boys at Srebrenica—that, in fact, he hadn't known about it until after the war. But as president, he said he took moral responsibility for "any crimes that had been committed by the citizens or armed forces of Republika Srpska." He also insisted, throughout, that it was not he, Karadžić, who stood accused by the Tribunal, but the Serbian people.

Waiting in the little room, I could hear the guards down the hallway, chitchatting in a language I couldn't quite make out. I could hear the melody, not the words. Oddly calming. I thought of the chitchat of the adults I often heard outside the closed door of my bedroom as a child, which I sometimes found comforting. For the guards, it was business as usual. There was nothing out of the ordinary about spending their day among the world's most notorious villains.

Then a new sound: men shuffling down the hallway toward the guard post. I heard Karadžić's booming "Allo!"—all friendliness to the guards, the voice of a man confident of his place in society, even when in a prison.

It came to me that these UN guards and their charges, the "old men" (average age sixty-two), were getting old together. One of the guards accompanied Karadžić to the room where I was waiting, then seated himself just outside the door.

Karadžić entered the little room, carrying a heavy black milk crate filled with food. In court, he had worn a dark suit, a pressed white shirt, and a blue tie. In the Detention Unit, which had been his home for six years, he was closer to disheveled, wearing a light maroon shirt he might have slept in, and a ratty old-man sweater. But he was confident, towering above his domain with affable cordiality. I had dressed with care, in black pants, a black jacket, and pearls, wanting to look respectful if not cheerful.

I have always had to fight shyness, and sometimes fall into silence, especially in the presence of gregarious people. It is a trait I find particularly annoying in myself when I'm trying to establish the authority of my role. I remember the sensation of taking in his presence. Tall. Polite. That hair. Striking features. Prominent bone structure. I could sense him trying, even if unconsciously, to draw me in, to persuade me that he was a regular, friendly person. But I felt wary. Something stopped me from looking straight into his eyes. I wondered if it was only what I knew about him or if it was something in his eyes that scared me.

I had my list of questions on the table. It began with: "What are you most proud of?" I had hoped that would put him at ease. But it was immediately clear that it was not going to be necessary to put this man at ease; he was far more socially adept than I. For a few minutes, we made small talk about the weather. Then he wanted to know if it was okay if he asked about me.

I was taken aback. "Ask anything you want," I said.

His first question was about my ethnicity. "Stern. What kind of name is that?"

Even when I've spoken with neo-Nazis or jihadists, I always tell the truth if asked this question. "German Jewish," I answered.

Is it possible he really didn't know that? I waited for the anti-Semitic shadow of disgust to flash across his face, which would be the typical reaction of the sort of person who inquires about my name. But he seemed entirely in control of his features and of whatever anti-Semitism he might harbor.

He mentioned right away that his father had fought the Nazis.

Right, I thought, some of my best friends . . .

Later I would learn that many Serbs do feel themselves to be members of a despised ethnicity, like Jews, and that his father really had fought the Nazi-affiliated Ustasha (Croatian fascists) during the war.

"And you're from Harvard?" he asked.

Yes, I told him. I was teaching there at the time.

"I was at Harvard in 1975," he said. "I made a pilgrimage to see Albert Lord, the specialist in epic poetry."

"You knew Albert Lord!" I said, happy at the memory of that enchanting man, whom I barely knew but remembered well, nonetheless. Albert Lord had been a longtime professor of Slavic and comparative literature who died in 1991. He was a Boston native with a heavy accent, most famous for his work on the origins of epic poetry. I first met him in the 1970s. I found him delightful—his love of stories and song was contagious.

I saw that Karadžić was developing a roster of our affinities, which (so far) included his Nazi-fighting father, my Nazi-escaping one; the fact that we had both met the beloved professor Albert Lord; and that we had both spent time at a liberal, world-class center of learning, where the presumption of innocence until proven guilty was an especially well-established norm.

"You traveled to Harvard when you were in the U.S. for a year, studying at Columbia?" I asked.

Karadžić had spent a year at Columbia University studying poetry. "Yes," he said. "American youth are so healthy, so capable, so curious." So, he would have me believe, he even likes Americans, despite both the NATO bombing campaign carried out in Serb parts of Bosnia—which most Serbs blamed on President Bill Clinton—and America's role in the creation of the Court that was about to convict him of genocide.

"I visited three universities when I was in the United States," Karadžić said with pride. "Columbia, Harvard, and the University of California at Berkeley. I made one or two lectures at U.C. Berkeley about the construction of socialist realism." He was thirty years old at the time.

Once again, a cloud of suspicion passed through my mind. I had detected his seduction strategy: one of the weapons in his arsenal was to focus on experiences he was intuiting that we had in common. Even so, I was ready to believe everything he had said until now. But I found it hard to believe that he wouldn't remember the exact number of lectures he had given during such an exciting sojourn, his first time in California.

"Miłosz was in the audience," he said. "I saw him there."

In spite of my wariness, I found myself feeling excited.

I told him that my publisher at Ecco was a poet and a poetry editor, and that he'd edited Czesław Miłosz in English. I asked him if he had read Miłosz's last collection, *Second Space*. He had not. It was a book I had given to a number of people as a gift. I couldn't resist. I offered to send it to him. And when I got back to Cambridge, I did. That was the first time I fell in. It lasted for a while.

NOTES

1. Between the ICTY's establishment and the end of 2017, when it was formally closed down, 161 persons were indicted, of whom 90 were sentenced and 19 acquitted. Thirty-seven indictments were withdrawn, and 13 cases were referred to courts in the former Yugoslavia. "Info-

graphic: ICTY Facts & Figures," International Criminal Tribunal for the former Yugoslavia, http://www.icty.org/en/content/infographic-icty-facts-figures.

2. The ICTY Registry was in charge of administering the Yugoslav Tribunal. Responsibilities included keeping records, translating court documents, personnel management, transporting and accommodating witnesses, as well as the Detention Unit, where indictees were incarcerated during the period of their trial. The ICTY formally ceased to exist on December 31, 2017. The successor body is known as the International Residual Mechanism for International Criminal Tribunals, and is responsible for residual functions such as oversight of sentences and consideration of appeal proceedings. See also: "Detention," International Criminal Tribunal for the former Yugoslavia, http://www.icty.org/en/about/detention.

3. Philosopher Hannah Arendt reported on the war crimes trial of Adolf Eichmann in 1961. Eichmann was responsible for organizing the transportation of millions of Jews to concentration camps. Arendt saw nothing in Eichmann that marked him as inherently evil. In fact, she considered him "terrifyingly normal." In 1963, Arendt published *Eichmann in Jerusalem: A Report on the Banality of Evil.* According to Arendt, Eichmann was simply driven by a desire to succeed within the Nazi party. There was no ideological motivation underpinning Eichmann's facilitation of the deaths of millions of Jews. Arendt referred to Eichmann's belief that he was just following orders and doing his job as "the banality of evil." Hannah Arendt, *Eichmann in Jerusalem: A Report on the Banality of Evil* (New York: Penguin Books, 2006). There is a debate among scholars whether Arendt's description of Eichmann was accurate and whether he was actually motivated by anti-Semitism.

    For further reference on the latter view, see Bettina Stangneth, *Eichmann Before Jerusalem: The Unexamined Life of a Mass Murderer* (New York: Vintage, 2015).

4. I began approaching the ICTY Registry in 2011. The Registry repeatedly rebuffed my request to interview the detainees. Even after I received permission to interview Karadžić, the bureaucracy continued to resist and it wasn't until October 2014 that I was able to speak with him. I was told by Court personnel that "it is exceptional for a researcher to be allowed to meet with a detainee at the UNDU." I had to sign a contract obligating me to comply with certain rules: I was not allowed to interfere with the administration of justice or endanger

the "security or good order" of the Detention Unit. I was forbidden to interfere with or intimidate witnesses, or make false or defamatory statements about judges or staff members. Furthermore, I was not allowed to bring any recording devices, or even pen and paper, into the prison. My questions had to be approved in advance. Each time I arrived at the prison, a guard would give me a copy of my own questions, a pad of paper, and a pen. This book was reviewed by the Tribunal in advance of publication, to ensure that I had complied with these rules. The Registry required only a few small corrections, but also required a disclaimer stating that I am not affiliated with the International Residual Mechanism for Criminal Tribunals or with the United Nations, and that the content and views expressed in this book are mine alone, and not those of the Tribunal.

5. According to Article 28 of the Statute of the ICTY, "Imprisonment shall be served in a State designated by the International Tribunal from a list of States which have indicated to the Security Council their willingness to accept convicted persons." United Nations Security Council, Statute of the International Criminal Tribunal for the former Yugoslavia (As Amended on 17 May, 2002), May 25, 1993, http://www .icty.org/x/file/Legal%20Library/Statute/statute_sept09_en.pdf.

6. Marlise Simons, "U.N. Court, for First Time, Defines Rape as War Crime," *New York Times*, June 28, 1996, https://www.nytimes .com/1996/06/28/world/un-court-for-first-time-defines-rape-as-war-crime.html. The Foča case at the ICTY was the first international case to prosecute sexual violence exclusively. All three defendants in the Foča case were found guilty of rape as a form of torture, a crime against humanity. Heidi Nichols Haddad, "Mobilizing the Will to Prosecute: Crimes of Rape at the Yugoslav and Rwandan Tribunals," *Human Rights Review*, Vol. 12, No. 1 (2011), pp. 109–132.

7. Steven L. Burg and Paul S. Shoup, *The War in Bosnia-Herzegovina: Ethnic Conflict and International Intervention* (Armonk, NY: M. E. Sharpe, 1999), pp. 170–171; Amnesty International, "Bosnia-Herzegovina: Rape and Sexual Abuse by Armed Forces," report, January 1993, https://www.amnesty.org/download/Documents/188000/eu r630011993en.pdf. Accessed August 15, 2018.

8. Experts from UNHCR put the number of rapes at 12,000, whereas the Bosnian Interior Ministry claims 50,000 cases. The European Union claims 20,000 cases of rape, and the United Nations Commission of Experts identified 1,600 cases. Alexandra Stiglmayer, ed., *Mass Rape:*

The War Against Women in Bosnia-Herzegovina (Lincoln, NE, and London: University of Nebraska Press, 1994); Steven L. Burg and Paul S. Shoup, *The War in Bosnia-Herzegovina: Ethnic Conflict and International Intervention* (Armonk, NY: M. E. Sharpe, 1999), pp. 170–171.

9. International Criminal Tribunal for the former Yugoslavia, *Prosecutor v. Dragan Zelenović—Judgement Summary*, Case No. IT-96-23/2-A, October 31, 2007, http://www.icty.org/x/cases/zelenovic/acjug/en/071031_Zelenovic_summary_en.pdf.

10. Memorandum from John Hocking, Registrar, to Judge Theodor Meron, President, dated October 19, 2012 ("19 October Memorandum"), transmitting a Letter from the Belgian Ministry of Justice, dated October 16, 2012, with attachments ("Custodial Report," "Psychosocial Report," and "Anthropological Report," respectively), cited in International Criminal Tribunal for the Former Yugoslavia, *Prosecutor v. Dragan Zelenović—Decision of President on Early Release of Dragan Zelenović*, Case No. IT-96-23/2-ES, November 30, 2012, http://www.icty.org/x/cases/zelenovic/presdec/en/121130.pdf.

    Jessica M. Kelder, Barbora Hola, and Joris van Wijk suggest rehabilitating war criminals upon their release. Jessica M. Kelder, Barbora Holá, and Joris van Wijk, "Rehabilitation and Early Release of Perpetrators of International Crimes: A Case Study of the ICTY and ICTR," *International Criminal Law Review*, Vol. 14 (2014), pp. 1177–1203, http://www.whenjusticeisdone.org/articles/Kelder_Hola_VanWijk2014.pdf.

11. My memory is very hazy here. Upon rereading what I've written, I'm concerned I may have been too dissociative to capture the details related to his scars.

12. Zelenović admitted guilt, he said, because "Carla Del Ponte gave me a choice: Admit your guilt to these charges and you'll get fifteen years in Europe, or I'll send you to Bosnia and you'll get thirty years." He also said that he thought everyone in the UN Detention Unit was guilty except Momčilo Krajišnik. He claimed that everyone agreed that Krajišnik was innocent. The ICTY was informed by the Belgian Ministry of Justice that Zelenović was not fully regretful. Memorandum from John Hocking, Registrar, to Judge Theodor Meron, President, dated October 19, 2012 ("19 October Memorandum"), transmitting a Letter from the Belgian Ministry of Justice, dated October 16, 2012, with attachments ("Custodial Report," "Psychosocial Report," and "Anthropological Report," respectively), cited in International Criminal Tribunal for the Former Yugoslavia, *Prosecutor v.*

Dragan Zelenović—Decision of President on Early Release of Dragan Zelenović, Case No. IT-96-23/2-ES, November 20, 2012, http://www .icty.org/x/cases/zelenovic/presdec/en/121130.pdf.

13. "Detention," International Criminal Tribunal for the former Yugoslavia, http://www.icty.org/en/about/detention.

14. Radoša Milutinović, "Scheveningen—a Far from 'Normal' Prison," *Justice Report*, November 27, 2013, http://www.justice-report.com/en /articles/scheveningen-a-far-from-normal-prison.

15. The ICTY explains: "The unit houses those persons accused by the ICTY Prosecution after they have been transferred to The Hague to stand trial. . . . Like in all legal systems, accused before the Tribunal enjoy the presumption of innocence unless they are proven guilty in a court of law. . . . Persons convicted of crimes do not serve their sentence in the unit as it is not a penitentiary. They are transferred to a prison outside of the Netherlands to serve their time." "Detention," International Criminal Tribunal for the former Yugoslavia, http:// www.icty.org/en/about/detention.

16. Freddy Heineken and his driver were kidnapped for a ransom of 35 million Dutch guilders in 1983. Catching the kidnappers took several years. Two of the kidnappers, Cor van Hout and Willem Holleeder, were in France for over three years, first as fugitives, then in prison, then under house arrest, and then in prison again. Frans Meijer was a fugitive in Paraguay, where he was later caught and imprisoned. Later, he accepted his extradition back to the Netherlands, where he served the final part of his sentence. See also: Andrew Osborn, "Time's Up for Man Who Kidnapped Boss of Heineken," *Guardian*, May 24, 2001, https://www.theguardian.com/world/2001 /may/25/andrewosborn.

17. Classified documents, intercepted communications, and satellite imagery, which national governments normally keep secret for many decades, were turned over to the ICTY because they were needed to secure convictions of indicted war criminals. For example, classified records of Serbia's Supreme Defense Council meetings, which were eventually shared with the ICTY, were released in 2011 during the trial of Momčilo Perišić. Milošević tried very hard to hide his and Serbia's involvement in the war in Bosnia so as not to be implicated. But the SDC records make clear that Milošević had a remarkably large influence over the Bosnian Serb political and military leadership; that Serbia financed and equipped the Bosnian Serb Army (VRS) to

such a degree that some experts saw it as an extension of the Yugoslav army; that VRS officers (including those convicted of genocide in Srebrenica) were on Serbia's payroll; that Serbia sent its own units to fight in Bosnia; and (perhaps most damning) that Milošević was in contact with General Mladić during the attacks on Srebrenica and Žepa. For an excellent analysis of how these Serbian classified documents came to be released, see Geoffrey Nice and Nevenka Tromp, "International Criminal Tribunals and Cooperation with States," in Margaret M. Deguzman and Diane Marie Amann, *Arcs of Global Justice: Essays in Honour of William A. Schabas* (Oxford: Oxford University Press USA–OSO, 2018). Declassified CIA assessments make clear the extent to which the U.S. government was aware, not only of the terrible atrocities carried out by the Bosnian Serb Army, but also that Serbia was involved, noting that Serb officials were taking pains to avoid "overt signs that they have sanctioned or directed the ethnic cleansing" and that the "irregular" status of Serb paramilitary units afforded the Serbian leaders plausible deniability. See, e.g., DCI Interagency Balkan Task Force, "Bosnia: Serb Ethnic Cleansing," p. 12. EUR 94-10008C SC 00396/94 (December 1995, approved for release April 5, 2011), https://www.cia.gov/library/readingroom/docs/1994 -12-01a.pdf. Damaging divisions among Western governments have been slowly revealed over time. For example, President Clinton understood that the presence of UN troops in Bosnia was not necessarily helping the Bosniaks because the UN troops' fear of being taken hostage by the Serbs kept NATO from using air power to stop Serb aggression. See National Security Council and Records Management Office, "Declassifed Documents concerning Bosnia," Clinton Digital Library. Accessed August 1, 2019, https://clinton.presidentiallibraries. us/items/show/36589. On this point, see also David Rohde, *Endgame: The Betrayal and Fall of Srebrenica, Europe's Worst Massacre Since World War II* (New York: Farrar, Straus and Giroux, 1997). The U.S. government was aware that President Izetbegović was relying on assistance from some problematic sources, for example, Libya and Iran, both on the list of state sponsors of terrorism at the time. See Office of European Analysis, "Bosnia-Hercegovina: On the Edge of the Abyss." CIA Electronic Reading Room (December 19, 1991, approved for release October 1, 2013), https://www.cia.gov/library/readingroom /docs/1991-12-19.pdf, and National Intelligence Council, "Ending US Compliance With the Bosnian Arms Embargo: Military and Political

Implications." CIA Electronic Reading Room (August 1994, approved for release October 1, 2013), https://www.cia.gov/library/reading-room/docs/1994-08-01.pdf.

A number of books and articles based on both leaked and declassified information make clear that the Bosniak leadership relied on jihadi partners to bolster its defense. For example, see J. M. Berger, *Jihad Joe: Americans Who Go to War in the Name of Islam*, 1st ed. (Washington, DC: Potomac Books, 2011). For an overview of what Western intelligence agencies knew during the war, see Cees Wiebes, *Intelligence and the War in Bosnia, 1992-1995*. (New Brunswick, NJ: Transaction Publishers, 2003). Wiebes was given access to classified intelligence information while researching the manuscript. An update was published in Dutch in 2016. See also Charles Lane and Thom Shanker, "Bosnia: What the CIA Didn't Tell Us," *New York Review of Books* 43, No. 8 (1996): 10. A large cache of classified documents related to the role of outside governments and the UN was declassified in 2015. They are available at https://nsarchive.gwu.edu/project/genocide-documentation-project. In a classified history that I was able to obtain via a freedom-of-information request, the U.S. Joint Chiefs of Staff admitted that the debate inside the Clinton administration was often driven by media atrocity stories rather than more sober assessments based on intelligence, leading, ultimately, to more military involvement than was favored by military advisors, and an unworkable Dayton Accord. The history notes that the "military and political provisions of the accord appear incompatible," and that none of its goals "appear attainable without the massive use of force." It observes that while "most US officials insist that the Dayton Accord insures a unitary Bosnian State," in fact, the military provisions of the Accord "have had the practical effect of consolidating ethnic enclaves," suggesting that "ethnic reconciliation may be a long way off." See Joint Chiefs of Staff, Joint History Office, "The Evolution of US Policy Toward the Former Republic of Yugoslavia and Bosnia Since 1990," September 1997, U.S. Department of Defense, Freedom of Information Division, FOIA Ref: 16-F-0858, p. 11, declassified March 29, 2019. After the loss of over 100,000 lives, the Dayton Accord gave the Muslims less territory than had the Lisbon Agreement, a plan put forward by the European Community (EC). The Lisbon Agreement would have created a confederation of three ethnic regions in a so-called soft partition, which the European mediators saw as the best way to avert war. Representatives of all three sides signed a Declaration of Principles on March 18, 1992. But as discussed in subsequent chapters, U.S. ambassador Warren Zimmerman would eventually admit that he urged Izetbegović to reject the Lisbon Agreement in the hope that a unitary Bosnia—a more favorable outcome for the Muslims—could eventually be obtained. See also "Lisbon Agreement—Chance for Peace or Plan to Destroy Bosnia?" *Sense Tribunal* (September 12, 2015, accessed August 2, 2019), http://www.sense-agency.com/icty/lisbon-agreement—chance-for-peace-or-plan-to-destroy-bosnia.29.html?news_id=16917.

Chapter Three

HATRED AND FEAR

On April 13, 2015, my fourth meeting with Karadžić, the guard brings me to a room set up for conjugal visits. I object. Could we please have our usual room, the one with the single table and two hard chairs? That room is busy, I am told.

Karadžić is not here yet, and I have time to examine the room where the guard has left me to wait. To the right of a small, low table is a cot-sized single bed with a bare green mattress. I notice the stains on the mattress. I will myself to look elsewhere. Two matching wooden chairs have been placed by the low table. It's a sort of coffee table, where cocktails might be served in another setting. The seats are covered in worn red wool. I notice more stains—food or vomit or semen, perhaps all three. My eyes are drawn back to the green mattress. I want to stand up and leave the room. I take myself in hand. Let's not think about that. The familiar odor of disinfectant imparts a hospital-like feeling. But I detect, as well, a strong odor of dirt. What is the odor of dirt? I must be imagining it. Dim, North Sea light comes through the open window, and a breeze from the prison yard flutters the dirty yellow curtains. Old-fashioned fluorescent tubes, here as in our usual room, flicker on and off.

The guard has left the door to the room open. The prison is bustling today. A prisoner I don't know rushes by with a big milk crate, just like the one Karadžić usually brings to our meetings. It is full of drinks and food for his visitor. I catch a glimpse of the prisoner's face and notice that his skin is pallid and swollen. Karadžić has told me that several of the detainees have cancer; perhaps this detainee is one of them. Now I see a guard walking by, a set of sheets draped over his arm and a pillow hugged to his chest. I am relieved to see that he is bringing the bedding to another room.

Finally, my war criminal appears, accompanied by a female guard. I had forgotten how tall Karadžić is, how good-looking.[1] Good-looking today, at least. He admonishes the guard. "Why this room? We are not going to sleep together."

I am relieved to hear his authoritative voice. The voice of a doctor, in charge of this mental hospital, used to getting his way. The voice of a president! But the guard knows who is boss, and it is not the doctor or even the president, at least not today.

"It's okay," she jokes, reassuring my war criminal. "You can leave the door open. I will keep you safe. I will be watching."

We are now together, sitting across from one another, in the conjugal visiting room. This time, I note, Karadžić looks untroubled by his life in the prison. He wears a white shirt, with a burgundy sweater draped over his shoulders, brown slacks, and scuffed loafers that might once have been burnt orange. He offers his hand to shake mine. I tell him I have a cold. But he is not put off; he takes my contaminated hand in his. He places the milk crate on the floor by his chair. First things first. Coffee or tea, he offers. I would like tea. A big fuss ensues. He leaves the room to put the kettle on. I hear him ask the guard for tea bags. Perhaps he neglected to add the usual tea bags to his crate. My heartbeat seems to slow as I hear these familiar pleasantries.

Karadžić had given me homework before our interview this time. He had asked me to read a short story, "A Letter from 1920," by Ivo Andrić (1892–1975), the celebrated Yugoslav writer and diplomat.[2] The story was published in 1946, and presumably reflects the devastating internecine violence inside Yugoslavia that Andrić

witnessed in the First and Second World Wars. It was remarkably
prescient about the 1990s wars. Andrić is one of Karadžić's favorite writers.[3]

Of course, I was determined to be a good student. I read "A
Letter from 1920" closely. The story is in the form of a letter written by a Jewish doctor to his childhood friend, explaining why he
was leaving his native Bosnia forever.[4] Bosnia is home to many
nationalities; no single ethnic group constitutes a majority.[5] The
letter is about the mutual fear and hatred among four different
ethnic groups in Bosnia: Catholic Croats, Orthodox Serbs, Muslims, and Jews.

Here is an excerpt:

> Bosnia is a country of hatred and fear.
>
> But leaving fear aside, which is only a correlative of
> hatred, the natural result of it, let us talk about hatred. . . .
> The fatal characteristic of this hatred is that the Bosnian
> man is unaware of the hatred that lives in him, shrinks from
> analyzing it, and hates everyone who tries to do so. And yet
> it's a fact that in Bosnia and Herzegovina there are more
> people ready in fits of this subconscious hatred to kill and
> be killed, for different reasons, and under different pretexts,
> than in other much bigger Slav and non-Slav lands. . . .
>
> But from time immemorial in Bosnian urban life there
> has been plenty of counterfeit courtesy, the wise deception
> of oneself and others by resounding words and empty
> ceremonies. That conceals the hatred up to a point, but
> doesn't get rid of it or thwart its growth. I'm afraid that in
> these circles, under the cover of all these contemporary
> maxims, old instincts and Cain-like plans may only
> be slumbering, and will live on until the foundations
> of material and spiritual life in Bosnia are altogether
> changed. And when will that time come, and who will

have the strength to carry it out? It will come one day, that I do believe. . . .

This uniquely Bosnian hatred should be studied and eradicated like some pernicious, deeply-rooted disease. Foreign scholars should come to Bosnia to study hatred, I do believe, just as scientists study leprosy, if hatred were only recognized as a separate, classified subject of study, as leprosy is.

I suppose I am one of those foreign scholars Andrić refers to, trying to understand the source of this hatred and fear.

"I read 'A Letter from 1920,'" I tell my war criminal. "Why did you want me to read it?"

"Because it explains our situation," he says. "The mutual suspicion and fear."

Is he talking about us? Or about Muslims and Serbs in Bosnia?

After reading my "homework," I found myself arguing with the brilliant Ivo Andrić, even though he'd won a Nobel Prize and many other literary awards; even though he'd been the Kingdom of Yugoslavia's ambassador to Germany and was recognized as a Grand Officer of the Legion of Honor, France's highest recognition of merit. I want to tell this great man, I am an advanced student of fear, and I know this: fear gives rise to hatred, not the other way around, as your letter writer suggests. And sometimes shame augments the transformation of fear into hate.

I was afraid of Zelenović, the convicted war rapist. So, naturally, now, I hate him. I dissociated both fear and hate, which are, for me, shameful feelings. I knew there was fear in the room, but I didn't really feel it in the moment. It would be very hard to bear being locked in a room with a rapist if I was aware that I felt petrified. And shame (an emotion that feeds on itself, inducing still more shame) made it hard for me to recognize the terror I would have felt, if I hadn't developed this trick of dissociation and denial.

Andrić's letter writer doesn't speak explicitly of shame, but he knows that fear and hatred are often disavowed, hidden under "counterfeit courtesy." I want to say to the great writer-ambassador: it is not just the Bosnian man who is unaware of the hatred that lies dormant within him, but many of us. It is a good thing, Ambassador Andrić, to keep that hate in a dormant state. When a leader makes it okay to let loose our hate, when he weaponizes fear, woe betide us.

It is not only Bosnia that is susceptible to being flooded by hate. Don't we all have the capacity to hate and fear the Other? Wouldn't you see that now, Ambassador Andrić, in my country, if you were with us? My country, too, is overrun by hate and fear, and is now deeply divided. Just as happened in Bosnia during the 1990s war, a leader appeared who knew how to weaponize and intensify our fears, who knew to put names to the objects of our hatred. We are now divided between those who want to maintain America's "white European" majority, and those who hate the people who cling to the superiority of their "white European culture."[6] We are led by a president who seems to sympathize with white supremacists.

My hunch, Ambassador Andrić, is that one pathway to hatred is when a dominant ethnic group fears losing its status and privileges. Just as Bosnian Serbs feared losing their status as the dominant demographic group as Yugoslavia began to fall apart, so, too, some white Americans fear losing their dominant demographic status.[7] Starting in 2013, more nonwhite babies than white babies were born in the United States, and by 2043 America will be majority minority.[8] Ambassador Andrić—don't you see the similarity?

—

Perhaps the most extreme manifestation of hate and fear was the Srebrenica genocide. On July 11, 1995, units of the Bosnian Serb Army, under the command of General Ratko Mladić, captured

the town of Srebrenica.[9] Mladić announced that he was "presenting this city to the Serbian people as a gift," and that "the time
has come to take revenge on the Turks in the region," referring
to an 1804 Serb rebellion that was savagely crushed by the Ottoman rulers.[10] The Bosnian Serb forces separated out the men
of military age. They loaded the women, children, and elderly
onto overcrowded buses and sent them across the front lines into
Muslim-held territory. As the men were attempting to flee the
area, thousands of them were taken prisoner and executed. An estimated eight thousand were murdered in the worst mass slaughter in Europe since the Second World War, all of them after the
town had surrendered.[11] The ICTY and the International Court of
Justice ruled that the mass murder involved a systematic attempt
to destroy the Muslim population in the area and was therefore a
genocide.[12]

The horrors of Srebrenica stayed with Charles Allen, who
served in the CIA for forty years and was at that time national intelligence officer for warning. He told me, "It still haunts me. Still
sticks in my mind. We know the horrors of the Holocaust. But to
see that in modern times—it left me deeply disturbed. The world
pretty much ignored it. I was a five-year-old kid during World
War II. I remember hearing from my mother about the terrible
things that were happening. But now it was happening again."[13]

I also spoke with former Special Advisor to the Prosecutor of
the ICTY William Stuebner, who said, "Have you ever visited a
mass grave? No? Well, if someone tells you that they visited one
and that what they remember is that it looked awful, don't believe
them. It smells awful. The smell, not the sight, is what you can
never forget."[14]

NOTES

1. A Bosniak woman told me that, to a Bosniak eye, Karadžić looked disheveled and unstable.
2. Ivo Andrić is one of the Balkans' greatest contributions to world literature, but he is now viewed by many Bosniaks as anti-Muslim, and has been viewed as anti-Croat as well. An alternative reading, voiced by a number of prominent scholars of Slavic literature, is that the Bosnia that Andrić writes about is symbolic of all of humanity. According to literature scholar E. D. Goy's reading of "A Letter from 1920," "Superficially Andrić might seem to be a regional writer. Here again there is so much reality that the symbolical meaning might well be lost. Yet Andrić's Bosnia is a Bosnia of his own mind. As [Tomislav] Ladan remarks: 'He does not portray Bosnia through his works but rather his works through Bosnia.' Andrić employs Bosnia with its oriental and very original character, its four faiths, its customs and beliefs, as a general symbol of human life rather than merely as a regional background to his stories." Tomislav Ladan, *Ivo Andrić-stvarnost i djelo* (Belgrade: Knjizevnik, 1961), p. 30, cited in E. D. Goy, "The Work of Ivo Andrić," *The Slavonic and East European Review*, Vol. 41, No. 97 (June 1963), p. 313. See also: Andrew B. Wachtel, "How to Use a Classic," in John Lampe and Mark Mazower, eds., *Ideologies and National Identities: The Case of Twentieth-Century Southeastern Europe* (Budapest: Central European University Press, 2004), pp. 139–140.
3. Andrić was an ethnic Croat, but he self-identified as a Serb. He adopted the Ekavian dialect of Serbia in most of his writing, rather than using the Ijekavian dialect of his native Bosnia or Croatia. I wondered if Karadžić got the idea to do the same when he published his first book of poetry in Ekavian in 1968.

   In part because of his choice of dialect, he is generally considered to be a Serbian writer, even a Serb nationalist, rather than Croatian. His work was blacklisted in Croatia soon after it broke away from Yugoslavia, but has since been reclaimed.
4. Ivo Andrić, "A Letter from 1920," trans., Lenore Grenoble (1946), accessed: https://www.thefreelibrary.com/%22A+Letter+from+1920%22 .-a0165021316.
5. In 1948, around the time "A Letter from 1920" was published, the ethnic makeup of Bosnia was as follows: 34.5 percent of Bosnians

identified as Muslim, 41.5 percent identified as Serbs, and 23 percent identified as Croats. Steven L. Burg and Paul S. Shoup, *The War in Bosnia-Herzegovina: Ethnic Conflict and International Intervention* (Armonk, NY: M. E. Sharpe, 1999), p. 27.

6. Jared Taylor, "What Is the Alt Right?" *American Renaissance*, October 11, 2016, https://www.amren.com/news/2016/10/what-is-the-alt -right-jared-taylor/.

     Peter Cvjetanovic, a white nationalist at the University of Nevada who attended the white nationalist rally in Charlottesville, Virginia, in August 2017, defended his presence at the march by saying, "I came to this march for the message that white European culture has a right to be here just like every other culture." David Edwards, "'I'm Not the Angry Racist They See': Alt-Righter Became Viral Face of Hate in Virginia—and Now Regrets It," *Raw Story*, August 13, 2017, https://www .rawstory.com/2017/08/im-not-the-angry-racist-they-see-alt-righter -became-viral-face-of-hate-in-virginia-and-now-regrets-it/.

7. Diana C. Mutz, "Status Threat, Not Economic Hardship, Explains the 2016 Presidential Vote," *Proceedings of the National Academy of Sciences*, Vol. 115, No. 19 (May 8, 2018), http://www.pnas.org/content/115/19 /E4330.

     All ethnic groups in Yugoslavia were minorities; however, the concept of "minority" was not recognized by the Yugoslav government. The Serbs made up the largest single ethnic group in Yugoslavia at 36.3 percent of the total population. Instead of looking at ethnic groups in terms of majorities and minorities, "the official classification differentiated between '(constitutive) nations' (*narodi*) and 'nationalities' (*narodnosti*)." In an independent Bosnia, Serbs would be relegated from *narodnosti* to just another minority—one that was outnumbered by Muslims. Dejan Jović, "Fear of Becoming Minority as a Motivator of Conflict in the Former Yugoslavia," *Balkanologie*, Vol. 5, No. 1–2 (December 2001), pp. 21–36.

8. T. J. Raphael, "America Will Become Majority-Minority in 2043—But in Many Ways That New America Has Already Arrived," *Public Radio International*, October 3, 2014, https://www.pri.org/stories/2014-10-03 /america-will-become-majority-minority-2043-many-ways-new -america-has-already; United States Census Bureau, "U.S. Census Bureau Projections Show a Slower Growing, Older, More Diverse Nation a Half Century from Now," December 12, 2012, https://www.census .gov/newsroom/releases/archives/population/cb12-243.html.

In fact, the U.S. Census Bureau, in 2017, released statistics showing "an absolute decline in the nation's white non-Hispanic population—accelerating a phenomenon that was not projected to occur until the next decade." Moreover, "for the first time, minorities outnumber whites nationally for each age under 10." William H. Frey, "US White Population Declines and Generation 'Z-Plus' is Minority White, Census Shows," Brookings Institute, June 22, 2018, https://www.brookings.edu/blog/the-avenue/2018/06/21/us-white-population-declines-and-generation-z-plus-is-minority-white-census-shows/. See also: United States Census Bureau, "Midwest Home to Most of the Counties with Decreases in Median Age," June 21, 2018, https://www.census.gov/newsroom/press-releases/2018/popest-characteristics.html.

9. The soldiers involved were members of the Drina Corps, one of six units of the VRS. The Scorpions, a Serbian paramilitary unit, were also involved. Srebrenica had been designated by the UN Security Council as a UN-protected "safe area," in which military action of any kind was prohibited. Nonetheless, the Bosnian Muslim forces were launching attacks on the Bosnian Serb Army from the area. In response to the Bosnian Army troops and weapons still hidden in the enclaves, Karadžić issued Directive 7 on March 8, 1995, calling for the Drina Corps to "[carry] out offensive activities" to "split apart the enclaves of Žepa and Srebrenica, and to reduce them to their urban areas." The directive also ordered the "physical separation of the Srebrenica and Žepa enclaves," even preventing communication between them, and the creation of an "unbearable situation of total insecurity, with no hope of further survival or life for the inhabitants of Srebrenica or Žepa." The VRS Main Staff ordered the Drina Corps to undertake operation Krivaja 95 to fulfill the directive. Krivaja 95 was launched on July 6, 1995, against the Bosniak army. The Bosnian Serb operation ended the three-year-long siege of Srebrenica, and led to the massacres in the eastern enclaves.

10. Quoted in Richard Holbrooke, *To End a War* (New York: The Modern Library, 1998), p. 69.

11. Based on Vladimir Petrović, personal communication, June 2, 2019.

12. The trial of Radislav Krstić was the first time that the ICTY ruled the massacre at Srebrenica a genocide. International Criminal Tribunal for the former Yugoslavia, *Prosecutor v. Radislav Krstić—Judgment*, Case No. IT-98-33-A, April 19, 2004, p. 16, accessed: http://www.icty.org/x/cases/krstic/acjug/en/krs-aj040419e.pdf#page=16.

In 2007, the International Court of Justice upheld the ICTY finding of genocide. International Court of Justice, *Application of the Convention on the Prevention and Punishment of the Crime of Genocide (Bosnia and Herzegovina v. Serbia and Montenegro)—Summary of the Judgment of 26 February 2007*, Case No. 2007/2, February 26, 2007, accessed: https://www.icj-cij.org/files/case-related/91/13687.pdf.

The legal definition of genocide involves both an *intention* "to destroy, in whole or in part, a national, ethnical, racial or religious group," and the *physical acts* of "(a) Killing members of the group; (b) Causing serious bodily or mental harm to members of the group; (c) Deliberately inflicting on the group conditions of life calculated to bring about its physical destruction in whole or in part; (d) Imposing measures intended to prevent births within the group; (e) Forcibly transferring children of the group to another group." The intention constitutes the *mens rea*, and the physical acts the *actus reus* of genocide.

The first international tribunal to deliver verdicts in relation to genocide, and the first to interpret the definition, was the International Criminal Tribunal for Rwanda, in 2003. "The ICTR in Brief," United Nations International Residual Mechanism for Criminal Tribunals, http://unictr.irmct.org/en/tribunal.

Although the intention in formulating the Genocide Convention was clearly to prevent future atrocities, it has turned out to be a problematic legal category in practice. The legal scholar Marko Milanović calls the definition of genocide "morally completely arbitrary" and "a product of political compromise." Marko Milanović, "The Shameful Twenty Years of Srebrenica," *EJIL: Talk! Blog of the European Journal of International Law*, July 13, 2015, https://www.ejiltalk.org/the-shameful-twenty-years-of-srebrenica/; Marko Milanović, "ICTY Convicts Radovan Karadzic," *EJIL: Talk! Blog of the European Journal of International Law*, March 25, 2016, https://www.ejiltalk.org/icty-convicts-radovan-karadzic/. It has proven difficult to distinguish, in the Bosnian War, between "ethnic cleansing" and genocide; to prove the latter requires showing evidence of a perpetrator's genocidal (as distinct from malign) thoughts. How we distinguish genocide from other, lesser war crimes can be quite confusing, as the treaty does not set a threshold for the number of persons murdered, only that the *intention* be to destroy a particular group in whole or in part. Thus, murdering hundreds of thousands of persons might not rise to the level of genocide if the perpetrator's intent was judged malign but not genocidal,

while murdering a hundred could be judged a genocide. Several scholars have questioned whether the Srebrenica massacre in particular
should be called a genocide. For example, legal scholar William Schabas argues that the ICTY conflated genocide with ethnic cleansing.
According to Schabas, while ethnic cleansing and genocide may have
the same goals, they have "two quite different specific intents. One
is intended to displace a population, the other to destroy it." Schabas wrote that "ethnic cleansing is also a warning sign of genocide to
come," as genocide is "the last resort of the frustrated ethnic cleanser."
William Schabas, *Genocide in International Law: The Crime of Crimes*
(Cambridge, UK: Cambridge University Press, 2000), p. 234.

Legal scholar and judge Kai Ambos refutes these arguments. He
points out that the Chamber noted that although the Bosniaks "constituted a numerically small percentage of the Bosnian Muslim population," Srebrenica was strategically important and had a "symbolic
stature as a refuge for Bosnian Muslims." Therefore, the Chamber
argued that the Bosniak population of Srebrenica was a "substantial
part" of the greater Bosniak population. International Criminal Tribunal for the former Yugoslavia, *Prosecutor v. Karadžić—Judgment*, Case
No. IT-95-5/18-T, March 24, 2016, para 5672, http://www.icty.org/x
/cases/karadzic/tjug/en/160324_judgement.pdf, cited in Kai Ambos,
"Karadzic's Genocidal Intent as the 'Only Reasonable Inference'?"
EJIL: Talk! Blog of the European Journal of International Law, April 1,
2016, https://www.ejiltalk.org/karadzics-genocidal-intent-as-the-only
-reasonable-inference/.

13. Charlie Allen, interview with author, July 18, 2018.
14. William Stuebner, interview with author, December 13, 2018.

Chapter Four

VICTIMS

I sought a lot of advice about how best to interview Karadžić. One idea, suggested to me by the eminent scholar of Slavic literature Andrew Wachtel, was to ask Karadžić to interpret his own poems. Karadžić and I went through many of his poems. Some are astonishingly violent. I was most intrigued by our discussion of his poem "Goodbye, Assassins."[1] It begins with the lines:

> Goodbye Assassins, it seems from now on
> The gentlefolks' aortas will gush without me.
> The last chance to get stained with blood
> I let go by.

I have no idea how to interpret this poem. Perhaps it is because I am reading it in translation, I tell him.

He explains that the poem is about Gavrilo Princip, the Bosnian Serb who shot Archduke Franz Ferdinand, precipitating the events that led to World War I.

Karadžić reminded me of the history. With the Treaty of Berlin in 1878, Serbia had finally achieved independence from the Ottoman Empire. Bosnia was liberated from the Ottoman Empire at the same time, only to be commandeered by Austria-Hungary.[2]

"Croats and Muslims both found a way to benefit during the Habsburg occupation," Karadžić said, sounding as resentful as he would have been had these events occurred the day before. "In 1914 Princip fought for *all* Bosnians [including Bosnian Muslims and Croats], not just Bosnian Serbs! But Muslims glorify the Archduke."

In truth, Bosnian Muslims are somewhat divided in relation to Princip. Prior to Bosnia's independence, Princip was viewed as a hero for fighting to liberate Bosnia from Habsburg rule, and the Communist-era plaque placed on the spot where the murder occurred celebrated him: "The youth of Bosnia and Herzegovina dedicate this plaque as a symbol of eternal gratitude to Gavrilo Princip and his comrades, to fighters against the Germanic conquerors."[3]

During the 1990s wars, when Bosnia was fighting for its independence from Yugoslavia, the view of Princip changed. He was seen as a terrorist, a participant in a Serb plot against Bosnia. The memorial plaque was smashed. After the 1990s wars were over, a new plaque was put up, with a more neutral telling of the same history. It reads, "From this place on 28 June 1914 Gavrilo Princip assassinated the heir to the Austro-Hungarian throne Franz Ferdinand and his wife Sofia."[4]

A number of terrorist groups formed in opposition to the Austrian occupation. Princip was a member of Young Bosnia (Mlada Bosna), a group of young, anti-Austrian zealots, and a "Yugoslavist" who favored uniting the South Slavic nations.[5] Some of the terrorist groups formed at the time promoted the unification of all ethnic Serbs into a Greater Serbia.[6] Suspicion that the pro-Serbian Black Hand, a secret society established by Serbian military personnel, had provided assistance to Young Bosnia infuriated Austria and played a big role in the start of the war: if the Black Hand were involved, the assassination could not be blamed on student zealots, but on Serbia itself.[7] Austria-Hungary blamed Serbia. A month after the assassination, Austria-Hungary attacked Serbia, initiating World War I.

—

"Archduke Franz Ferdinand had just made an extremely pro-vocative move," Karadžić told me. "He came to review Austrian troops' military maneuvers in occupied Bosnia on June 28, 1914, on St. Vitus Day." St. Vitus Day is the anniversary of the Serbs' military defeat at Kosovo in 1389 and the beginning of the Otto-man occupation of Serbia, which lasted for five centuries.[8] "This was a provocation similar to when Miloš Obilić killed Sultan Mu-rad," he added, his voice louder now. (Miloš Obilić, a Serb, is said to have killed the Ottoman sultan Murad by slashing him with a dagger, knowing that he would be killed himself. However, his-torians are not entirely certain that Obilić existed.) He seemed genuinely angry, not only at the thought of the Archduke's 1914 "provocation," but also at the "memory" of what the terrible Turks had done to Serbia in 1389. Karadžić was implying that when Franz Ferdinand reviewed military maneuvers of Austrian troops in occupied Bosnia on June 28, it was a kind of "martyr-dom operation," and that the Archduke was at least as much of a terrorist as his murderer.

Who was the victim and who was the aggressor?

I marveled at how fresh these historical wounds seemed to be.

Karadžić seemed to read my thoughts. "Historic peoples like Jews and Serbs don't think that historical figures lived in a differ-ent time from our own," he said. "Historic peoples believe in the existence of eternity. Serbs think of Princip as a contemporary." I have no idea what he meant by "historic peoples," or "believing in the existence of eternity." I didn't stop him to demand an explana-tion. But I did notice he was finding a way to link Serbs and Jews again.

These coincidental dates—Franz Ferdinand's visit to Bosnia on St. Vitus Day, the day the Serbs were defeated at Kosovo—get him thinking about other strange chronological concurrences.[9]

"Bosnia was awarded independence on April 6, 1992, on the anniversary of the day that Hitler attacked Yugoslavia in 1941. April 6 was also the day of the liberation of Sarajevo in 1945," he said.

"I don't really believe in numerology or synchronicity," he alleged, but then launched into a list of chronological coincidences that occurred in his own family, regarding the birth of his father, son, and various grandchildren.

I am relieved when we return to the poem.

"Princip had two natures," Karadžić said. "He was not just an assassin, but also a poet." I hadn't realized that.

"Before the 1970s, we all read Princip's poetry. I was thinking, Who is this guy who writes poetry, who also assassinated the Archduke?" The revolutionary movement, Young Bosnia, he said, didn't just plot the assassination, but held literary meetings.

"Princip had a double nature. There is Princip the poet, a member of the intelligentsia. And there is Princip the assassin, who feels compelled to shoot at senseless decoration."

I assume he means the trappings of the fading Austro-Hungarian empire.

"Princip has a conflict within himself. In my poem, he is saying: let someone else be the assassin," Karadžić said. "The poet is trying to get rid of Princip the fighter. He wasn't interested in business affairs or in fighting or killing. He is saying, I will answer the call to be a poet. He loves the mountains and streams."

The thought of mountains and streams gets Karadžić thinking about Montenegro. "When you go to Montenegro, you must go see the Monastery at Ostrog," he says, going off on a tangent again. "It was built in honor of Saint Basil, who was buried there. Lots of miracles happened at that monastery. Ostrog Monastery is built into the side of a mountain, which made it inaccessible to the Turks."

Who said I would go to Montenegro?

He returns to the poem again.

Goodbye, assassins, a rare thought of
genesis enters my mind. Of knowing the heaven.
And blood, that ugly word, violent and dark,
Angers Milutin, the ancestor asleep,
gentle even in death, as if in times of fasting.

"Gentle . . . as if in times of fasting," says Karadžić, explaining the words.

"When people are fasting, they are so gentle. The most important of our saints could live entirely on water."

An image of a monastery built into a stony mountainside comes to my mind. The gentle saints pray there so much they can exist on water alone. I want to see this.

"Princip is saying, 'I cannot share in this madness, this violence.' The poet knows that something terrible is about to happen. He senses disaster. He understands the futility of plotting the assassination. Everything is going in the wrong direction. Heading toward war, toward a target or bullet."

Karadžić continues at great length, interpreting nearly every line of his own poem, which I had sent to him in English translation. He takes short breaks to go on tangents about spiritual matters. I am most interested in what he describes as the split within Princip, between the poet and the assassin.

Until now, I've not crossed my war criminal in any way. It's not my job, I think to myself. I'm here to learn about how he came to be the man he is today, the man convicted of genocide. But a thought comes to me and I utter it before having a chance to worry he'll turn against me, tell me never to return.

"This poem is about you," I say. "About the split in you between poet and assassin. Those green mountains and streams you were referring to, you told me about them, in Petnjica. The mountains and streams of your childhood."

Silence.

Have I really just called him an assassin?

I see a new look on his face, which I have trouble interpreting. "Why didn't you tell me that you studied so much psychoanalysis?" he asks, now looking like a petulant child who has been tricked.

He doesn't say, *Get out of my prison and never come back.* Instead he says, "You're scaring me."

I am ashamed to admit that I was gratified to hear this. Flattered. Delighted. I sensed my whole body relax—both because he didn't kick me out, which would have made it harder for me to finish my book, and because he noticed my great insight. But this moment of pleasure would not last long.

"I'm just interpreting a poem," I said. "You told me that you let your unconscious run free when you write poems." He did, in fact, tell me that.

"You're scaring me," he said, a second time. But I saw from his eyes that he had already recovered the upper hand. He saw that I was flattered by his words.

Here's the odd thing. Often, if someone I don't know well compliments me, I have a perverse reaction; I assume they are lying, trying to manipulate me. This man never told me, "You look nice today," or "I read your book about terrorism and liked it," or used any of the more obvious ways to flatter me. But in the brief moment I let down my guard, he had figured out one of the few tributes, coming from him, that would mean something to me.

He would repeat this phrase, "You're scaring me," many times over the remaining year and a half that we met in the prison. But as soon as I realized he was trying to flatter me, "You're scaring me," become a useless weapon in his arsenal of seduction.

How many pinpricks of persuasion was I unaware of? How many affected me unconsciously?

I believe that the first time he said, "You're scaring me," he probably meant it. But the second, and third, and fourth times, what I think he meant was, *I've got you.* I had noticed the division within him—he, too, was a poet assassin—and in the moment I brought that observation into the room, I believe he hated me. But he still wanted to use me. He hoped against hope that I might tell his story as he wanted it told. The narrative he would like to see spread is that he was a "man of peace" and a "true friend of Muslims" who was determined to avoid war. The war started because Bosnian Serbs were under threat from the Bosnian Muslims, who were determined to create an "Islamic state in the heart of Europe." He became a martyr to the Serb cause. "It is the Serb people who stand accused," Karadžić repeatedly said at his trial.[10] He told the Court, "There hasn't been a situation where so many decent, innocent people, mostly Serbs, were sentenced to high prison sentences that they are serving in different European countries outside their homeland; and, on the other side, so many perpetrators of crimes against Serbs, murderers, were set free."[11]

—

It is hard to understand the beginning of the 1990s war, and Karadžić's role, without being reminded of some of the history. Yugoslavia came into existence just after World War I, in 1918, as the Kingdom of the Serbs, Croats, and Slovenes. The new state combined the independent states of Serbia and Montenegro with territories that had most recently been a part of the Austro-Hungarian Empire, including Bosnia-Herzegovina, Croatia, and Slovenia.[12] In 1929, the Kingdom was renamed Yugoslavia, after the *južnoslovenski* (South Slavic) peoples that had come together to form the state. The Kingdom was dominated by Serbs: the Serbian royal house ruled the new state, and Serbs controlled the senior positions in government and the officer corps.

At the end of World War II, the monarchy relinquished power to the Communists, who controlled the country for nearly five decades.[13] The Communists, under Josip Broz Tito, were determined to emancipate the non-Serb nations from Serb domination, and to do so, they created a federation of six republics. Although all of Yugoslavia's ethnic groups lived throughout Yugoslavia, Croats, Macedonians, Montenegrins, Serbs, and Slovenes were granted eponymous republics. They were referred to as *narodi*, or constitutive nations, and were all of equal status.[14] (Thus, Montenegrins, who constituted about 3 percent of the population of Yugoslavia, were politically equal to Serbs, at 35–40 percent.)[15] Bosnia was unique among the six republics in that no single ethnic group constituted a majority.[16]

Despite the creation of republics and other efforts to equalize the status of nationalities, Yugoslavian nationalism was in tension with the particularist nationalisms of its component parts. Long before Yugoslavia began to fall apart in the 1990s wars, there was a tension between ethnic groups wanting to maximize their autonomy and the need to integrate the various ethnic groups into a cohesive political unit.[17] But, as political scientist Jasna Dragović-Soso points out, "peaceful coexistence and even cooperation between the Yugoslav peoples was just as much a characteristic of the region as periods of conflict."[18]

Over time, however, partly because of growing economic disparities between the republics, centrifugal forces increased.[19] Even before the 1991 breakup of the Soviet Union, Yugoslavia's constituent republics had begun asserting their independence. In 1991, Slovenia and Croatia became the first to declare independence. Slovenian independence was achieved in the space of ten days, with minimal violence. But there was a significant Serb minority living in Croatia, and the Yugoslav armed forces immediately intervened to prevent Croatia's secession. It was only after a seven-month war that left 10,000 dead and 700,000 displaced that an independent Croatia was recognized internationally.[20]

Bosnia-Herzegovina was a mixed region, often described as a mini-Yugoslavia because of the presence of so many nationalities living together in the small republic. At the time the war began, 43 percent of Bosnia's citizens identified themselves as Muslim, 35 percent as Orthodox Serbs, and 18 percent as Catholic Croats, with the remainder identifying themselves as Yugoslavs, or other, even smaller minorities.

In socialist Yugoslavia, no ethnic group was considered a minority, regardless of the size of its population or territory, and the word "minority" had developed a negative or even insulting connotation.[21] Instead of classifying ethnic groups as majorities and minorities, they were classified as constitutive nations (*narodi*) and nationalities (*narodnosti*). At 36.3 percent of the total population, the Serbs made up the largest single ethnic group in Yugoslavia. In an independent Bosnia, they would lose that status.

When socialism fell away, and terms such as *narodi* and *narodnosti* lost their former significance, Bosnian Serbs (and Croats) were suddenly in danger of becoming relegated to the demeaning status of lesser "minorities." Moreover, many Bosnian Serbs feared being subject to "ethnic outvoting," or majoritarian rule. According to political scientist Dejan Jović, this fear of being relegated to minority status was an important driver of ethnic nationalism throughout the region.[22] Franjo Tudjman and Slobodan Milošević, the respective wartime leaders of the Bosnian Croat and Serb "parent" republics, deliberately exaggerated the negative aspects of becoming a "minority."[23] If Bosnia achieved independence, Serbs would be outnumbered by Muslims and relegated from *narodnosti* to just another minority.[24] As economist Vladimir Gligorov wrote, "We do not want to be a minority in your state, fairness or no fairness (but if you want, you are welcome to be a minority in our state)."[25]

A referendum on Bosnia's independence was held between February 29 and March 1, 1992. Nearly all of those who went to the polls voted in favor of secession. The majority of ethnic Serbs, however, wanted Bosnia to remain within Yugoslavia (where they would still be the most numerous ethnic group), and had largely boycotted the referendum.[26]

Soon after the referendum, tensions between the Bosnian Serbs, Croats, and Muslims rose to a flash point. By late spring of 1992, Serb forces laid siege to Sarajevo, Bosnia's capital city, a symbol of multiculturalism where Muslims, Catholics, and Orthodox Christians had long lived together in peace.[27] This was the beginning of the war in Bosnia.

In Sarajevo, gas, water, and electricity were cut off. According to the ICTY, "the attacks on Sarajevo civilians were often unrelated to military actions and were designed to keep the inhabitants in a constant state of terror." For forty-four months, Serb military forces used sniping and shelling to kill, maim, and terrorize the civilian inhabitants of Sarajevo.[28]

This was early in the age of televised war. For the residents of Sarajevo, venturing outside their homes to acquire food or water became a game of chicken. TV cameras captured pictures of unarmed civilians running through the streets, dodging sniper fire as they raced to get food and water for their families. Their misery drew so much attention from the global media, and from artists and intellectuals, that Sarajevo under siege became an "icon of contemporary atrocity."[29] Journalists were excited by how the city's "cultural syncretism, religious pluralism and ethnic diversity" could engage their audience's sympathy. In addition to journalists, a "rotating roster of intellectuals, politicians and celebrities, whose appearances generated additional media events," created a hall of mirrors, with filmmakers filming each other.[30]

The poet Semezdin Mehmedinović wrote:

I'm running across an intersection to avoid the bullet of a sniper from the hill when I walk straight into some photographers: they're doing their job, in deep cover. If a bullet hit me they'd get a shot worth so much more than my life that I'm not even sure whom to hate: the Chetnik sniper or these monkeys with Nikons. For the Chetniks I'm just a simple target but these others only confirm my utter helplessness and even want to take advantage of it.[31]

Later, it would become clear that Sarajevo's Muslims were being shot at—not only by Serbian snipers, but also occasionally by their own leadership, some of whom (like their Serbian counterparts) were making money off the war at their own population's expense. And the media coverage of besieged Sarajevo was useful to the Bosniak leadership.[32] In one of the most egregious examples of media manipulation, during the winter of 1993–1994, Fred Cuny, an American civil engineer who served as a disaster-relief worker, discovered an important source of water—a cistern at the top of a hill. But Sarajevo government officials prevented Cuny from pumping the water into the city's empty lines. According to General Michael Hayden and others, this was likely because Bosniak military personnel were making a profit from reselling UN fuel donated to help deliver the water by truck. And the image of Sarajevans queuing up at water distribution points, sometimes under sniper fire, drew international sympathy, which the Bosniaks hoped would lead to Western intervention on their side.[33]

—

Karadžić often told me that during the Ottoman occupation, many Bosnian Muslims who had been members of the Serbian elite converted from Christianity to Islam. The Ottoman Empire occupied much of the Balkans for more than five hundred years—from the fourteenth century until the early twentieth century. Converting to Islam meant that wealthy Christians could avoid paying the dhimmi taxes imposed by the Turks on non-Muslims. The more "courageous" Serbs, Karadžić said, were not so easily manipulated by lucre. They refused to convert. They were, he said, poor but faithful Christians—forced to live in the hills above Sarajevo rather than in the center of town. Karadžić wanted to take the city back from those "Turks," the term he often used for Bosnian Muslims, and return it to its "rightful owners." (Contemporary historians do not believe that it was only wealthy Christians who converted to Islam. But it is true that conversion to Islam conferred special privileges and status, and those who converted gained a higher standard of living than those who did not.)[34]

Serb military operations involved not only sniping at the residents of the city, but also destroying cultural institutions.[35] The National Library was razed. According to an investigator from Harvard University, before the fire, which lasted three days, the library had held 1.5 million volumes, including 155,000 rare books; it was the largest single incident of deliberate book burning in modern history.[36] The Oriental Institute was demolished. Islamic and Jewish manuscripts—in Arabic, Persian, Hebrew, and Aljamiado (Bosnian Slavic written in Arabic script)—and many thousands of valuable documents from the Ottoman period were destroyed.[37]

The United Nations had imposed an embargo on military assistance to any side in the war with the hope of minimizing bloodshed. But Serb forces had inherited weaponry and personnel from Yugoslavia's armed forces; the embargo had minimal impact on the Serbs but left the Muslims essentially defenseless.[38] From their hillside outposts, some thirteen thousand Serb troops encircled Sarajevo and assaulted it with tanks and artillery. Seventy thousand Bosnian Muslim troops remained inside the city, but they were poorly armed.

On May 27, 1992, two mortar rounds were fired into a crowd of people waiting for bread. Twenty-two people were killed. This incident became known as the Breadline Massacre. After that, for twenty-two days, a lone cellist, Vedran Smailović, appeared in evening dress at precisely four o'clock, risking his own life to play Albinoni's mournful Adagio in G Minor, in honor of those who had died in the massacre.[39] The lone cellist became the subject of poetry, plays, novels, and music. David Wilde's *Cellist of Sarajevo*, "a lament in rondo form," was recorded by Yo-Yo Ma. This was despite some initial uncertainty on the part of UN officials as to whether this particular mortar attack was carried out by Serb forces or by local residents as part of a propaganda campaign to persuade the international community to intervene militarily.

There were a number of cases in which investigators concluded that the Bosnian Muslim leadership had carried out attacks staged to look as if they were carried out by the Serbs, and still others in which the evidence remains uncertain. In the judgment at the end of Karadžić's trial, the Court conceded that "the Bosnian Muslim side was intent on provoking the international community to act on its behalf and, as a result, at times, engaged in targeting UN personnel in the city or opening fire on territory under its control in order to lay blame on the Bosnian Serbs. However, the evidence indicates that the occasions on which this happened pale in significance when compared to the evidence relating to SRK [a Serb military corps based in Sarajevo] fire on the city."[40]

The siege of Sarajevo lasted 1,425 days. It resulted in nearly 14,000 fatalities, of which 5,434 were civilians. During much of the period that Sarajevo was besieged, "moral entrepreneurs" flocked to the city.[41]

Despite the siege, you could still drive around Sarajevo "at the price of a good scare," journalist Emmanuel Carrère explained, and Sarajevo was awash with reporters and filmmakers.[42] The city became a cause célèbre. Although there was violence all over Bosnia, journalists flocked to Sarajevo, and besieged Sarajevo was mostly what we heard about.

NOTES

1. Quoted in Jay Surdukowski, "Is Poetry a War Crime? Reckoning for Radovan Karadzic the Poet-Warrior," *Michigan Journal of International Law*, Vol. 26, No. 2 (2005), p. 686.

2. From 1878 until 1908, Bosnia was formally still part of the Ottoman Empire, but governed by Austria-Hungary. In 1908, Austria-Hungary annexed Bosnia.

3. In 1916, a plaque was placed at the scene of the assassination of Archduke Franz Ferdinand, identifying Princip as a "murderer" and commemorating the deaths of Archduke Franz Ferdinand and Duchess Sophie of Hohenberg, along with a monument in their honor. In 1918, the plaque and monument were removed. In 1930, another plaque was placed by the Yugoslav government—this time to commemorate Gavrilo Princip and his expression of "the longing of people to be free." Ari Shapiro, "The Shifting Legacy of the Man Who Shot Franz Ferdinand," *NPR*, June 27, 2014, https://www.npr.org /sections/parallels/2014/06/27/326164157/the-shifting-legacy-of-the -man-who-shot-franz-ferdinand; Paul Miller, "Compromising Memory: The Site of the Sarajevo Assassination," East European Studies Program of the Woodrow Wilson International Center for Scholars, Meeting Report 333, July 7, 2011, https://www.wilsoncenter .org/publication/333-compromising-memory-the-site-the-sarajevo -assassination.

   This plaque was removed upon the arrival of the Germans in Bosnia and given to Hitler for his fifty-second birthday. After the Second World War, another plaque was erected in 1945, and Princip was honored for liberating Sarajevo "from oppressive German rule." Robert J. Donia, *Sarajevo: A Biography* (Ann Arbor, MI: The University of Michigan Press, 2006), p. 209. In 1953, the Yugoslav government installed the "Assassination Steps," indicating where Princip stood when he shot the archduke and his wife, underneath the already existing plaque commemorating Princip. Quentin Stevens and Mirjana Ristic, "Memories Come to the Surface: Pavement Memorials in Urban Public Spaces," *Journal of Urban Design*, Vol. 20, No. 2 (2015), pp. 273–290. In 1992, the footsteps were destroyed. At that point in history, Princip was seen as a strictly Serbian hero by Bosnian Muslims and Croats. Finally, in 2004, the Bosnian Muslim government erected a neutral and tourist-friendly commemorative plaque. Tea Sindbaek Andersen, "Lessons from Sarajevo and the First World War: From Yugoslav to National Memories," *East European Politics and Societies and Cultures*, Vol. 30, No. 1 (February 2016), pp. 34–54.

4. Paul Miller, "Compromising Memory: The Site of the Sarajevo Assassination," East European Studies Program of the Woodrow Wilson International Center for Scholars, Meeting Report 333, July 7, 2011, https://www.wilsoncenter.org/publication/333-compromising-memory-the-site-the-sarajevo-assassination.

5. "The political union of the Yugoslavs . . . was my basic idea . . . I am a Yugoslav nationalist, aiming for the unification of all Yugoslavs, and I do not care what form of state, but it must be free from Austria," said Gavrilo Princip during his trial. Neven Andjelic, *Bosnia-Herzegovina: The End of a Legacy* (London and Portland: Frank Cass, 2003), p. 11.

6. These included Garašanin network, 1844–1867 (focused on intelligence and propaganda); Matija Ban's (an ethnic Croat) Belgrade Committee, 1860–1861 (focused on guerilla warfare); the officer conspiracy of 1903; Narodna Odbrana (People's Defense), 1908–1914; Ujedinjenje ili smrt (Unification or Death, also known as the Black Hand), 1911–1914; and most important, Mlada Bosna (Young Bosnia). David MacKenzie, "Serbian Nationalist and Military Organizations and the Piedmont Idea, 1844–1914," *East European Quarterly*, Vol. 16, No. 3 (Fall 1982), pp. 323–344.

7. David MacKenzie argues that while Black Hand promoted a greater Serbia, by the time the organization was near its end in 1914, a few of its members favored a Yugoslav state led by Serbia. The only confirmed member of both Black Hand and Young Bosnia was Vladimir Gaćinović, who was the founder of Young Bosnia. As described by MacKenzie, the two organizations were quite different: most members of Black Hand were politically conservative, while most members of Young Bosnia were atheists and either socialist or republicans. Historians are still uncertain as to whether Princip received assistance from the Black Hand. David MacKenzie, "Serbian Nationalist and Military Organizations and the Piedmont Idea, 1844–1914," *East European Quarterly*, Vol. 16, No. 3 (Fall 1982), pp. 323–344.

8. It is also the date that Serbian leader Slobodan Milošević gave his Gazimestan speech, delivered at Kosovo Polje, the site of the battle, on its six hundredth anniversary, exacerbating preexisting tensions between Serbs and Kosovars.

9. According to political scientist Vladimir Petrović, there is a school of thought that believes that Franz Ferdinand visited Sarajevo on St. Vitus Day deliberately to offend the Serbs.

10. Julian Borger, "Radovan Karadžić Tells War Crimes Trial There Was No Ethnic Cleansing in Bosnia," *Guardian*, October 1, 2014, https://www.theguardian.com/world/2014/oct/01/radovan-karadzic-war-crimes-trial-no-ethnic-cleansing-bosnia.

11. International Criminal Tribunal for the former Yugoslavia, *Prosecutor v. Radovan Karadžić—Defense Closing Statement*, Case No. IT-95-5/18, October 1, 2014, http://www.icty.org/x/cases/karadzic/trans/en/141001ED.htm.

12. Croatia was part of the Habsburg monarchy from 1527 to 1918 as the Kingdom of Croatia, which comprised modern-day Croatia and much of modern-day Bosnia and Herzegovina. Austro-Hungarian rule lasted in Bosnia-Herzegovina from 1878 until 1918, when World War I ended. Much of Slovenia had been under Habsburg rule from the fourteenth century until the Austro-Hungarian Empire's dissolution in 1918.

    After the two Balkan wars in 1912 and 1913 and the subsequent dissolution of the Ottoman Empire, the former Ottoman territories were divided between Bulgaria, Greece, and Serbia. Serbia also annexed the area comprising modern North Macedonia, which was renamed Southern Serbia and was subjected to "Serbianization," often violently. Philip J. Cohen, *Serbia's Secret War: Propaganda and the Deceit of History* (College Station: Texas A&M University Press, 1996), p. 11. The Bulgarians, however, "felt cheated over the territorial spoils" and attacked Montenegro, Greece, and Serbia. Tim Judah, *The Serbs: History, Myth and the Destruction of Yugoslavia*, 3rd ed. (New Haven, London: Yale University Press, 2009), p. 71.

13. At the end of World War II, Yugoslavia acquired three small territories from Italy. In 1946, the Communists renamed the country the Federal People's Republic of Yugoslavia and in 1963 renamed it again as the Socialist Federal Republic of Yugoslavia (SFRY).

14. Historian Marko Attila Hoare explains very well why the new (post–World War II) Yugoslavia was resented by the Serbs. Hoare argues that in stark contrast to the interwar period, after World War II, Serbia had the strongest reasons for rebellion against the center, which they did in the 1990s, under Milošević. It was a rebellion, he says, not just against the 1974 constitution, which granted much greater auton-

omy to the republics, but also against the settlement of the Yugoslav national question in the 1940s, which favored non-Serbs. Marko Attila Hoare, "Slobodan Milošević's Place in Serbian History," *European History Quarterly*, Vol. 36, No. 3 (July 2006), pp. 445–462.

According to political scientist Mladen Mrdalj, Serbs especially resented the 1974 constitution because of its failure to secure the human rights of Kosovo Serbs.

15. Gale Stokes, "Independence and the Fate of Minorities (1991–1992)," in Charles Ingrao and Thomas A. Emmert, eds., *Confronting the Yugoslav Controversies: A Scholar's Initiative* (West Lafayette, IN: Purdue University Press, 2013), p. 83.

16. Between 1879 and 1971, the most numerous nationality in Bosnia was Serb. After 1971, Muslims became the dominant group in Bosnia. Robert J. Donia and John V. A. Fine Jr., *Bosnia and Hercegovina: A Tradition Betrayed* (New York: Columbia University Press, 1994), p. 87.

After 1968, Muslims were considered both an ethnic group, equal in status to the five other *narodi*, and a religious group. Most of Yugoslavia's numerous other ethnic groups were classified as *narodnosti*, or nationalities and not "minorities," although they enjoyed rights usually associated with minority rights. Gale Stokes, "Independence and the Fate of Minorities (1991–1992)," in Charles Ingrao and Thomas A. Emmert, eds., *Confronting the Yugoslav Controversies: A Scholar's Initiative* (West Lafayette, IN: Purdue University Press, 2013), p. 83.

17. Duško Sekulić, Garth Massey, and Randy Hodson, "Who Were the Yugoslavs? Failed Sources of a Common Identity in the Former Yugoslavia," *American Sociological Review*, Vol. 59, No. 1 (February 1994), pp. 83–97.

18. Jasna Dragović-Soso, "Why Did Yugoslavia Disintegrate? An Overview of Contending Explanations," in Lenard J. Cohen and Jasna Dragović-Soso, eds., *State Collapse in South-Eastern Europe* (West Lafayette, IN: Purdue University Press, 2008), p. 3. For another overview of the causes of the war, see Nebojša Popov and Drinka Gojković, eds., *The Road to War in Serbia: Trauma and Catharsis* (Budapest, New York: Central European University Press, 1999).

19. Even before its formation as a state, there were both centripetal and centrifugal forces at play in the lands that became Yugoslavia. The Yugoslav Partisans, who took power at the end of World War II in Yugoslavia, condemned "particularist" nationalism as a divisive force, hoping to strengthen allegiance to the new state. All Yugoslavs who

were alive during the war remembered not only the partitioning of Yugoslavia, but also the internecine warfare that claimed hundreds of thousands of lives. Duško Sekulić, Garth Massey, and Randy Hodson, "Who Were the Yugoslavs? Failed Sources of a Common Identity in the Former Yugoslavia," *American Sociological Review*, Vol. 59, No. 1 (February 1994), pp. 83–97. Thus, Yugoslav nationalism was strengthened by "the desire to forget the trauma of World War II," and to identify as a Yugoslav "was to condemn the forces that betrayed the memory of the war and to identify with the efforts of the Partisans to create a progressive, socialist society." Reconciliation was promoted under the banner *bratstvo i jedinstvo* (brotherhood and unity). Alexander J. Motyl, ed., *Encyclopedia of Nationalism*, Vol. 2 (San Diego, CA: Academic Press, 2001), p. 598.

Since the end of the war, Yugoslavia's economy had grown rapidly. Citizens had enjoyed a steadily improving lifestyle, unusual for planned economies. Urbanization and higher rates of education "were expected to reduce the political strength of nationalism, leaving in its place cultural traditions and ethnic pride held in common by all South Slavic people." See Sekulić, Massey, and Hodson, "Who Were the Yugoslavs?" This did not occur, however. A new constitution, put in place in 1974, created an even looser federation by establishing a collective presidency. Now each republic had the right to veto decisions by the presidency. Republic-level Communist party leaders began to see identification with the republics, rather than the federation, as a means to consolidate power. Especially given economic resentments, the weak federation enshrined in the 1974 constitution became a liability rather than a strength. Jasna Dragović-Soso, "Why Did Yugoslavia Disintegrate? An Overview of Contending Explanations," in Lenard J. Cohen and Jasna Dragović-Soso, eds., *State Collapse in South-Eastern Europe* (West Lafayette, IN: Purdue University Press, 2008), p. 10. Political scientist Valerie Bunce writes that the loosening of the federation created nation-like republics and provided them with the "institutions, elites, boundaries, and, ultimately, incentives and opportunities they needed to mount nationalist movements, to liberate themselves from regimes and states, and to construct new regimes and sovereign states in their place." Bunce attributes the severity of the violence during Yugoslavia's breakup to the effectively confederal government, which sowed dissension between the newly emboldened republics. Valerie Bunce, *Subversive Institutions: The Design and Destruc-*

tion of Socialism and the State (Cambridge, UK: Cambridge University Press, 1999), p. 147.

Yugoslavia was highly dependent on imports of oil and consumer goods, and the state borrowed from the International Monetary Fund (IMF). During the oil crisis, the country found itself owing more money to the IMF than it could easily repay. At that time, IMF policy dictated structural reform and harsh austerity. Expert on Balkan affairs Susan Woodward argued that these austerity policies turned ordinary economic tensions between the richer and poorer republics into a threat to the federation. Wealthier republican governments began refusing to meet their obligations to the center, and to question the utility and legitimacy of the state. Susan Woodward, *Balkan Tragedy* (Washington, DC: Brookings, 1995), pp. 79–80. With the IMF-imposed structural reforms, and the enforced reduction in ordinary citizens' wages, citizens' lifestyles were suddenly cut back. By 1989, inflation had reached more than 2,500 percent, and living standards declined by at least a quarter. See Sekulić, Massey, and Hodson, "Who Were the Yugoslavs?" At the Fourteenth National Congress in January 1990, tensions between the Serbian delegation—which proposed a tighter union—and the Slovenian one—which favored a looser federation—reached their peak. Soon after that, the League of Communists of Yugoslavia—which had ruled Yugoslavia for eighty-one years—was dissolved, opening the way for free elections. Thus, for Woodward, Slovenia's actions were as important as the actions of outside powers. See Woodward, *Balkan Tragedy*, pp. 115–116. See also David N. Gibbs, *First Do No Harm: Humanitarian Intervention and the Destruction of Yugoslavia* (Nashville: Vanderbilt University Press, 2009); Steven L. Burg and Paul S. Shoup, *The War in Bosnia-Herzegovina: Ethnic Conflict and International Intervention* (Armonk, NY: M. E. Sharpe, 1999).

20. Both Slovenia's and Croatia's independence was formally recognized by the United Nations in January 1992. Bosnia and Herzegovina, Croatia, and Slovenia were all admitted to the UN on May 22, 1992. Krajina, a largely Serb enclave in Croatia, declared itself the Republika Srpska Krajina (RSK) with the assistance of Serb military forces, independent of Croatia. The RSK served as a model for the creation of a separate Serb entity inside Bosnia, called Republika Srpska (RS). But the temporarily independent RSK would be brutally crushed in Operation Storm in August 1995.

21. Gale Stokes, "Independence and the Fate of Minorities (1991–1992)," in Charles Ingrao and Thomas A. Emmert, eds., *Confronting the Yugoslav Controversies: A Scholar's Initiative* (West Lafayette, IN: Purdue University Press, 2013), p. 83.

22. Dejan Jović, "Fear of Becoming Minority as a Motivator of Conflict in the Former Yugoslavia," *Balkanologie*, Vol. 5, No. 1–2 (December 2001), pp. 21–36. See also Alina Mungiu-Pippidi, "Lessons Learned: From Nationalism to State Building After Communism," East European Studies Program of the Woodrow Wilson International Center for Scholars, Meeting Report 303, July 7, 2001, https://www.wilsoncenter. org/publication/303-lessons-learned-nationalism-to-state-building-after-communism. Cited in Gale Stokes, "Independence and the Fate of Minorities (1991–1992)," in Charles Ingrao and Thomas A. Emmert, eds., *Confronting the Yugoslav Controversies: A Scholar's Initiative* (West Lafayette, IN: Purdue University Press, 2013).

23. Dejan Jović, "Fear of Becoming Minority as a Motivator of Conflict in the Former Yugoslavia," *Balkanologie*, Vol. 5, No. 1–2 (December 2001), pp. 21–36; Dejan Jović, "Communist Yugoslavia and Its 'Others,'" in John R. Lampe and Mark Mazower, eds., *Ideologies and National Identities: The Case of Twentieth-Century Southeastern Europe* (Budapest: Central European University Press, 2004), pp. 277–302.

24. Dejan Jović, "Fear of Becoming Minority as a Motivator of Conflict in the Former Yugoslavia," *Balkanologie*, Vol. 5, No. 1–2 (December 2001), pp. 21–36.

25. Vladimir Gligorov, "What If They Will Not Give Up?" *Eastern European Politics and Societies,* Vol. 9, No. 3 (Fall 1995), p. 510.

26. Serbs had voted earlier to create their own ethnically defined state within Bosnia-Herzegovina. On November 9 and 10, 1991, a referendum on independence was held among Serbs. The majority voted to remain inside Yugoslavia. In late January 1992, Serbs agreed to a referendum on Bosnia's independence, but only after a Serb entity was established within Bosnia. The Bosniaks rejected this.

27. According to a declassified U.S. Department of Defense document, "The Bosnia Serbs [sic] therefore enjoyed a significant advantage in heavy weapons, but the largely Muslim Bosnian government forces outnumbered them 2 to 1 in infantry. The Serbs' shortage of infantry meant that they could not usually take the larger towns by direct assault, but had to adopt siege tactics, hoping that shelling and cutting off utilities, food and supplies would drive out the population." U.S.

Department of Defense, Freedom of Information Division, Joint History Office, "The Evolution of US Policy Toward the Former Republic of Yugoslavia and Bosnia Since 1990," September 1997, FOIA Ref: 16-F-0858, p. 4. Declassified March 29, 2019.

28. International Criminal Tribunal for the Former Yugoslavia, *Prosecutor v. Karadžić—Amended Indictment*, Case No. IT-95-5/18, April 28, 2000, http://www.icty.org/x/cases/karadzic-mladic/ind/en/kar-ai000428e.htm.

  Serbs controlled parts of Sarajevo, including the neighborhood of Grbavica, until the end of the war. But many of Sarajevo's Serbs left the city by the end of the war, because they were afraid of Muslim revenge strikes. Robert J. Donia, *Sarajevo: A Biography* (Ann Arbor, MI: The University of Michigan Press, 2006), p. 283.

29. David Campbell, "Atrocity, Memory, Photography: Imaging the Concentration Camps of Bosnia—The Case of ITN Versus Living Marxism," *Journal of Human Rights*, Vol. 1, No. 1 (2002), p. 6, cited in Dragana Obradović, *Writing the Yugoslav Wars: Literature, Postmodernism, and the Ethics of Representation* (Toronto: University of Toronto Press, 2016), p. 38.

30. Dragana Obradović, *Writing the Yugoslav Wars: Literature, Postmodernism, and the Ethics of Representation* (Toronto: University of Toronto Press, 2016), p. 38.

31. Semezdin Mehmedinović, *Sarajevo Blues*, trans. Ammiel Alcalay (San Francisco: City Lights Books, 1998), p. 36. Chetniks were monarchists who defended the Yugoslav Kingdom against the Nazis and Nazi allies and collaborators during the Second World War.

32. Joint Chiefs of Staff, Joint History Office, "The Evolution of US Policy Toward the Former Republic of Yugoslavia and Bosnia Since 1990," September 1997, U.S. Department of Defense, Freedom of Information Division, FOIA Ref: 16-F-0858, p. 4. Declassified March 29, 2019.

33. Scott Anderson, *The Man Who Tried to Save the World: The Dangerous Life and Mysterious Disappearance of Fred Cuny* (New York: Doubleday, 1999); Michael Hayden, interview with author, November 12, 2015. Michael Hayden is a retired United States Air Force four-star general and served as both director of the National Security Agency and CIA. Fred Cuny died in Chechnya in 1995, and was therefore unable to verify this story.

34. One theory is that the Bosnian-Herzegovinian gentry converted in order to protect their wealth and privileged status during the Ottoman period. This theory is the one that Karadžić frequently disclaimed

to me. It comes in two variants. The first, to which Serb nationalists naturally subscribe, claims that the Bosnian Muslims were formerly Orthodox Serbs. The second is that they were formerly Croat Catholics. Each of these theories has its pet historians. According to Tone Bringa, these theories oversimplify the process of conversions—not only who converted, but why. Those who converted came from a broad cross section of society. Bringa argues that the Bosnian gentry were among the first to convert to Islam, perhaps to protect their property and privileges, but that the peasants converted soon after. Another popular theory, also rejected by contemporary historians, is that Bosnia's Muslims were Bogomils who converted to Islam. Bogomilism was a sect of Christianity founded in the tenth century which pushed against ecclesiastical hierarchies, resisted church and state authorities, and rejected the material world as the work of Satan. Tone Bringa, *Being Muslim the Bosnian Way* (Princeton: Princeton University Press, 1995), pp. 14–15. See also: John V. A. Fine, *The Bosnian Church: A New Interpretation* (New York: Columbia University Press, 1975), p. 385.

Historian and political journalist Noel Malcolm argues that the Bosnian Church had disappeared prior to the Ottoman invasion, and that the identification of the Bosnian Church as Bogomil turns out to be based on "wishful thinking." In Malcolm's view, twentieth-century Bosnian Muslims are attracted to the Bogomil theory because "instead of being seen as mere renegades from Catholicism or Orthodoxy (to which, at various times, Croats and Serbs have suggested that they should 'return'), they could now be regarded as descendants of the membership of an authentically and peculiarly Bosnian Church; and their turning to Islam could be described not as an act of weakness, but as a final gesture of defiance against their Christian persecutors." But, he says, modern scholarship has demolished the theory that the Islamicization of Bosnia consisted of a mass conversion of the Bosnian Church. Noel Malcolm, *Bosnia: A Short History* (New York: New York University Press, 1994), pp. 27, 29.

35. No religious institutions were destroyed in Sarajevo, but in Bosnia as a whole 1,180 mosques were destroyed, in addition to 580 Croatian and 290 Serbian churches. Helen Walasek, *Bosnia and the Destruction of Cultural Heritage* (New York: Routledge, 2016), pp. 152–154.

36. András Riedlmayer, "Erasing the Past: The Destruction of Libraries and Archives in Bosnia-Herzegovina," *Middle East Studies Association*

Bulletin, Vol. 29, No. 1 (July 1995), available at https://web.archive.
org/web/20120118204551/http://fp.arizona.edu/mesassoc/Bulletin/
bosnia.htm; András J. Riedlmayer, "The Destruction of Cultural Heritage in Bosnia-Herzegovina, 1992–1996: A Post-War Survey of Selected Municipalities," *Bosnia-Herzegovina Cultural Heritage Report* (2002).

37. András Riedlmayer, "Erasing the Past: The Destruction of Libraries and Archives in Bosnia-Herzegovina," *Middle East Studies Association Bulletin*, Vol. 29, No. 1 (July 1995), available at https://web.archive
.org/web/20120118204551/http://fp.arizona.edu/mesassoc/Bulletin
/bosnia.htm.

38. With the breakup of the SFRY, the JNA ceased to exist. Its personnel and equipment were divided into three separate but still interconnected Serb armies, the Army of Yugoslavia, the Serbian Army of Krajina, and the VRS (the Bosnian Serb Army). This last was formed in RS. Thus, the UN-imposed arms embargo affected only the Bosniaks, not the VRS, which was extremely well equipped. Nevenka Tromp, *Prosecuting Slobodan Milošević: The Unfinished Trial* (London and New York: Routledge, 2016), p. 142.

39. Ironically, the cellist would be "dragooned" to dig trenches by an infamous member of a Bosniak organized-crime gang, Caco Topalović, in 1993. While any man—especially Serb but also Muslim—could be rounded up by Caco's men, "Caco's favorite targets were Sarajevo artists and intellectuals, whom he regarded as soft and cowardly." Smailović was forced to dig trenches for seven weeks, "within shooting range of Serb snipers." Smailović was freed after forty-seven days. Tom Gjelten, *Sarajevo Daily: A City and Its Newspaper Under Siege* (New York: HarperCollins, 1995), pp. 100, 196.

40. International Criminal Tribunal for the former Yugoslavia, *Prosecutor v. Karadžić—Judgment Summary*, Case No. IT-95-5/18, March 24, 2016, http://www.icty.org/x/cases/karadzic/tjug/en/160324_judgement_
summary.pdf; Leonard Doyle, "Muslims 'Slaughter Their Own People': Bosnia Bread Queue Massacre Was Propaganda Ploy, UN Told," *Independent*, August 22, 1992, http://www.independent.co.uk/news
/muslims-slaughter-their-own-people-bosnia-bread-queue-massacre
-was-propaganda-ploy-un-told-1541801.html.

See also: International Criminal Tribunal for the former Yugoslavia, *Prosecutor v. Karadžić—Judgment*, Case No. IT-95-5/18, March 24, 2016, http://www.icty.org/x/cases/karadzic/tjug/en/160324_judgement.pdf; David Owen, *Balkan Odyssey* (New York: Harcourt Brace,

1995), p. 112; Philip Corwin, *Dubious Mandate: A Memoir of the UN in Bosnia, Summer 1995* (Durham: Duke University Press, 1999), pp. 39, 97.

For an excellent analysis of VRS general Ratko Mladić's approach to propaganda, and a discussion about the arbitrary distinction between ethnic cleansing and genocide, see Edina Bećirević, "The Issue of Genocidal Intent and Denial of Genocide: A Case Study of Bosnia and Herzegovina," *Eastern European Politics and Societies,* Vol. 24, No. 4 (Fall 2010), pp. 480-502. Bećirević quotes Mladić, "We cannot . . . [use] a sieve to sift so that only Serbs . . . stay, or [so] that the Serbs fall through and the rest leave. . . . I do not know how Mr. Krajišnik and Mr. Karadžić would explain that to the world. That would be genocide." He also said, ". . . We are not going to say that we are going to destroy the power supply pylons or turn off the water supply, no, because that would turn America out of its seat, but . . . one day there is no water at all in Sarajevo. [Why] it is we do not know . . . and the same with electrical power . . . we have to wisely tell the world it was they who were shooting, hit the transmission line and the power went off, they were shooting at the power supply facilities. . . . That is what diplomacy is." International Criminal Tribunal for the Former Yugoslavia, *Prosecutor v. Momčilo Krajišnik – Judgment,* Case No. IT-00-39-T, September 27, 2006, http://www.icty.org/x/cases/krajisnik/tjug/en/kra-jud060927e.pdf. Cited in Edina Bećirević, "The Issue of Genocidal Intent and Denial of Genocide: A Case Study of Bosnia and Herzegovina," *Eastern European Politics and Societies,* Vol. 24, No. 4 (Fall 2010), pp. 480-502.

41. The term "moral entrepreneur" was coined by American sociologist Howard S. Becker. A moral entrepreneur is any person, group, or organization that attempts to influence groups within a society to adopt or maintain a societal norm. Moral entrepreneurs can generate moral panics around behaviors perceived as undermining the norm they seek to uphold. The pro-choice and pro-life movements are examples of two groups of moral entrepreneurs on opposing sides of the same issue, i.e., abortion.

42. Emmanuel Carrère, *Limonov: The Outrageous Adventures of the Radical Soviet Poet Who Became a Bum in New York, a Sensation in France, and a Political Antihero in Russia,* trans. John Lambert (New York: Farrar, Straus and Giroux, 2014), p. 217.

Chapter Five

PETNJICA

Radovan Karadžić was born in a tiny hamlet in the Durmitor Mountains, close to a UNESCO-designated wilderness in north-western Montenegro. The name of the village is Petnjica. Every time he mentioned the place during our prison talks, there was a tiny pause in the speed of my writing, as I was unsure how to spell it. Eventually, he took matters in hand. He grabbed my notebook and spelled it out for me, in big block letters, as if for a small child. He pressed so hard with the cheap pen the guards had given me that he made tiny holes atop the *j* and *i*. Now the spelling of the village is etched into my mind.

Karadžić, the eldest of his parents' five children, spoke of Petnjica with a kind of reverence. He told me about running up and down the hills, the profusion of fruit trees, the mighty oaks where family members had been shot by the Communists. "We had three springs, with very good water. We had very good plums," he said. Before a highway was built, it was nearly impossible to get out of the village in winter. But to build the highway, oak trees—which many Serbs consider sacred—had to be destroyed, and for Karadžić, the village was changed forever.[1] After the highway was built, Petnjica became "a broken nest," he wrote in a poem he later published, as if "there were no childhood," as if "the bad spirit has passed this way."

Karadžić's mother, Jovanka, was born in 1923, one of six

children, in the nearby village of Dobra Sela. She was a "scrappy, energetic peasant girl" with no formal education.[2] Jovanka had met Radovan's father, Vuko, when she was in her late teens, and married him in 1943. (Radovan's father's formal name was Vuk. I use the name Vuko, which is a nickname, because that was how Radovan referred to his father.)

"She used to recite epic poetry for me every night," Karadžić told me. Then he demonstrated how she chanted. I didn't understand the words, but the sound was moving.

There was a change in the atmosphere of the room. He was getting excited.

"I learned many of these poems by heart before I learned to read," he said.

Vuko was born in 1912 in Petnjica, the youngest of thirteen children. Radovan told me a number of times that, as a result, his father was "spoiled." According to Radovan, Vuko had breastfed until he was seven years old; soon after that, he started to smoke. His father, Radovan said, had "an oral fixation." Radovan did not seem to be quite as fond of his father as he was of his mother. It would be a couple of years before I understood what this antipathy might have been about.

The Karadžić men were famous for their skill at playing the *gusle*—a lyre-like instrument that accompanies the *guslar*'s recitation of epic poems or ballads. Most of the epic poems tell stories about the Ottoman occupation and the Southern Slavs' struggle to achieve their freedom. Vuko was an especially accomplished *guslar*, Radovan said. "My friends and I once asked my late father how it was possible to know so many poems by heart. And my father said that if a singer forgets a line, he can substitute a new one. If the new line is better than the old one, other singers will continue to use the new one. This is why our epic poetry is so great; it was always being improved upon." The great folklorist Albert Lord compared Serbian epic poetry to Homeric ballads and referred to Prince Marko Kraljević—a heroic character found in many of the ballads—as Serbia's Hercules.[3]

The Karadžić clan were Chetniks, monarchists who defended the Yugoslav Kingdom against the Nazis and Nazi allies and collaborators during the Second World War. The Chetniks also fought the Communists for control of postwar Yugoslavia, at times collaborating with the Axis powers, and lost. There was a civil war at the same time World War II was under way. Before Radovan was born, his father was sent to eastern Bosnia to fight the Bosniak Ustasha (Muslims who were Nazi collaborators).[4] When Vuko came back from the front, he was shot and almost killed, and then imprisoned by the Communists for the first five years of his eldest son's life. Radovan told me the story of his father's capture five different times, each time slightly differently. I am not sure if he thought I wouldn't remember the story, or if he was reciting it, both for me and for himself, like a ballad, the same way *guslars* recite epic poems. I would also hear slightly different versions of the story from Radovan's brother, Luka, when I met him in a Belgrade bar in 2017, and later, from his cousin in Montenegro. Radovan's mother told a version of the story of Vuko's encounter with the Partisans to an interviewer for the newspaper *Svedok*, while also sending a message to her son, who was then the most wanted man in Europe.

While he was a fugitive, Karadžić was sought by NATO forces, the Yugoslav Tribunal, and a special intelligence unit in Belgrade. Remarkably, his mother urged him to commit suicide if he were captured by any of these hunters. "Do not surrender to them alive, Radovan, my son; better to be dead than a traitor. Do not yield; may your courageous heart never betray you!" she said.[5]

A translation of the interview was later published on a U.S.-based white nationalist website called Stormfront. In the interview, Jovanka says that she believed that it would be a betrayal of Serbdom for Radovan to submit to the judgment of international law, as faithless and cowardly an act as the treacherous acts of Vuk Branković, the most famous traitor in Serbian folklore. Branković is said to have betrayed his father-in-law, Prince Lazar, in the famous Battle of Kosovo, which took place on June 28, 1389, at Kosovo Polje (Field of Blackbirds).[6] Although Prince Lazar and Vuk Branković are historical figures, historians are not sure that this betrayal actually occurred.

The notion that historical animosities, including the Battle of Kosovo in 1389, were responsible for the start of the war was in fashion in the West early in the Yugoslav wars, when Western governments were reluctant to intervene. This is the "ancient hatreds" hypothesis. Robert Kaplan's book *Balkan Ghosts*, which promulgated the idea, was famously read by President Bill Clinton.[7] In the words of President Clinton's secretary of state, Warren Christopher, "It's really a tragic problem. The hatred between all three groups—the Bosnians and the Serbs and the Croatians—is almost unbelievable. It's almost terrifying, and it's centuries old. That really is a problem from hell. . . . The United States simply doesn't have the means to make people in that region of the world like each other."[8]

Kaplan's book was rejected by scholars of Yugoslavia as well as by political scientists, sparking an entirely new body of literature, a kind of anti-Kaplan industry.[9] I have come to believe that there is more truth to Kaplan's hypothesis than political scientists have claimed. The myths and memories of historical animosities don't, in and of themselves, explain the outbreak of the war. But leaders were able to use these myths and memories to their advantage. This is true not only of the 1389 Battle of Kosovo (evoked by Serbia's President Milošević in his famous 1989 speech), but of more recent wounds.[10] During World War II, more Yugoslavs were killed in internecine battles by fellow Yugoslavs than by outside powers. Political scientist Lenard Cohen observed that in attempting to explain Yugoslavia's demise, analysts lurched from an "ancient hatreds" paradigm (which justified inaction by Western governments) to a "loathsome leaders" one (which justified intervention), neither of which he considered to be valid.[11] Cohen's words strike me as correct.

While it is impossible to measure the impact, Radovan Karadžić heard a great deal about the antipathy between Serbs and Muslims from his mother, mostly via the epic poetry she recited for him.

"It is nothing new in his family to perish for Serbdom," Radovan's mother said in the published interview, in which she urged her son to commit suicide rather than be rendered to the international Tribunal. "And Radovan would not be the first among his lineage to meet with this fate." Then she launched into the story about the Communists' attempt to murder her Chetnik husband at the end of the World War II, the story I was to hear so many times.[12]

Radovan's mother told the interviewer, "I remember three men came to the front of the house, right at twilight. They asked: who is Vuko Karadžić and is he here. He [Vuko] answered; he had no reason to hide. They led him away by some footpaths, one in front and two behind him. At that time, members of the Yugoslav secret police had the habit of singing when they were taking someone to be executed. Vuko saw what awaited him and attempted to escape. They shot him from an automatic rifle and wounded him in several places. He pretended to be dead and they, seeing him all covered in blood, believed him to be dead. When they left, he somehow managed to get back home and we treated his wounds. And he lived. Nevertheless, after that he was arrested and spent five years in prison."[13]

Jovanka said that Radovan inherited his sense of obligation toward the Serbian people from his father and his ancestors. "His father fought for the same thing," she said.[14]

—

Radovan had no memory of seeing his father during the first five years of his life. What he did remember was the beauty of Petnjica, which he recounted for me many times. Most of the villagers drove cows up the Durmitor Mountains in the summer. He said that he and his mother both loved farm animals, and they insisted on keeping cows even when the family moved to a bigger town.

All the children in the village would take fruit from the trees in the orchards, but Vuko's children were held to a higher standard: forbidden to take a single plum. Telling me this reminds Radovan of how his mother raised him to be respectful and polite at all times, more so than the other villagers. "If someone came into a room, we were taught to stand up. Even children from the neighborhood. We never ate from the same plate, as other families did. Another family axiom: you always leave the bigger portion for others."

Radovan maintains these habits of politeness even in the prison. "I keep wine so that if a priest comes here, I can offer it to him. We always offer whatever we have to others; we always offer the bigger part." He was unceasingly polite even with me, always offering me food and drink.

"In the first five years of my life," he said, "I was never beaten. I was never hit. My mother never kicked me." I noted the wistful look that came over his face. Over time, I would come to associate this look with his thinking of his mother.

He seemed to be implying, perhaps inadvertently, that when his father got out of prison, he beat and kicked his first son. When I asked, he said, "My father was a strict disciplinarian. But he hit me less than he hit my siblings. I was afraid that my father was very harsh with the other children. My father did beat me. But he didn't beat me that much." Then he added, "I don't believe in being harsh with children. I never beat my own children."

Was he worried that I might draw conclusions about the supposed connection between authoritarian child-rearing practices and the creation of authoritarian personalities, a subject much studied after World War II? Radovan had told me that he had spent time with a small group of psychiatrists when he visited Columbia University on an International Research and Exchanges scholarship in 1974–1975.[15] He had also studied at the London Institute of Group Analysis, which offered courses in Zagreb. I tried to find every one of the professors he mentioned by name, or others I knew would have taught him or known him. The only one who remembered him well was the Croatian psychiatrist, Dr. Angel. We were sitting together in her Zagreb apartment. She told me that Dr. Bertram Schaffner, an expert on authoritarian child-rearing practices in prewar Germany whom she had met at a psychiatry conference in Opatija, Yugoslavia, had spent time with Karadžić when he was visiting Columbia.[16] Dr. Angel said that Dr. Schaffner had stayed with Karadžić and his wife in their apartment in Sarajevo and attended grand rounds at Koscvo Clinic, where Karadžić was a staff psychiatrist. Schaffner and Karadžić had also traveled together around Yugoslavia. Schaffner had told Dr. Angel that his conclusion was that Serbian child-rearing customs—even in the 1970s—were still quite authoritarian and patriarchal, and not that different from prewar German practices. I wondered if Karadžić was remembering the observations of his deceased colleague, Bertram Schaffner, when he kept protesting that his father didn't beat him that much.

While I was thinking all this, I noticed that Karadžić was looking away. He too seemed to be dwelling on something.

"I didn't like it when my father got out of prison," he said.

I'm pretty sure he didn't mean to tell me that. I was surprised to see those words when I read my notes to type them up. Sometimes when people accidentally tell me revealing things, I deliberately don't think about what they've said, perhaps out of respect for their privacy.

Vuko had represented himself at his trial, just as Radovan had done at his trial in The Hague. "The Communists asked my father, 'Were you a good Partisan?' He said no. And they asked, 'Were you a good Chetnik?' and he said yes. Then they asked him, 'Would you have killed us if you could?' He said, 'Yes, I would like to have killed all of you.' He was crazy. He told the truth."

Was he crazy, I wondered, because he told the truth about his desire to murder his captors, or because he actually would have killed them in his rage?

"He was stubborn," Karadžić added. If Vuko had pled guilty, he would have received a shorter sentence. Instead, he defied the Court.

"My family was very prominent," Karadžić said. "Both my father and my younger brother Luka were very well known for playing the *gusle* and singing." Vuko's purported honesty and interest in justice, and the Karadžić family's prominence, were themes for Karadžić. He would repeat these claims many times, as if trying to persuade himself of their veracity.

NOTES

1. Oaks are thought to have special powers, Karadžić explained to me. Some of the trees they cut down to build the highway were seven hundred years old, he said. "Blasphemy," he called it. Even before the highway, "when the Communists came—that was a period of desecration," he said. In both Slavic and Norse mythology, oaks are very important. Serbian Orthodoxy incorporated pagan practices, including the reverence for oaks. On Orthodox Christmas Eve (called *Badnje veče*) village men pass from house to house with a burning oaken log, using it to light the hearth in each family's home.
2. Robert J. Donia, *Radovan Karadžić: Architect of Bosnian Genocide* (New York: Cambridge University Press, 2015), p. 23.

3. Albert Bates Lord, *Epic Singers and Oral Traditions* (Ithaca, NY: Cornell University Press, 1991).

Albert Bates Lord, "The Effect of the Turkish Conquest on Balkan Epic Tradition," in Henrik Birmbaum and Speros Vryonis Jr., eds., *Aspects of the Balkans: Continuity and Change: Contributions to the International Balkan Conference Held at UCLA, October 23–28, 1969* (The Hague: De Gruyter, 2018).

Novelist Marguerite Yourcenar wrote the story "Marko's Smile," based on the epic of Marko Kraljević. Marko is an interesting character in that he is forced to serve his Ottoman masters, but is often tricking them.

4. Robert J. Donia, *Radovan Karadžić: Architect of the Bosnian Genocide* (New York: Cambridge University Press, 2015), pp. 24–25.

5. Nikola Marković, "Jovanka Karadžić, Mother of the Former RS President, Sends a Message to Her Son Through 'Svedok,'" quoted in ktvrdi [pseud.], "Karadžić's Mother— Do Not Surrender, My Son," Stormfront (forum), September 19, 2003, https://www.stormfront .org/forum/t54165/.

6. Prince Lazar (1329–1389) was a medieval Serbian ruler who sought to resurrect the Serbian Empire. He was killed at the Battle of Kosovo on June 15, 1389, while at the helm of an army to stave off the encroaching Ottoman Empire. The Ottoman ruler, Sultan Murad I, was also killed in the battle. Prince Lazar is venerated by the Serbian Orthodox Church as a saint and a martyr.

7. Michael T. Kaufman, "The Dangers of Letting a President Read," *New York Times*, May 22, 1999, http://www.nytimes.com/1999/05/22/ books/the-dangers-of-letting-a-president-read.html?mcubz=0.

8. Thomas L. Friedman, "Bosnia Reconsidered; Where Candidate Clinton Saw a Challenge the President Sees an Insoluble Quagmire," *New York Times*, April 8, 1993, https://www.nytimes.com/1993/04/08 /world/bosnia-reconsidered-where-candidate-clinton-saw-challenge -president-sees.html.

9. Author Robert Kaplan's theory—that the conflicts in the Balkans were based on ancient hatreds between ethnic factions—was met with a variety of counterarguments, among them observations about the frequency of shared celebration of religious holidays, intermarriage, and political cooperation across ethnoreligious lines; claims that the "ancient hatreds" argument was essentialist, portraying the Balkans as a land of barbarians; or assertions that ethnic tensions

had been deliberately stoked by cynical politicians seeking to cement their hold on power. In response, some observers pointed out that the cooperation and even intermarriage that was often seen among the educated elite in urban areas was not necessarily as common in rural areas, leading another group of scholars to characterize the war as a rural-urban divide or "the revenge of the countryside." Based on the excellent summary in Jasna Dragović-Soso, "Why Did Yugoslavia Disintegrate? An Overview of Contending Explanations," in Lenard J. Cohen and Jasna Dragović-Soso, eds., *State Collapse in South-Eastern Europe* (West Lafayette, IN: Purdue University Press, 2008), p. 3.

10. On June 28, 1989, several hundred thousand Serbs assembled in Kosovo on the six hundredth anniversary of the Battle of Kosovo. For many weeks prior, the bones of Prince Lazar, who had died in the battle against Ottoman invaders, were taken on a tour of Serbia, Montenegro, and Bosnia. Serbs came to visit the Orthodox monastery outside Pristina, where stalls sold icon-style posters of Prince Lazar, Jesus Christ, and Slobodan Milošević standing side by side. Milošević told the crowd, "After six centuries we are again engaged in battles and quarrels. They are not armed battles, but this cannot be excluded yet." Misha Glenny, who witnessed the speech, observed that the message to the Slovenes, Croats, Muslims, and Albanians was this: "Look with what ease I can mobilize over 1 million Serbs." Misha Glenny, *The Fall of Yugoslavia: The Third Balkan War* (New York: Penguin Books, 1996), p. 35.

The speech, and the crowd's thunderous approbation, is largely considered in the literature to have been a symbolic turning point in the short history of the Yugoslav state, signaling the beginning of the end. Professor of history David Gibbs gathered several such observations he describes as "simplifications." David N. Gibbs, *First Do No Harm: Humanitarian Intervention and the Destruction of Yugoslavia* (Nashville: Vanderbilt University Press, 2009), pp. 45–46.

Interestingly, economic stress increased nationalism and ethnic hatred. According to polling carried out by the Consortium of Social Research Institutes of Yugoslavia in late 1989 and early 1990, ethnic tensions and hatred grew strongest in the richest regions, forced to subsidize the poorer ones, as well as in the poorest regions. The most vehement racist sentiments were measured among ethnic Albanians, who lived mostly in Kosovo. There, ethnic Albanian students began rioting in 1981, demanding greater autonomy from Serbia, leading to a harsh crackdown on the part of the Yugoslav government. Milošević, who became president of Serbia in 1989, began exploiting these ethnic tensions in 1987, while he was serving as the president of the Central Committee of the Serbian Communist party, most notably in his aforementioned famous speech, two years later, at the Field of Blackbirds on the six hundredth anniversary of the Battle of Kosovo. Randy Hodson, Duško Sekulić, and Garth Massey, "National Tolerance in the Former Yugoslavia," *American Journal of Sociology*, Vol. 99, No. 6 (May 1994), pp. 1534–1558, cited in Gibbs, *First Do No Harm*.

11. Lenard J. Cohen, *Serpent in the Bosom: The Rise and Fall of Slobodan Milošević* (Boulder, CO: Westview Press, 2001), pp. 451–455.

12. The story about the large number of Karadžić family members who were murdered in the region of Petnjica was confirmed by Milovan Djilas, the famous Yugoslav dissident who had fought with the Partisans during the war. He wrote that a large number of the men who were executed were "of the Drobnjak clan of Karadžići—the clan of the reformer of the Serbian language, Vuk Karadžić." Milovan Djilas, *Wartime*, trans. Michael Petrovich (New York: Harcourt Brace Jovanovich, 1977), p. 156.

13. ktvrdi [pseud.], "Karadžić's Mother—Do Not Surrender, My Son," Stormfront (forum), September 19, 2003, https://www.stormfront.org /forum/t54165/.

   In Radovan and Luka's version of their father's escape from the Communists, Vuko Karadžić put out his hand and deflected the bullet that was meant to have killed him. Instead of hitting his heart or his head, it hit his leg, wounding but not killing him. Also, according to Radovan, his father had whistled, and was carried home by his wife and another relative.

14. ktvrdi [pseud.], "Karadžić's Mother—Do Not Surrender, My Son," Stormfront (forum), September 19, 2003, https://www.stormfront.org /forum/t54165/.

15. Robert J. Donia, *Radovan Karadžić: Architect of the Bosnian Genocide* (New York: Cambridge University Press, 2015).

16. Dr. Bertram Schaffner also served as an army psychiatrist at the Nuremberg trials. See: Bertram Schaffner, *Father Land: A Study of Authoritarianism in the German Family* (New York: Columbia University Press, 1948).

Chapter Six

VISITING THE POET'S FAMILY

Vuko and Jovanka Karadžić had four more children after Radovan: Luka, Ivanka, Ivan, and Radosav. Radovan was closest to Luka, the sibling nearest to him in age.

I met Luka Karadžić in Belgrade in the summer of 2017, after my last interview with Radovan. It was a hot July afternoon in the middle of a heat wave. The sun was blindingly bright. I arrived at the bar of the Hotel Prague, an art deco structure designed in 1929. The bar was dark and cool, with wood-paneled walls. It was too late for lunch but still too early for drinks, and the bar was empty of customers, a respite from the hectic, sunny streets. Luka was late, as I had been warned was his habit.

Unlike his famous brother, Luka is relatively unschooled. He completed high school in Nikšić, Montenegro, and then worked there as a mailman.[1] During the war, he moved to the much larger capital city of Belgrade and transformed himself into a highly successful businessman with concerns in Bosnia, Serbia, and Montenegro. He acquired a lumber mill in Bosnia, got into commercial-scale bread-baking and fruit-juice manufacturing, and leased gas stations from a company called Jugopetrol in Serbia. After the war, when NATO and the UN began pressuring Serbia to assist in locating indicted war criminals, including Radovan, Luka complained that intelligence operatives were trying to hamper his business interests.[2] The U.S. government alleged, in 2002, that

Jugopetrol was using Luka as a conduit to funnel money to his fugitive brother, and under pressure from the United States, the company ended its contract with Luka.[3]

During the war, Radovan's position had conferred on his brother Luka access to both money and power. Luka has often been referred to as a war profiteer and reportedly had connections with organized crime.[4] At the time we met, Luka was still dealing with a drunk-driving case that had plagued him since 2005, when his car hit a twenty-one-year-old woman head-on, killing her. A year after our meeting, thirteen years after the accident, he was finally sentenced to two years in prison. (The maximum sentence is twelve years.) The deceased victim's father attributed the delay in the case to continuing political support for the Karadžić family among Serb nationalists. However, there were also problems with the way evidence was presented to the court, and the first case ended in a mistrial.[5]

While I was waiting for him, I thought about what I'd read about him in media reporting or heard about him from his brother. Luka has consistently been his brother's most staunch defender. While Radovan was a fugitive, trying to avoid being extradited to the Netherlands for trial, Luka reportedly communicated with him every day.[6] He had set up the International Committee for the Defense of Radovan Karadžić, which was said to be supported by Serb nationalist intellectuals, academics, and writers.[7] Luka repeatedly told reporters that he and his family felt betrayed by Washington's refusal to abide by a promise of immunity from prosecution that he and his brother both insist was offered by Richard Holbrooke, then U.S. special envoy to the Balkans. This promise was allegedly offered in exchange for Radovan Karadžić's retreating from political life, which he did in July 1996. At one point, Luka even told the media that the family had "photographic proof" of the guarantee of immunity. The alleged agreement was published in two Banja Luka newspapers in 2007, but according to former ICTY public affairs officer and French journalist Florence Hartmann, the signatures were obviously forged.[8] Luka said that the family didn't trust the international court in The Hague to give his brother a fair trial. But Radovan, he said, was more optimistic about his prospects than the rest of the family. Luka reported that his brother was convinced that if he were to be tried, "the truth" would come out, that "he was never an aggressor," and that "he tried to prevent the outbreak of war in Bosnia."[9] This is similar to what I heard many times from Radovan himself—that if the Yugoslav Tribunal were a "real court," he'd be acquitted and eventually rewarded for the number of people he had "protected" from harm.

Luka finally arrived. My first thought was how different he was from his older brother in appearance and manner. To begin with, their hairstyles. Luka is almost entirely bald, with sparse white hair lying flat on the sides of his remarkably round head. Unlike his tall elder brother, Luka is squat and muscular, with a kind of coiled power. He had a vague look to his eyes, which I associate with heavy drinkers. Knowing all I did about him, I felt shy to look straight at him, but when I did, his eyes shifted sideways, as if he didn't want to be too keenly observed. I noticed the tense cords in his thick neck. To my eye, he had a thuggish aspect. I was actually somewhat afraid of him and felt glad to have my translator with me. Luka could damage a person, I thought, if he were moved to punch. Radovan, in contrast, sought distinction as a member of the intelligentsia. He had adopted the style and mannerisms of a Central European gentleman of indeterminate origin. In court, and with me, Radovan was unimpeachably polite, with an almost aristocratic bearing. I still retain an image of him from a photograph taken early in the war, when he was involved in peace talks in Geneva. During those ill-fated negotiations, the future war criminal always wore a white scarf draped loosely about his neck, like a dandy dressed for the opera. In contrast, Luka had a furtive look. He seemed to want to fade into the background. He sported a carefully trimmed mustache, a symbol of waning Balkan patriarchy. He wore the kind of clothing you might have seen in Communist Yugoslavia: a faded, short-sleeved, button-down shirt and jeans. When I pressed my translator for his impressions, he said that Luka seemed like "a hunted animal that can't run away, so he decided to pretend he wasn't worth catching."

I asked Luka about his *gusle* playing, which his brother had told me about. He had recorded a couple of albums, he said, and added, "Most people learn history from *gusle*, not in school." I've heard Bosniaks say that of Serbs as a complaint about their poor understanding of history, not something to be boasted about, so I was surprised to hear Luka admit this.

"We were slaves under the Ottomans for five hundred years," Luka said. "What would you do if someone tried to boss you around in your own house? That is what the Turks did to us. It is normal to resist when someone is trying to impose his will on you."

Our tea arrived just as Luka's phone rang. He gave the phone a withering look as if trying to frighten it into silence. Then he picked it up, grunted a few words to the person obviously harassing him, and turned back to me.

He then said, seeming to contradict his previous statement, that the Serbs shouldn't have fought the Ottomans, especially not for such a long time. "If someone is stronger, make a deal." Is this the way his brother thought about the deal he claimed to have struck with Holbrooke, to leave political life in exchange for immunity?

The waitress came to our table again. My translator knew the manager of the hotel, and she had sent us a gift of crepes with fruit and whipped cream piled high.

What was your father like? I asked Luka. "He was just a regular guy trying to put food on the table," he said. These words rang false to me. Then he launched into the family myth about his father's having avoided death by deflecting a bullet with his hand.

"What year did your father get out of prison?" I asked.

I wasn't expecting to learn anything new from this conversation; I knew that Luka was more protective of Radovan's image than Radovan was himself. I was hoping for an introduction to a cousin who would be able to show us around Petnjica. I remember I was vaguely wondering how much older Luka was than I, noticing how white his hair was. I knew that Luka was born after his father got out of prison, and that his father had been imprisoned for five years. But I wasn't sure of the exact timing.

"Do you mean the first or second time?" he asked.

I was taken aback. Although his father's time in prison was one of the themes of my long-running conversation with Radovan, somehow he'd failed to mention that his father had been in prison more than once.

"I mean after the war," I said. I knew that Luka was born soon after that.

He didn't answer my question, and though I was very curious, something stopped me from asking about his father's first time in prison.

"The land in Petnjica is very harsh," Luka said. "It's very hard to live in Petnjica. The only thing you can do is tend cattle. The highlands are harsh and the people are tough."

Yes, I would discover that some of them, at least, are very tough indeed.

—

I thought Karadžić was romanticizing his birthplace when he described the beauty of Petnjica, so I wasn't really prepared to be moved when I traveled there with a translator in the summer of 2017. It felt wrong, somehow, to enjoy the stark mountain light.

It's a fairy-tale sort of spot, where you half expect to see elves popping out from behind the ancient oaks. The great Yugoslav dissident and writer Milovan Djilas referred to the highlands of Montenegro as "a wilderness and a seat of stone, but one lifted high upon a confusion of peaks, gashed by canyons and gorges, and gouged by gaping precipices burrowing into stone cracked by heat and frost."[10]

Montenegro is a tiny mountainous country, about the size of Connecticut, with a population of under 650,000. Petnjica, in the northwest of the country, is close to, but not part of, Durmitor National Park, which was selected by UNESCO as a World Heritage site. The park preserves the Durmitor massif, eighteen glacial lakes, the Tara canyon (Europe's deepest gorge), and the Sušica and Draga Rivers. Among UNESCO's reasons for selecting the Durmitor region as a World Heritage site is that it includes not only the mountain peaks but also an old-growth forest, subterranean rivers, "savagely contorted" limestone formations, and Montenegro's deepest underground cave, known as the Ice Cave. UNESCO also highlighted the presence of rare, endemic species of flora and fauna, and the alpine meadows—where I saw a profusion of many types of brightly colored butterflies and moths, pictures of which I brought back to show an entomologist friend.[11]

Beginning in the 1950s, it was common for rural Yugoslavs to move into cities.[12] Radovan and his mother lived in Petnjica for five years. Soon after his father got out of prison, the family moved to an only slightly larger village called Savnik. In 1956, they moved to Nikšić, the second-largest city in Montenegro after the capital, Podgorica. Nikšić is a major industrial center, with a steel mill, a bauxite mine, and a large brewery. But it was clear that Radovan felt most connected to Petnjica, where every resident is a Karadžić. The village consists of some twenty stone houses, a very small thirteenth-century church, and a graveyard. The last census, in 2011, reported twenty-eight residents.[13]

—

Simeon is Radovan Karadžić's cousin. I met him in a café in Petnjica on the side of the new highway that Radovan had spoken
about. The café was made to look like a mountain cabin—the
building and the tables were made of the same light wood, as
if mountaineers had constructed the entire thing from the sur-
rounding trees. During the war and its aftermath, while Karadžić
was in hiding, Simeon had spoken to journalists from all over the
world who had come to Montenegro to see Radovan Karadžić's
birthplace. Perhaps Simeon's social skills had gotten rusty since
then. I sensed a shyness between us that wasn't just on my side.
He launched into a practiced history of the village and the region,
which I'd already heard many times from Radovan in prison.

The 2010 highway, which connected the city of Nikšić with
the mountain resort town of Žabljak, divided Petnjica in half.
Simeon pointed across the highway to a small church. The church
had been there before the Karadžić clan came to the area. "It
dates from the thirteenth century," he said. I had already heard all
about this church from Radovan, and I was anxious to see it, but I
didn't interrupt Simeon.

A waiter brought a beer for Simeon, and tea for my translator
and me.

Montenegro was ruled by clans and tribes into the twentieth
century, long after such clans had disappeared from other Serbian
lands. Radovan Karadžić was deeply proud of his Montenegrin
heritage and the Drobnjak tribe's history of resisting domination.
That pride made more sense to me sitting here in the "fantastic
dream world" of limestone crags and deep canyons.[14] When the
Ottoman Turks swept over the Balkans in the fourteenth century, many Serbs fled to the Montenegrin highlands, where they
were partly protected by mountainous geography, but also by the
clan structure. Alfred, Lord Tennyson, celebrated the romance

of these rebellious clans, referring to Montenegrins as a race of savage mountaineers living in a "rough rock-throne of freedom," able to beat back "the swarm of Turkish Islam for five hundred years."[15]

The migrant Serbs reverted from their medieval civilization to a "primitive, patriarchal way of life" in Montenegro.[16] One of their goals was to avoid paying the dhimmi tax that was imposed on non-Muslims under Turkish rule. In Montenegro, "the resistance to exorbitant taxes and to serfdom was transformed into a religious and national movement," Djilas explains.[17]

Simeon said, "The Karadžić family produced a number of 'dukes'—prominent leaders of the clan." He pointed to one of the stone houses. "Over there is the house of Duke Sujo Karadžić."

I sipped my tea and waited for Simeon to finish this history, but I wanted to cross the highway to see the church and Sujo's house.

—

I had heard about Sujo Karadžić from Radovan many times. This is the story he told me. "We had our own aga [an aga was a local Turkish leader, defined variously as an Ottoman feudal lord or army general], Smail-aga Čengić, who tried to collect the dhimmi tax. He was constantly attacking us." In these historical stories Radovan relished, he used terms such as "our leader" and "us" as if he had personally experienced the fight against the Ottomans. "The aga was assassinated when he visited my area of Montenegro. One of the killers was my relative, Duke Sujo Karadžić," he said proudly.

The Death of Smail-aga Čengić is an epic poem written in the mid-nineteenth century by the Croatian writer Ivan Mažuranić. Along with Petar Petrović Njegoš's *The Mountain Wreath*, it is one of the most important works of South Slavic literature. Njegoš is often described as the region's greatest poet, analogous to Shakespeare. Radovan referred to these two poems frequently. When

he spoke about Serbian history, I wasn't always sure he was distinguishing between what the poets have imagined about the Ottoman period, and what historians believe to be true.

I made it a habit, when typing up my notes from our conversations, to look up everything Radovan said to me, on the
assumption that it was not a good idea to take at face value the
words of an indicted war criminal. I discovered that Sujo Karadžić
really *had* existed, that he really *was* a duke, and that he really *did*
play a role in the death of the famous Smail-aga Čengić. Among
the Montenegrin clans, "duke" was not a hereditary title but an
earned recognition of prominent fighters against the Ottoman
Turks. Sujo Karadžić was such a fighter. "The Turks were unable
to overcome the resistance of our clan," Radovan said. "People
escaped into caves. They tried to convert the people of our area,
but our people fought the Turks back."

I was able to confirm most of these claims, but historians dispute that any tribe was successful in permanently fending off the
Ottoman conquerors; it was an ongoing battle. Still, the tribes
nurtured what Djilas calls "an inner spiritual implacability" toward
the Turks, a resentment that was the result not only of transient
causes such as high taxes or violence. Djilas writes: "In their craggy
heights, bleached by sun and storm and bereft of everything that a
body needs, ceaseless struggle with the Turks was not only a way
of life, but a cult."[18] The beliefs of this "cult," according to Djilas,
included the notion of a doomed Serbia, the flight of its nobility
into Montenegro, the duty to avenge Kosovo, Miloš Obilić's sacrifice, and the irreconcilable struggle between Cross and Crescent.
This is what Radovan's mother, Jovanka, was referring to when
she spoke of her son having inherited a duty to promote the interests of the Serb people and protect them from outsiders.

In the café in Petnjica, Simeon continued this story. "The
Karadžić clan retained its integrity because all of them were Chetniks," he said. "Many of the clans in old Montenegro fought one

another in World War II. Some became Partisans. But not in this part of Montenegro. Here we were all Chetniks. Here we stuck together."

Karadžić's anti-Muslim sentiments would seem to have been bred in the bone.

Now that Simeon had rehearsed this history, he turned his attention to me, his American guest.

"When I was younger everyone loved America," he said. "Now everyone hates America even more than they hated the Communists. America used to be a symbol of democracy. Now America is a symbol of Western enslavement of the rest of the world, via globalization."

I smiled politely. This is a narrative I have heard from Radovan as well. Radovan said to me, "Globalization is just 'deculturization.' It helps no one except large corporations. It is about financial power. It is not healthy that the people at the top of the world dictate to the rest of the world."

Simeon added, "The educational reforms imposed by the European Union are even more senseless than the reforms required under Communism." Apparently, he held the United States—which he sees as the principal architect of globalization—responsible for those changes as well.

You can hear this nationalist, anti-globalization screed all over the world, whenever and wherever people feel their status is threatened by demographic shifts and "outsiders" taking something away from "us." While Simeon was talking, I was thinking about what had recently happened in my country—the surprising election of Donald Trump, who also claimed to oppose global trade. This is not the first time that fear of globalization has led to a resurgence of nationalism—there are periodic waves of anti-immigrant bias in the United States. Even the rise of the Nazis in interwar Germany can be seen as a "nationalist protest against globalization," according to historian Benjamin Hett.[19] The fear that "our" people and culture are under threat played a big role in the Brexit vote as well as in the election of Donald Trump. With these votes, people who felt attached to a specific culture and a specific place—those whom journalist David Goodhart refers to as "somewhere" people—were voicing their disapproval of the global elite who benefit from globalization, the "anywhere people." Today, those voting against economic integration and for populist leaders tend to feel threatened by the rapid pace of change initiated by the information revolution. They feel displaced by ethnically fluid, borderless societies.[20] In the United States, at least, the populist vote is not necessarily a reflection of economic anxiety, but of fear of diminished status.[21] Even if economists tell us that unimpeded global trade and movement of workers result in pareto-efficient outcomes, they nonetheless pose a genuine threat to something of value—and that something includes fairy-tale villages like Petnjica, in which there is a very specific culture that cannot be duplicated anywhere else. (In a "pareto-efficient" arrangement, if the winners compensate the losers for whatever they lose, everyone would still be at least as well off, and no one would be worse off. While this concept assumes the greatest possible efficiency in the allocation of resources, it does not necessarily imply equality.)

I ask Simeon about his life here. His mother is one hundred years old, he says, and cannot leave the house anymore. He doesn't live in Petnjica year-round now, but he is here taking care of her. I express sympathy. I'm also disappointed: in this moment, I have a childish wish to believe that it is possible to thrive as a shepherd in a place like Petnjica. It is not.

Finally, Simeon wanted to show us around. It was early evening, and one of the villagers was returning to the village with his three cows. He smiled at Simeon and I noticed he was missing some teeth, though he is a young man, perhaps in his twenties. The cows ambled across the two-lane highway as if it were a small road.

Globalization has even come here. We saw a number of campers who had set up tents not far from the café, and we heard snippets of French, Spanish, and Hebrew. This part of northern Montenegro has become popular with tourists seeking "high adrenaline" outdoor adventures, including rock climbing, white-water rafting, and canyoning—a sport that involves traveling through the deep canyons by walking, swimming, climbing, and rappelling. Close to the campground, we came upon a small but deep gorge that was barely marked. Had Simeon not been with us to point it out, it would have been easy to fall into the chasm. I'm not at all sure it would have been possible to get out of that gorge if I had fallen in.

—

The week before our arrival in Petnjica, there had been a literary festival that attracted many visitors to the tiny village. There were still candles on the stone walls and other remnants of the festivities in evidence. Literary festivals are held here in Petnjica frequently, Simeon said, to celebrate the family's most famous ancestor, Vuk Karadžić (1787–1864), the nineteenth-century linguist and philologist. Vuk Karadžić was the major reformer of the Serbian language.[22] He is internationally known: UNESCO named 1987, the two hundredth anniversary of his birth, the year of Vuk Karadžić.

Vuk created a grammar for a new written form of the Serbo-Croatian language and wrote the first dictionary. He is most celebrated, especially outside the Balkans, as a folklorist. His collection of fairy tales and epic poems caught the attention of Jacob Grimm and Johann Wolfgang von Goethe, both of whom used some of the poems Vuk Karadžić collected as inspiration for their own work. The "wild tales" collected by Karadžić became a "fever," an "obsession," for the cultured people of the West. "The effect on the weary literature of the time was magical. "Here was something strange and compelling!" a 1922 treatise on Vuk Karadžić's collection of ballads explains.[23] Goethe's Werther said that the Serbian epics had superseded Homer in his heart.[24] Jacob Grimm was so thrilled by the stories in Vuk Karadžić's collection of ballads that he decided to learn Serbian so he could read them in the original.[25] Among Vuk Karadžić's collection of songs was a book of one hundred ballads and poems he heard as a child and was able to write down from memory—something Radovan Karadžić told me he could also do.

—

On the second day of my visit to Montenegro, Simeon told me that he had written a ballad for his cousin Radovan. *Guslars* sing their history in the style of a dirge. They wail the lyrics, often matching their tone to the limited notes of the horsehair string, which itself evokes the sound of human moaning. At first, the grief of the *guslar* feels theatrical. But if you listen for a while, the lamentation begins to evoke some kind of universal sadness, perhaps about our inability to understand God's purpose in allowing human suffering or our frustration with the problem of evil. During the war, the *gusle* became an instrument of Serb nationalism. I am partial to the strange, mournful sound, a fondness that feels wrong.

After Simeon discovered that he and I could communicate in rusty Russian, he dismissed my translator, telling him to take our rental car to the lower part of the village. Then he took me to the top of a hill from where we could get a good view. I noted the damson plum trees that Radovan had told me about. There were wildflowers at our feet, and a dry, herbaceous scent that I associate with mountain climbing. Then he led me into the tiny church that Radovan had told me about and that I was excited to see. He said that a traveling priest sometimes came to perform services, but I found it hard to imagine how this would work, as there were no chairs in the church, and there was room for only a very small number of people to stand—perhaps ten if they stood closely packed. It was cold and strangely moist inside the church, with an unhealthy-seeming odor of cold, damp stone. Just behind the church was the small graveyard, where I saw that every stone was marked with the name Karadžić.

Much to my surprise, Simeon walked me over to his own small stone house, where he introduced me to his mother. He called out to my translator, who was waiting for us nearby, to come join us. Simeon's mother was reclining on a bed that had been set up in the kitchen. She did not get up to greet us but was all smiles. It was late morning. Simeon offered us some brandy he had made from the plums that grow in the village. My translator doesn't drink, but I thought it important to say yes. The clear liquid was bracing: harsh on the tongue, but also sweet, more like an eau-de-vie than a sweet liqueur. As we left, Simeon's mother took my translator's hand, but not mine. Perhaps she knew I was American.

—

I was haunted by the new information that Radovan's brother Luka had shared—that their father was imprisoned twice—not only just after the war, for serving as a Chetnik fighter, but also before the war, for some other crime. I was too shy to press Luka for an explanation, but I was more comfortable with Simeon. I asked him if he knew about the first time that Radovan's father had been imprisoned. Simeon told me the story.

When Radovan's father, Vuko, was a boy, he fell in love with a girl who was his fifth cousin. She, too, lived in Petnjica. The King-dom of Yugoslavia allowed marriage between third cousins, so a marriage was possible under the law. Under the dictates of the Serbian Orthodox Church, marriages among fourth cousins were permitted but discouraged. Even marriage among fifth cousins was frowned upon. The girl, however, did not love Radovan's father back. One day, the girl accompanied Vuko as he was herding cattle. He had a firearm with him, Simeon said, as if it were common for cowherds to carry guns, as if everyone knows this. Radovan's father tried to kiss the girl. She rebuffed him. The gun went off accidentally and hit an artery in her thigh. Radovan's father tried to help her by stanching her wounds with tobacco. That was what people did back then when someone had a cut, Simeon explained. But the tobacco failed to stanch the wound, and she bled to death.

The first people on the scene were Vuko's mother and the mother of the girl. The girl's family understood that the shooting was accidental, Simeon said. But still, Vuko was sent to prison for the death of the girl he loved.

I did not immediately express my doubts about the veracity of this story. It sounded to me like a family myth, rather than an episode from Radovan's father's biography. It reminded me of the story of Radovan's father deflecting a Partisan bullet with his hand. I asked my translator to see if we could get documents detailing the charges against Radovan's father. Over the next year, he tried a number of archives—both in Montenegro and in Serbia. A Montenegrin diplomat to the United States who teaches at my university tried to help us. The archivists were unable to find the documents. But my translator did find an article from a Belgrade paper, *Pravda*, dated January 2, 1934, which provided another version of the shooting incident.

The article says that Radovan's father, Vuko, then twenty-one and a descendant of his namesake, the famous folklorist Vuk Karadžić, was tending cattle with his cousin, Jela. The two cousins drove the cattle every morning to fresh pasture and drove them home to Petnjica every evening. Eventually they fell in love. Vuko wanted to marry Jela. Her parents insisted that the cousins wait until Vuko had completed his military service. Jela promised to marry Vuko, but, in keeping with her parents' wishes, insisted on delay. Vuko, on the other hand, wanted to get married immediately. One day Jela asked Vuko to meet her at the top of the large hill above the village. Vuko went to meet his cousin, as requested. He brought a revolver as well as the cows. He pressed, once again, for Jela to marry him. When Jela refused, he shot her. The bullet went through both of her thighs, damaging the blood vessels. She died soon afterward, due to the loss of blood.

Vuko did not confess to the crime but told the court that the shooting was accidental. He testified that his revolver had fallen out of his pocket as he was seating himself next to his cousin Jela. He said that Jela had asked him, "Why are you carrying that devil with you?" Then she grabbed the gun and threw it away from where they were sitting. Vuko testified that the gun hit a rock, and accidentally discharged, fatally wounding Jela in the thigh. The court did not accept Vuko's version of what transpired.

The court had access to a letter that had been found in Jela's bag. Vuko confessed that he had written the letter, in which he threatened to kill Jela as well as himself if she refused to marry him immediately. It read in part, "Dear Jela: If our marriage cannot be proclaimed, then thank you for burying both of us in the black ground." Vuko testified that the letter was intended to scare Jela into marrying him right away.

According to the court, Vuko ran off when he saw villagers rushing to the crime scene. He waited until the next day to surrender to the authorities. The Nikšić County Court found that Vuko had killed his cousin intentionally. He was convicted of murder and sentenced to twenty years' imprisonment and a "permanent loss of honorable rights," which meant he had lost the right to hold public office, earn an academic degree, receive a medal, or serve in the government. This murder, which had taken place in a tiny hamlet in diminutive Montenegro, made it into a big-city paper in the Kingdom of Yugoslavia's capital city, perhaps because of Vuko's famous namesake.[26]

Vuko was released from prison around the time that the Axis powers invaded the Kingdom of Yugoslavia, on April 6, 1941, as the law at that time required releasing prisoners if the country was invaded. King Peter went immediately into exile. The Yugoslav Army collapsed nearly at once, within a week and a half of the invasion. Vuko would join the Chetniks and would be sent back to prison by the victorious (and apparently vindictive) Partisans at the end of the war.

NOTES

1. Luka Karadžić said that he trained as a lawyer, but it is not clear why he worked as a mailman if that were the case. Ivana Vranešević, "BIA mi je upropastila biznis," *Glas javnosti*, August 10, 2008, http://www .glas-javnosti.rs/clanak/tema/glas-javnosti-10-08-2008/bia-mi-je -upropastila-biznis. N.N., "Radovan Karadžić, heroj u rodnom selu," *Nezavisne novine*, March 22, 2016, http://www.nezavisne.com/novosti /drustvo/Radovan-Karadzic-heroj-u-rodnom-selu-FOTO/360917.
2. Ivana Vranešević, "BIA mi je upropastila biznis," *Glas javnosti*, August 10, 2008, http://www.glas-javnosti.rs/clanak/tema/glas-javnosti -10-08-2008/bia-mi-je-upropastila-biznis.

3. "'Reporter': 'Jugopetrol' finansijski pomaze Karadzica," *B92*, February 25, 2002, https://www.b92.net/info/vesti/index.php?yyyy=2002&mm=02&dd=25&nav_category=1&nav_id=56688; "Luka Karadzic imao u zakupu pumpu, ugovor vise ne vazi," *B92*, February 26, 2002, https://www.b92.net/info/vesti/index.php?yyyy=2002&mm=02&dd=26&nav_category=1&nav_id=56712.

4. Julian Borger, *The Butcher's Trail: How the Search for Balkan War Criminals Became the World's Most Successful Manhunt* (New York: Other Press, 2016), p. 139. According to Biljana Plavšić, a Bosnian Serb leader during the war and later president of the RS, Milošević told Plavšić that wartime RS parliamentary speaker Momčilo Krajišnik's brother controlled border smuggling in eastern Bosnia toward Serbia and Radovan Karadžić's brother Luka controlled smuggling in eastern Herzegovina toward Montenegro. See: Biljana Plavšić, *I Testify*, Vol. 2 (Banja Luka: Trioprint, 2005), pp. 212, 284. Excerpts translated by political scientist Mladen Mrdalj.

Soon after being accused of his criminal activity by the Serbian Orthodox Patriarch, Luka gave an interview to the newspaper *Reporter* bragging about his business successes. See Plavšić, *I Testify*, Vol. 2, p. 275. Excerpts translated by political scientist Mladen Mrdalj.

Ratko Mladić wrote in his diary that Luka was selling gas donated to the Army of Republic of Srpska in 1994. S. Marjanović, "Ekskluzivno, dnevnik Ratka Mladića iz '95: Karadžić i Krajišnik pokrali milione!" *Press Online*, June 20, 2009, http://www.pressonline.rs/info/politika/69500/ekskluzivno-dnevnik-ratka-mladica-iz-95-karadzic-i-krajisnik-pokrali-milione.html.

5. M.D.V., "Dve godine zatvora Luki Karadžiću," *Danas*, May 8, 2018, https://www.danas.rs/drustvo/dve-godine-zatvora-luki-karadzicu/. The usual sentence is twelve years for fatal drunk-driving accidents. See V. Z. Cvijić, "BRUKA Političari zaštitili Luku Karadžića," *Blic*, August 28, 2016, https://www.blic.rs/vesti/hronika/bruka-politicari-zastitili-luku-karadzica/6pbqfjd.

6. Ivana Vranešević, "BIA mi je upropastila biznis," *Glas javnosti*, August 10, 2008, http://www.glas-javnosti.rs/clanak/tema/glas-javnosti-10-08-2008/bia-mi-je-upropastila-biznis.

7. John Phillips, "On the Run, Accused Serbian War Criminal Writes Poems," *Christian Science Monitor*, March 6, 2002, https://www.csmonitor.com/2002/0306/p07s01-woeu.html.

8. "Luka Karadzic: My Brother Tells Truth About Deal With Hol-

brooke," *Russia Today*, August 2, 2008, https://www.youtube.com/watch?v=sHCgHLxMBW0.

(Note that *Russia Today* is a Russian government organ and would be generally pro–Serb nationalist, but in this case we're interested in what Luka said, not in an analysis of his position.) On the forged signatures, see: Florence Hartmann, *Paix et Châtiment: les guerres secrètes de la politique et de la justice internationales* (Paris: Flammarion, 2007), p. 170.

9. John Phillips, "On the Run, Accused Serbian War Criminal Writes Poems," *Christian Science Monitor*, March 6, 2002, https://www.csmonitor.com/2002/0306/p07s01-woeu.html.

10. Milovan Djilas, *Njegoš: Poet, Prince, Bishop*, trans. Michael B. Petrovich (New York: Harcourt, Brace & World, 1966), p. 14.

11. "World Heritage List—Durmitor National Park," United Nations Educational, Scientific and Cultural Organization, http://whc.unesco.org/en/list/100.

12. Robert J. Donia, *Radovan Karadžić: Architect of the Bosnian Genocide* (New York: Cambridge University Press, 2015), p. 27.

13. The census reports 38 "structures," but that would seem to include sheds and other structures that are not houses. Statistical Office of Montenegro (MONSTAT), *First Results: Census of Population, Households and Dwellings in Montenegro* (Podgorica, Montenegro: MONSTAT, 2011), https://www.monstat.org/userfiles/file/popis2011/saopstenje/knjiga_prvi%20rezultati(1).pdf.

14. Milovan Djilas, *Njegoš: Poet, Prince, Bishop*, trans. Michael B. Petrovich (New York: Harcourt, Brace & World, 1966), p. xvii.

15. Alfred, Lord Tennyson, "Montenegro" (1877).

16. Milovan Djilas, *Njegoš: Poet, Prince, Bishop*, trans. Michael B. Petrovich (New York: Harcourt, Brace & World, 1966), p. xx.

17. Milovan Djilas, *Njegoš: Poet, Prince, Bishop*, trans. Michael B. Petrovich (New York: Harcourt, Brace & World, 1966), p. 20.

18. Milovan Djilas, *Njegoš: Poet, Prince, Bishop*, trans. Michael B. Petrovich (New York: Harcourt, Brace & World, 1966), p. 10.

19. Benjamin Carter Hett, "The Hunger Chancellor," in *The Death of Democracy* (New York: Henry Holt, 2018). In the Middle East, I heard people refer to globalization as McDonaldization or Westoxification, beginning in the 1980s. Jessica Stern, *Terror in the Name of God* (New York: HarperCollins, 2003).

20. David Goodhart, *The Road to Somewhere: The Populist Revolt and the Future of Politics* (New York: Oxford University Press, 2017).

21. This finding was captured by a study for the National Academy of Sciences, referring to the United States. Diana C. Mutz, "Status Threat, Not Economic Hardship, Explains the 2016 Presidential Vote," *Proceedings of the National Academy of Sciences*, Vol. 115, No. 19 (May 8, 2018), http://www.pnas.org/content/115/19/E4330.

22. Vuk Karadžić's grandfather, Joksim Karadžić, had lived in the village of Petnjica and moved to Tršić in western Serbia (then part of the Ottoman Empire) around the time of the Austro-Turkish War of 1737–1739.

23. *The Ballads of Marko Kraljević*, trans. D. H. Low (New York: Greenwood Press, 1968), p. x.

24. Johann Wolfgang von Goethe, *The Sorrows of Young Werther*, trans. R. Dillon Boylan, accessed: https://www.gutenberg.org/files/2527/2527-h/2527-h.htm.

   Ossian is the narrator and supposed author of the South Slavic epic poems, translated into English, in James MacPherson, *Fragments of Ancient Poetry Collected in the Highlands of Scotland and Translated from the Gaelic or Erse Language* (Edinburgh, 1760). *The Ballads of Marko Kraljević*, trans. D. H. Low (New York: Greenwood Press, 1968).

25. Nada Milošević-Dordević, "The Oral Tradition," in Pavle Ivić, ed., *The History of Serbian Culture* (Edgeware, Middlesex, UK: Porthill, 1995).

26. "Vuk St. Karadžić Sentenced to 20 Years in Prison," *Pravda*, January 2, 1934, p. 14.

Chapter Seven

THE POET BECOMES A POLITICIAN

When I first read the report of Radovan Karadžić's father's conviction for murder, I let it wash over me like a story. Like the libretto of an opera. But then I started thinking about what it might mean to the very real people involved. How did Radovan's mother, Jovanka, feel about marrying a man who had murdered the first woman he had wanted to marry? Why would Jovanka marry a convicted murderer? Wasn't she frightened of her fiancé's capacity for violence?

If I allow myself truly to feel what it might have been like for twenty-year-old Jovanka to marry a murderer, I find myself getting strangely anxious. So, as is my habit, I escape into facts, tracing the order of events. Radovan's mother, Jovanka, married a man twelve years her senior, a man with a murderous temper. She had to have known Vuko was a murderer. He'd gotten out of prison only because of a law that released prisoners during wartime. Two years later, she gave birth to Radovan, their first child. Soon after Radovan's birth, when Vuko was imprisoned for a second time—this time by the Communists he despised—he left his young wife and infant son to fend for themselves in impoverished postwar Montenegro.[1] Jovanka was left alone to raise her young son, to plow the fields, and to plant the potatoes and grain.[2] "It was a struggle," she said in a television interview. "I had no wages, nothing. I'd been pushed out," punished because her husband had been a Chetnik, although members of her own family had fought on the side of the Communist Partisans. Under the leadership of Josip Broz Tito, the Partisans had won the *civil war in Yugoslavia that occurred at the same time as World War II and penalized the defeated monarchists as well as others who had fought them. "I was given a very bad time," she said. She had tried not to share her growing hatred for the Communists with her children.*[3]

Now that I've got these facts straight, it seems that I can bear, once again, to wonder about the young mother's feelings. Was Jovanka truly in love with the murderous man she married? Was he truly in love with Jovanka? Was Jovanka second-best? According to Radovan, the true divide in his part of Montenegro was not among ethnic Serb, Muslim, and Croat, but between the royalist Chetniks and the Communist Partisans. And the Partisans, he insisted, were generally of "lower class." Did Vuko feel himself to be marrying down when he married the young Jovanka, an illiterate girl from a neighboring village? Jovanka must have barely known her husband until seven years into their marriage; before that, he was either serving as a Chetnik soldier or living behind bars. Was Radovan's closeness to his mother partly a function of his suspicion that Jovanka was not her husband's first choice? I have also wondered: how much of this story about their father's conviction for murder did Radovan and his siblings know? What would it be like to pretend not to know that one's father had murdered his own cousin?

—

When Radovan Karadžić was fifteen years old, he moved, by himself, to Sarajevo, the biggest city in neighboring Bosnia. At that time, Sarajevo would have seemed as exotic, and nearly as far away, as America. "Most Montenegrins would have gone to Belgrade to study," he told me. Belgrade was the capital of Yugoslavia and a more obvious choice. But Sarajevo was the most ethnically and religiously diverse city in all of Yugoslavia. "It was a twenty-three-hour train ride away back then," he said.

When he arrived in the big city, some of the Sarajevo residents who met him saw the teenage Karadžić as a country bumpkin.

He was tall, good-looking, and obviously intelligent. But a former neighbor told an interviewer, "He was provincial, a typical peasant lost in the big city."[4] Another neighbor, a barber who used to play poker with Karadžić, said, "He had a hillbilly kind of haircut, very fashionable in his village. When I tried to make a suggestion, he'd say, 'No, no, I like long hair.'"[5]

Karadžić attended a medical high school, followed by medical school. He excelled as a student and was seen by the faculty as a star.[6] He was happy there. "It was Sarajevo's golden age," Karadžić said.[7]

In 1967, he married a fellow medical student, Ljiljana Zelen, who came from an upper-class Bosnian Serb family. Their daughter, Sonja, was born in 1967, and their son, Aleksander, in 1972.

In 1968, when Radovan was still in medical school, he got involved in student protests against the Communist regime. Like other students around the world, the University of Sarajevo's protestors carried pictures of the Argentine revolutionary Che Guevara and considered themselves to be part of a global movement protesting capitalist (and, in their case, nationalist or socialist) elites. Karadžić's involvement in the protests was extraordinary, historian Robert Donia explained to me, since medical students were viewed by those in the department of philosophy (home to the humanities and some social sciences) as conventional and staid.[8] They were often children of Sarajevo's most privileged families.

Karadžić was different in many ways from the typical medical student. Not only was he from faraway rural Montenegro, but he came from an impoverished family, and he had a strong interest in literature and politics. A friend from that period explained, "We were dreamers, and we lived for literature. Literature was the most important thing on the planet, in the universe. Karadžić was at the medical faculty, and he was someone [of] whom you could say, 'Well, he, too, dabbles in writing, so let him be with us.'"[9]

He dressed in the style of "flower children," with "groovy clothes," according to a fellow student who had also been involved in the protests. "Inside," however, "he remained what he always was, a peasant who came to the big city."[10]

—

Karadžić was the only medical student to assume a leading role in the infamous massive one-day protest at the University of Sarajevo. When he spoke about this period in his life, Karadžić seemed to be escaping from the prison surroundings into pleasant memories. "I was prominent in the student movement against the Communist regime," he told me proudly. "I climbed up on the roof of the faculty building to give a speech."

He was bringing his younger self into the room—the tall, thin Byronic hero I've seen in photographs. *Was he an idealist back then, or just a social climber?*

Almost as if he had read my mind, he continued, "As a result of my involvement in the movement, I started spending time with the Serbian elite in Bosnia. They were all dissidents, working in opposition to the regime." Karadžić's involvement in the student protest movement was an important part of his entrée into Sarajevo's literary society.[11] His first book of poetry was published that year—not in the Bosnian dialect, but in the dialect spoken in Serbia. He told me, "The publisher didn't like it that I wanted to publish in Ekavian. The Bosnian authorities didn't like it either." *Was this an early sign of his later transformation into a Serb nationalist?* None of his friends seemed to notice at the time.

Karadžić's father, Vuko, was a staunch anti-Communist. Karadžić told me that when he was still living at home, he often argued with his father, defending the Communist regime against his father's resolute opposition to the victorious Partisans who had incarcerated him for the first five years of his son's life. "My father told me how many people Tito killed during the war. . . . I quarreled with my father—who was opposed to Tito."

I couldn't help but wonder, were these arguments really about something else—a form of "metacommunication"—the term Karadžić had used the first time we met?

After Karadžić got involved in the student protest movement in Sarajevo, father and son switched sides, he told me. "My father worried about my becoming a dissident because he feared that I could find myself in political trouble, just as he had. After 1968, I realized that my father had been right all along." Karadžić resigned from the presidency of the student (Communist) Central Committee.

The political trouble Vuko had gotten into would haunt him throughout his life, as the Communists had made it hard for him to get a good job. Radovan would find other ways to get into political trouble. Eventually, he would pursue a Chetnik dream similar to his father's, but he would make more progress toward achieving it.

Some of Karadžić's friends from his dissident period suspected that he was actually paid by the security services to be a political informant.[12] One of his friends, Marko Vešović, a prominent poet and writer, began referring to himself as a former friend, due to his conviction that Karadžić had been a police informant, spying on his friends, the other dissidents.[13] To add to the confusion, when Karadžić lived in New York City in 1974–75, he presented himself as a staunch supporter of the Tito regime. According to his former friend Vešović, Karadžić's writer friends thought he had gone to New York to study medicine, and his doctor colleagues thought he had gone to study literature. "That's a secret we were never able to solve," Vešović said.[14]

When he arrived in New York, Karadžić lodged with a man named Barry Farber, whom he remembered as a radio host who went to his office at the radio station seven days a week. It turns out that Barry Farber is a famous conservative talk-radio host, named by *Talkers* magazine as the ninth-greatest radio host of all time.[15] With that information, I was able to track down Karadžić's American landlord from 1974, when Karadžić was twenty-nine years old.

In 2017, I went to see the landlord in his vast, rent-controlled apartment in the glamorous Apthorp building on the Upper West Side. I found him in good humor, though nearly blind. He was no longer able to read due to his failing eyesight and had no idea that Karadžić had recently been convicted of genocide. But the nearly ninety-year-old Farber remembered his former tenant well. He'd been ardently pro-Tito, Farber recalled, while Farber had been an anti-Communist activist, just as Karadžić had been only a few years earlier. "We lived in the Normandy, a building on the corner of Riverside Drive between Eighty-Sixth and Eighty-Seventh," Farber told me. "We advertised to trade a room for a houseboy, and a young Yugoslav, a poet who was also a physician, applied for the job." Farber was delighted, since he wanted to practice his Serbo-Croatian, one of many languages he was trying to master. To Farber's surprise, the young socialist came with his own maid from the Caribbean, and the maid helped to set Karadžić up in his room. He did a good job as a houseboy, Farber said, and was nice to Farber and his family. But Farber found Karadžić's pro-Tito stance hard to understand at the time. "I walked in on one of his parties and they were singing songs about Tito," Farber recalled. "They were ridiculously banal."[16]

I asked Farber: was Karadžić playing a role for the benefit of his Yugoslav-government minders? (I assumed that there would have been spies monitoring Karadžić during that era, though I could be wrong.) Farber wasn't sure. But he added, "I should have seen that Radovan would not remain just a poet. He was much too smart and forceful a character. I could see him running a country. He was formidable. He looked the part."

This word "formidable" would stick with me, as would Karadžić's apparent ability to present himself, even to close observers, as holding very different views from one day to the next, and possessing very different traits. To some he was a dissident, to others a stooge, and to others an ardent champion of Tito; those who watched him closely over time recognized that he was capable of "instantly mutat[ing] his personality and mood to suit the needs of the moment."[17] He had a capacity for "instant transformation," said historian Robert Donia, who testified at Karadžić's trial and was subjected to Karadžić's cross-examination over twelve days.[18] He was a "chameleon," Donia concluded.[19] Marko Vešović described him this way: "He knew exactly what to say, a different story for everyone, with perfect knowledge of what people want to hear."[20]

Perhaps this is part of why I always felt so manipulated by Karadžić in our two-year conversation, even though he was unfailingly polite and never tried to persuade me of his innocence, or of anything else.

More "metacommunication"?

Karadžić graduated from medical school at the University of Sarajevo in 1971. Some of his colleagues reported that it wasn't clear if he saw himself as a poet dabbling in medicine, or a psychiatrist dabbling in poetry. He found a job as a staff psychiatrist at the Koševo Clinic in Sarajevo. His supervisor was Dr. Ismet Cerić, the head of the clinic. When I asked Karadžić to name the persons he most admired in the world, he included Dr. Cerić on the short list. Dr. Cerić was Muslim.

Karadžić had come to the hospital as a very young doctor. Even starting out, he was bizarrely boastful, so much so that Dr. Cerić assumed he was joking when he spoke of his accomplishments. The young doctor referred to himself as an "excellent psychiatrist," "the third best poet in Serbian history," and even an "excellent businessman in the Communist system," Dr. Cerić said to an interviewer. Over time, Dr. Cerić and other clinic personnel came to understand that Karadžić really believed himself to be excellent in all these ways.

In fact, Karadžić was not an excellent doctor, Dr. Cerić said, on account of his laziness. He got along well with the other clinic staff, but he didn't take much interest in his work. He didn't seem to care about his patients' well-being. "He tried to find the easy way for everything," Cerić observed.[21] He was not an excellent poet, either, Dr. Cerić said. Karadžić won a lot of poetry prizes during the Communist era, but the poet Christopher Merrill confirmed Dr. Cerić's assessment of Karadžić when he said that "the literati viewed him as an ambitious, untalented boor."[22] The Pulitzer Prize–winning Serbian-American poet Charles Simic said that Karadžić's poetry "stinks." "I never met any poet there who thought otherwise," he told me.[23] "He doesn't live in reality," Dr. Cerić declared.[24] His boasting was so extreme that Marko Vešović concluded that everything Karadžić did or said was done with the aim of "self-glorification."[25]

Another aspect of Karadžić's character, evident to Dr. Cerić and other clinic personnel, and even to friends who spoke with the media during the war, was that he had "a thousand different faces," a thousand sides to his personality.[26]

Dr. Cerić said that in all the years he had known Karadžić, he had never seen signs of his nationalism, nor his love of gambling, though others report that he was a regular gambler. For example, Biljana Plavšić, who served in the Republika Srpska government with Karadžić and replaced him as president in 1996, referred in her memoir to his frequent gambling.[27] Others said that even during the worst fighting of the war, he would often be found gambling at the Hotel Metropol Palace in Belgrade, rather than in his office in Pale.[28]

Soccer was another one of Karadžić's passions. He managed to get himself hired as a team psychologist—first for Sarajevo, and later for Red Star, the best professional club in Yugoslavia. The captain of the Sarajevo team reported that at one point, Karadžić instructed team members to lie down together in a darkened room and imagine themselves to be bumblebees, flying from flower to flower. The captain recalled the players' responses: "Someone was sleeping, someone snoring, someone else was farting, and someone cursing about bumblebees. The whole bumblebee thing was a huge joke to us."[29] For the Red Star position, he moved to Belgrade, leaving his family behind for a year in 1983. Karadžić was as boastful about his skill as a team psychologist as he was about everything else. Vešović recalled that if the team scored a point, Karadžić felt that the point was due to his "psychotraining" of the players. "He said he could make the Red Star the best team in the world."[30]

During our interviews, I came to notice that Karadžić showed me a particular side of himself. Whatever the topic of conversation, he would inevitably drift to one of several of his pet obsessions: history, literature, mysticism. He must have intuited that I would find him more fascinating on these topics than on the subjects of sports or gambling, his other passions, which he never brought up during our many conversations, not even once.

—

Karadžić was arrested for embezzlement and fraud in 1984 and spent eleven months in prison. According to the prosecutor, half a million deutsche marks were missing from the accounts of a state-run company, while large sums of money had been found in Karadžić's account.[31] The court found Karadžić guilty, and he spent nearly a year in jail. But later, mysteriously, all charges were dropped. The prosecutors said the evidence against him was overwhelming, and that the acquittal was politically motivated. But Karadžić insisted that the opposite was the case—that the charges against him were politically motivated.[32] "They thought I'd come

back to Bosnia from Serbia with instructions from the Serb nationalist Dobrica Ćosić to start an uprising in Bosnia-Herzegovina,"
Karadžić declared in an interview.[33] Dr. Cerić was shocked when
Karadžić was sent to prison for embezzlement—something he
hadn't thought Karadžić capable of—and was equally surprised
to discover that Karadžić had friends powerful enough to get him
released from prison and rehired at the clinic.[34] He was dishonest,
and "he hasn't a feeling of guilt," Cerić concluded.[35] *Was he suggesting Radovan Karadžić might be a psychopath?*

—

The celebrated Bosniak poet Semezdin Mehmedinović also knew
Karadžić during the period up until the war when he was working as a psychiatrist. Mehmedinović is the author of the book *Sarajevo Blues*, published during the war and translated into thirty
languages. He has quite a bit to say about Karadžić in the book,
much of it flattering. Like the other poets cited here, however,
Mehmedinović said that few serious poets of his generation
thought much of Karadžić's poetry. Karadžić seemed to understand this, the younger poet said, but he wasn't bitter about it.

Karadžić seldom spoke when the Sarajevo poets hung out as a
group in cafés, Mehmedinović wrote. He just listened. And when
he did join a conversation, his words were "calm and reassuring,
perhaps because of his years as a psychiatrist." Karadžić gave the
impression of being a "peace-loving and good-natured fellow,"
showing a very different side of himself from the side he showed
during the war. No one among their literary circle suspected that
he would eventually be a candidate for political office, let alone a
war criminal. Later, people realized that "the hatred so evident in
his early poetry" had, somehow, escaped their notice.[36] A line from
one of Karadžić's poems: "Take no pity let's go / kill that scum in
the city," would later become a slogan for the war project.[37]

After the 1980 death of Marshal Tito, and especially after the

1989 collapse of the Soviet Union, Communist rule in Yugoslavia began to erode. According to historian Robert Donia, Karadžić was enthralled by the political opportunities developing, but was uncertain how to exploit them.[38] He began his political career as a member of the Green Party. "That seemed quite in character," the poet Mehmedinović said, because founding a party in the Balkans in the late 1980s "represented more of an artistic performance than true political engagement."[39] Soon after the party was formed, the Greens draped plastic bags over the limbs of acacia trees, presumably to demonstrate concern about the pernicious effects of plastics on the environment. But a few months after this, Karadžić joined forces with a group of prominent intellectuals who had been involved in the 1968 student protest movement.[40]

In the days of the student movement, Karadžić and his cadre of friends were critical of "nationalist jargon," complaining that Yugoslavia had become a "battlefield on which nationalist oligarchies fought to enhance their socialist prestige."[41] But with the Communist regime on its last legs, this group of former dissidents was not sure what sort of policies to promote, other than advancing the Serb cause. Eventually they settled on a nationalist agenda that was not only pro-Serb, but also anti-Muslim and anti-Croat.

"We formed the SDS [Srpska Demokratska Stranka—the Bosnian Serb nationalist party] in response to a bunch of Muslim extremists creating a militant Islamist party in 1990, called the SDA [Stranka Demokratske Akcije—or Party of Democratic Action]," Karadžić said to me in January 2015. "There was a sense of paranoia among Serbs." Islamism is an Islamic revivalist movement that seeks to center Islamic values in all facets of life. Islamists tend to be religious conservatives who follow a literal interpretation of Islamic texts.

At the time he said this, I assumed he was making up the story about "Muslim extremists" out of whole cloth as a way to rationalize the war and the Serb atrocities. He must have been exaggerating. At the time the party first formed, Serbs and Muslims were not enemies at all.

Karadžić did not seem to have a personal animus against Muslims prior to the war. Most of his friends were Muslim, Dr. Cerić said.[42] That was during the period that Karadžić was posing as an urban sophisticate. "Izet Sarajlić was the godfather to my son," Karadžić told me. (Izet Sarajlić, a Bosniak, was Bosnia's most widely celebrated poet after World War II and the former Yugoslavia's most widely translated poet.) In June 1990, Karadžić told an interviewer, "The Serbs and Muslims do not have conflicting interests in any field whatsoever." He also noted that there were no "Islamic fundamentalists" in Bosnia. He even praised Alija Izetbegović, the leader of the Muslim party, who, he said, had once declared himself an Islamicized Serb.[43] But after the elections in November 1990, and especially after Bosniaks began pushing for independence, Karadžić began speaking of an Islamist threat.

On February 6, 1990, the Bosnian parliament passed a law allowing the creation of non-Communist political parties. The law explicitly forbade parties to be organized on the basis of ethnicity. Subsequent legislation in June and July of 1990, however, allowed such national parties to form, creating the potential for ethnonationalist conflict.[44] Even before the law was changed, however, all three nationalities—Serbs, Croats, and Muslims—had found a way around the prohibition of nationalist parties, calling their organizations cultural rather than political.[45] Interestingly, researchers have shown that when authoritarian states transition to democracies, they are vulnerable to terrorist violence and ethnoreligious conflict.[46] According to a study by political scientists Edward Mansfield and Jack Snyder, democratizing states are at elevated risk of war due to institutional weaknesses that can be leveraged by elites fearing loss of status.[47]

Karadžić and the group of former anti-Communist dissidents were unsure what a Bosnian Serb political party should promote.

The group relied on two well-known Serbs to advise them: the Belgrade-based politician and celebrated novelist Dobrica Ćosić, and the Croatia-based distinguished academic and politician Jovan Rašković. Ćosić and Rašković were renowned and extraordinarily accomplished members of the Yugoslav elite. The two of them helped the group of Bosnian Serb intellectuals and former dissidents find an appropriate platform and leadership, eventually settling on the model of the Serb nationalist party that Rašković had created in Croatia.

I spoke with Karadžić many times about both of these eminent advisors. Dobrica Ćosić (1921–2014) viewed Yugoslavia's increasing decentralization, which began in the 1960s, as threatening to Serbia and to ethnic Serbs living in other republics. Ćosić was a member of the prestigious Serbian Academy of Sciences and Arts and would serve as the president of Yugoslavia from 1992 to 1993; Serb admirers refer to him as the "father of the nation." The fact that such a prominent Serb from Belgrade was so involved in the founding of the Bosnian Serb nationalist party was not something the Bosnian Serbs spoke much about in public: the image they tried to project was that their movement was indigenous—a reaction to policies that were harmful to Bosnian Serbs, not a nationalist movement orchestrated and controlled by Belgrade.[48]

Karadžić said to me that he and Dobrica Ćosić had become friends in 1967. He was showing off a bit. "Ćosić visited my family in Montenegro, where he heard my father play the *gusle*. He was interested in me as a young poet."

I asked if Karadžić considered Ćosić to be a mentor. He said no, making me curious about the nature of their relationship. Why wouldn't Karadžić claim Ćosić as a mentor?

Jovan Rašković (1929–1992) was an ethnic Serb from Croatia, who, like Karadžić, was a psychiatrist. Rašković was known for his attempts to explain ethnic tensions in Yugoslavia by referring to Freud's theory of the Oedipus complex. Freud was still in fashion in psychiatric circles in Yugoslavia at the time that Rašković (and even Karadžić, who was younger) were trained.[49] Rašković was on the faculty of universities in both Croatia and Slovenia, and a visiting professor at universities in Italy, the United Kingdom, and the United States. Like Ćosić, he was a member of the Serbian Academy of Sciences and Arts. Karadžić was not.

Rašković founded the Serbian Democratic Party of Croatia (SDS) and persuaded Karadžić, whom he knew from psychiatric circles, to found an analogous, Serb nationalist party in Bosnia with the same name. In Croatia, unlike Bosnia, the ethnic Serb minority was unquestionably under threat from the dominant Croatian nationalist party, which had expropriated fascist symbols from the time when Croatia had been part of the Independent State of Croatia (NDH), the Nazi puppet state established during the Second World War.[50]

Rašković argued that the genocide against the Serbs, carried out by the pro-Nazi regime in wartime Croatia, was a collective trauma for ethnic Serbs. Under Tito's Communist rule, the impact of that collective trauma was repressed, leading, according to Rašković, to a dangerous, if suppressed rage, and "ethnic madness."[51] The sudden release of these memories could lead Serbs to submit to the "collective will of the mob" in massive acts of revenge, he warned, even "a dangerous and genocidal campaign of vengeance against the Croats and Muslims, a tendency that could be monitored and controlled only by a skilled psychiatrist in touch with the Serb collective unconscious. He saw himself in this role, as a sort of shepherd leading his people through the labyrinth of the unconscious and helping them to avoid the temptations of violence."[52] Unfortunately, Rašković did not succeed in this role of violence-preventing shepherd. What was missing from Rašković's account is that elites play a major role in weaponizing these memories.

—

"So, we started the same party," Karadžić told me. "Why invent hot water when it already exists?" The Bosnian SDS party was founded on July 12, 1990. "Party elections were expected in November, only five months after the party was founded. We needed a lot of preelection activities. We needed to develop a propaganda campaign. I was traveling around Bosnia making speeches maybe five times a day. Like a circus bear! People thought I was a good speaker. I was always speaking extemporaneously. I would look out at the audience to see who was listening. I would see on their faces who understood me. I gave thousands of speeches. Millions of sentences. I hadn't written a single word in advance." I was reminded of his earlier surprising claim, that he could control a mob with his eyes.

"Rašković was a colleague. But I knew Ćosić better," Karadžić said. "We talked about literature and Titoism. He had the highest position a writer can have in the Tito regime, but then he turned against it." Ćosić had turned against the Communist regime in the 1960s as a result of his perception that it was favoring other nationalities over Serbs, especially as the federation continued to loosen.

"Ćosić was a little bit nineteenth century," Karadžić explained. "He was old-fashioned. He created a picture of Serbian society and wars and destiny. . . . A great writer, but not to my taste. He wrote extensive works, mild and longer. I like intensive writing, poetry."

Rašković was twenty years older than Karadžić. "Rašković was more of a father figure to me," Karadžić said. "He was like a lamb! He was so sweet. He had the attitude of a caring parent." And, he added, "He had a blind spot for Chetniks."

Karadžić speaks excellent English, but once in a while he got idiomatic expressions slightly wrong. I think he meant a "soft spot" for Chetniks. Was he referring to himself as a Chetnik, or was he saying that Rašković gave him some kind of credit for being the son of a Chetnik?

Karadžić then commenced a confusing soliloquy that began with what I thought was a non sequitur, followed by a series of seemingly unrelated topics. He did this now and then, and I came to understand that I should listen closely when I saw him look away and start talking as if to himself. Sometimes I could figure out what he meant by trying to trace his apparently unconnected associations. But it was often hard, as happened that day, to catch every word when he went off on such tangents.

"Aggression is often sublimated and resolved through humor. . . . But if it's not sublimated you will get violence. . . . But it is always elites who create war. State of mind is very important. If it is corroborated with real events, ontological feelings of insecurity . . . Three brothers may have different feelings of security. If one is presuming he will be killed, he will kill. Readiness for aggression exists particularly in oppressive societies."

Karadžić was explaining the role of elites in stirring up fear and violence, I would later realize.

—

Karadžić was not the first choice to run the party, but the fourth, the "last ditch choice."[53] Ćosić had offered the leading position of the SDS to a series of prominent intellectuals, but they all refused. However, according to political scientists Gerard Toal and Adis Maksić, it soon became apparent that Karadžić was nonetheless well suited for the job:

> Karadžić was an effective public speaker, with an affective makeup that enabled him to connect with rural Serb mores and habits of thought. Furthermore, he was a true believer, an authentic cultural nationalist with a grandiose sense of his own leadership. Finally, Karadžić was an effective propagandist who gravitated by behavioral disposition and psychological condition to demagogic rhetoric.

He advocated positions with passionate vigor and, like many politicians, resorted to convenient truths and useful falsehoods in his advocacy. Put differently, he could be an effective and skillful dissembler.[54]

"Ćosić and Rašković together forced me to accept the leadership position," Karadžić said to me. The two of them made a big effort to "make me a politician," he explained. "To have well-educated people involved in politics—this is a good thing."

It took me some time to understand why he used the word "forced." I believe he chose it deliberately, as it was the same word he used every time he described how he'd come to be leader of the party over the two-year period we spoke. He was developing a narrative about his own martyrdom on behalf of the Serb people.[55]

"In 1990 I was very happy," he said. "I didn't want to be the leader of the party. I didn't want to run for office. I was satisfied with my life. Why would I need to run the party? I was still working as a psychiatrist. Every morning I was working in the clinic, and every afternoon I was working pro bono for the party."

Another time he said, "All of my actions were dictated by my duty to my community." He also said, "I did not have any personal incentives or interests during the war. My family got so poor due to my decision to enter politics."

These were statements that do not appear to be true, as he reportedly enriched himself during the war.[56] He even said, "I was a respected and beloved psychiatrist," a claim that Dr. Cerić refuted.

Another time he seemed to be blaming Milošević. "I knew it was dangerous to accept the leadership of the party—I knew I would not last long as the leader. But I did not think it would go so far, that I would be indicted by The Hague. But I was obedient to Milošević."

I listened to these claims and thought to myself, He is Prince Lazar, a martyr for the Serbian people.

—

According to the poet Mehmedinović, as soon as Karadžić got involved in nationalist politics, he became a new man, seemingly overnight. In order to fit into his new role, he would stand in such a way that observers could see that the psychiatrist and poet was carrying a pistol under his jacket. "The transformation was fundamental," Mehmedinović wrote in his book. "His expression turned wild and he was no longer the same person I had once known. His unassuming look evaporated, like the soul leaving the body of a dead man."[57] According to Mehmedinović, Karadžić developed a "psychiatric strategy" for the war, which General Ratko Mladić (his chief of staff of the Republika Srpska Army) called "mind bending," involving the constant humiliation of the Muslim people of Bosnia.[58] According to political scientist Adis Maksić, Karadžić was preferred as the leader of a future Bosnian Serb party because of his "credentials as a psychiatrist, a skill they believed would translate into an ability to understand and connect with mass sentiments."[59]

Karadžić told me that he studied at the London Institute of Group Analysis, which offered courses in Zagreb. This school was known to offer good training for running therapy groups, he said. There was a permanent staff there, and visiting faculty came in from London. I called some of the faculty whose names Karadžić mentioned, but none of them, except Dr. Angel, had noticed anything unusual about Karadžić at the time.[60]

Karadžić did run therapy groups in his work at the Koševo Clinic. But he was also interested in pursuing a grand intellectual synthesis of group psychology and "our folk poetics," a close friend and fellow poet told historian Robert Donia.[61] By "folk poetics," the friend presumably meant Serbian epic poetry. Karadžić considered pursuing a PhD in this subject after he finished his MD. He never managed to formalize his study of this grand intellectual synthesis, but in many ways his leadership style combined group psychology with what political anthropologist Ivan Čolović calls "war-propaganda folklorism"—the use of Serbian folk traditions as a political instrument, a means of demonstrating that the Serb nationalist party arose in response to the people's needs (vox populi), not the leaders' wishes.[62] "People needed my leadership because they were afraid," Karadžić told me. He said in a 1990 interview, "We waited for the moment when the last Serb was frightened—not by our activity, but by our inactivity."[63]

Karadžić developed a mobilization style that emphasized less what was said and more what was felt, using what Toal and Maksić call "affective inducement," including the symbolic importance of his famous ancestor, Vuk Karadžić. As Toal and Maksić explain, "Heightened drama and paranoia were never far from his rhetoric. Like many revivalist nationalist movements, its stock metaphorical images and story line featured a supposedly humiliated, victimized and oppressed people slowly awakening and re-masculinizing itself for struggle as its historic enemies gather to plot against it. . . . Visceral appeals, existential threat language and direct appeals to 'emotions': all help to prime and organize an affective foundation for ethnopolitical identity."[64]

On May 13, 1992, in Pale, Radovan Karadžić was voted president of the Republika Srpska. Under his newfound authority was the command of the Republika Srpska army and the ability to appoint, promote, or otherwise remove officers in the army.

Dr. Cerić thought that Karadžić didn't really want to be commander in the terrible civil war. All he wanted was to be important—a view I heard from other friends of Karadžić's. "But step by step, month by month he became engaged and believed that he's the big leader, that he's the great historical leader of the Serbs," Dr. Cerić said. "And I believe that he now has the idea of having a place in history for himself—not as an excellent poet but as a war criminal."[65]

—

Jovan Rašković would eventually come to regret his role in forming a Serb nationalist party.[66] In a 1992 interview with the Croatian periodical *Vjesnik*, he said, "I feel responsible because I made the preparations for this war, even if not the military preparations. If I hadn't created this emotional strain in the Serbian people, nothing would have happened. My party lit the fuse of Serbian nationalism not only in Croatia but everywhere else in Bosnia and Herzegovina. It's impossible to imagine an SDS in Bosnia and Herzegovina or a Mr. Karadžić in power without our influence. We have driven this people and we have given it an identity."[67]

I was determined, I am embarrassed to confess, to somehow get Karadžić to feel, and to express, a similar regret about the war. But it would be many months before I was able to ask him about this.

NOTES

1. "The World's Most Wanted Man," script, written and directed by Kevin Sim, *Frontline*, PBS, May 26, 1998, https://www.pbs.org/wgbh/pages/frontline/shows/karadzic/etc/script.html.
2. Robert J. Donia, *Radovan Karadžić: Architect of the Bosnian Genocide* (New York: Cambridge University Press, 2015), p. 25; Jovanka Karadžić, interview in "The World's Most Wanted Man," script, written and directed by Kevin Sim, *Frontline*, PBS, May 26, 1998, https://www.pbs.org/wgbh/pages/frontline/shows/karadzic/etc/script.html.
3. Jovanka Karadžić, interview in "The World's Most Wanted Man," script, written and directed by Kevin Sim, *Frontline*, PBS, May 26, 1998, https://www.pbs.org/wgbh/pages/frontline/shows/karadzic/etc/script.html.
4. Tracy Wilkinson, "Bosnians Recall Karadzic, a Neighbor Turned

Enemy," *Los Angeles Times*, July 23, 1995, http://articles.latimes.com/1995-07-23/news/mn-27059_1_bosnian-serb.

5. Tracy Wilkinson, "Bosnians Recall Karadzic, a Neighbor Turned Enemy," *Los Angeles Times*, July 23, 1995, http://articles.latimes.com/1995-07-23/news/mn-27059_1_bosnian-serb.

6. Robert J. Donia, *Radovan Karadžić: Architect of the Bosnian Genocide* (New York: Cambridge University Press, 2015), p. 30.

7. It is worth noting that Serbs outnumbered Muslims in Bosnia at the time Karadžić first moved to Sarajevo. The 1961 census reported 1,406,057 Serbs, 842,248 Muslims, and 711,665 Croats living in Bosnia. By 1971, self-identified Muslims exceeded the number of Serbs. Robert J. Donia and John V. A. Fine Jr., *Bosnia and Hercegovina: A Tradition Betrayed* (New York: Columbia University Press, 1994), pp. 87, 178.

8. Robert J. Donia, telephone interview with author, June 27, 2018; Robert J. Donia, *Radovan Karadžić: Architect of the Bosnian Genocide* (New York: Cambridge University Press, 2015), pp. 31–32.

9. All quotes from Marko Vešović in this text are from an interview for the PBS *Frontline* documentary "The World's Most Wanted Man." Marko Vešović, interview in "The World's Most Wanted Man," script, written and directed by Kevin Sim, *Frontline*, PBS, May 26, 1998, https://www.pbs.org/wgbh/pages/frontline/shows/karadzic/etc/script.html.

10. Vladimir Srebrov, interview in "The World's Most Wanted Man," script, written and directed by Kevin Sim, *Frontline*, PBS, May 26, 1998, https://www.pbs.org/wgbh/pages/frontline/shows/karadzic/etc/script.html.

11. Mirko Arsić and Dragan R. Marković, *'68. Studentski bunt i društvo* ['68. Student uprising and society], 3rd ed. (Belgrade: Istrazivacko izdavacki centar SSO Srbije, 1988), p. 100, cited in Robert J. Donia, *Radovan Karadžić: Architect of the Bosnian Genocide* (New York: Cambridge University Press, 2015), pp. 31–32.

12. Semezdin Mehmedinović, *Sarajevo Blues*, trans. Ammiel Alcalay (San Francisco: City Lights Books, 1998).

    Historian Robert Donia explains that it was common practice at the time for the security services to speak with intellectuals, and that just speaking to the security services would not make a person an informant. Robert J. Donia, *Radovan Karadžić: Architect of the Bosnian Genocide* (New York: Cambridge University Press, 2015), p. 32.

13. Karadžić's good friend Marko Vešović said that he stopped being friends with Karadžić when he realized Karadžić was spying on the

group of student protestors for the police. Marko Vešović, interview in "The World's Most Wanted Man," script, written and directed by Kevin Sim, *Frontline*, PBS, May 26, 1998, https://www.pbs.org/wgbh/pages/frontline/shows/karadzic/etc/script.html.

14. Marko Vešović, interview in "The World's Most Wanted Man," transcript, *Frontline*, PBS, https://www.pbs.org/wgbh/pages/frontline/shows/karadzic/interviews/vesovic.html.

15. "The 25 Greatest Radio and Television Talk Show Hosts of All Time," *Talkers Magazine*, September 2002, http://www.talkers.com/greatest/.

16. Barry Farber, interview with author, April 8, 2017.

17. Robert J. Donia, *Radovan Karadžić: Architect of the Bosnian Genocide* (New York: Cambridge University Press, 2015), p. 5.

18. Balkan Investigative Reporting Network, "Karadzic Completes Donia Cross-Examination," *Balkan Transitional Justice*, June 11, 2010, http://www.balkaninsight.com/en/article/karadzic-completes-donia-cross-examination/1458/81.

19. Robert J. Donia, *Radovan Karadžić: Architect of the Bosnian Genocide* (New York: Cambridge University Press, 2015), p. 6. Remarkably, "chameleon" was precisely the word that interrogator Joseph Maier used to describe Hermann Goering. The Nuremberg Nazis claimed to see a chameleon in the Rorschach inkblots, in much higher numbers than is the norm for that test. This finding has not yet been explained by Rorschach experts. Joel E. Dimsdale, *Anatomy of Malice: The Enigma of the Nazi War Criminals* (New Haven: Yale University Press, 2016).

20. Marko Vešović, interview in "The World's Most Wanted Man," script, written and directed by Kevin Sim, *Frontline*, PBS, May 26, 1998, https://www.pbs.org/wgbh/pages/frontline/shows/karadzic/etc/script.html.

21. Ismet Cerić, interview in "The World's Most Wanted Man," transcript, *Frontline*, PBS, https://www.pbs.org/wgbh/pages/frontline/shows/karadzic/interviews/ceric.html. Every quote from Ismet Cerić in this book has been taken from the PBS *Frontline* documentary "The World's Most Wanted Man."

22. Christopher Merrill, *Only the Nails Remain: Scenes from the Balkan Wars* (Lanham, MD: Rowman & Littlefield, 2001), p. 155.

23. Charles Simic, email correspondence with author, August 22, 2016.

24. Ismet Cerić, interview in "The World's Most Wanted Man," transcript, *Frontline*, PBS, https://www.pbs.org/wgbh/pages/frontline/shows/karadzic/interviews/ceric.html.

25. Marko Vešović, interview in "The World's Most Wanted Man," script, written and directed by Kevin Sim, *Frontline*, PBS, May 26, 1998, https://www.pbs.org/wgbh/pages/frontline/shows/karadzic/etc /script.html.

26. Ismet Cerić, interview in "The World's Most Wanted Man," transcript, *Frontline*, PBS, https://www.pbs.org/wgbh/pages/frontline /shows/karadzic/interviews/ceric.html.

27. Biljana Plavšić, *I Testify*, Vol. 2 (Banja Luka: Trioprint, 2005), pp. 212, 284. Excerpts translated by political scientist Mladen Mrdalj. Plavšić made three references to Karadžić's gambling habits, on pages 59, 65, and 208.

28. Julian Borger, "How Radovan Karadžić Embraced Evil," *Daily Beast*, March 24, 2016, https://www.thedailybeast.com/how-radovan-karadzic -embraced-evil.

29. As reported in Julian Borger, "How Radovan Karadžić Embraced Evil," *Daily Beast*, March 24, 2016, https://www.thedailybeast.com /how-radovan-karadzic-embraced-evil.

30. Marko Vešović, interview in "The World's Most Wanted Man," script, written and directed by Kevin Sim, *Frontline*, PBS, May 26, 1998, https://www.pbs.org/wgbh/pages/frontline/shows/karadzic/etc /script.html.

31. According to Robert Donia, Karadžić was briefly an entrepreneur. He engaged in some petty corruption, but never enough to enrichen himself. Robert J. Donia, *Radovan Karadžić: Architect of the Bosnian Genocide* (New York: Cambridge University Press, 2015), p. 40. Karadzic and Momćilo Krajišnik were arrested on suspicion of embezzling public funds in order to build homes for themselves in Pale. Denis Dzidic, "Radovan Karadzic: Psychiatrist, Poet, Politician, Convict?" *Balkan Insight*, March 21, 2016, https://balkaninsight.com/2016/03/21/radovan -karadzic-psychiatrist-poet-politician-convict-03-21-2016/.

32. "The World's Most Wanted Man," script, written and directed by Kevin Sim, *Frontline*, PBS, May 26, 1998, https://www.pbs.org/wgbh /pages/frontline/shows/karadzic/etc/script.html.

33. Radovan Karadžić, interview in "The World's Most Wanted Man," script, written and directed by Kevin Sim, *Frontline*, PBS, May 26, 1998, https://www.pbs.org/wgbh/pages/frontline/shows/karadzic/etc /script.html.

34. Robert J. Donia, *Radovan Karadžić: Architect of the Bosnian Genocide* (New York: Cambridge University Press, 2015), pp. 39–40.

35. Ismet Cerić, interview in "The World's Most Wanted Man," transcript, *Frontline*, PBS, https://www.pbs.org/wgbh/pages/frontline/shows/karadzic/interviews/ceric.html.

36. Semezdin Mehmedinović, *Sarajevo Blues*, trans. Ammiel Alcalay (San Francisco: City Lights Books, 1998), pp. 15-16.

37. Semezdin Mehmedinović, *Sarajevo Blues*, trans. Ammiel Alcalay (San Francisco: City Lights Books, 1998), pp. 15–16.

38. Robert J. Donia, *Radovan Karadžić: Architect of the Bosnian Genocide* (New York: Cambridge University Press, 2015), p. 50.

39. Semezdin Mehmedinović, *Sarajevo Blues*, trans. Ammiel Alcalay (San Francisco: City Lights Books, 1998), p. 16.

40. Robert J. Donia, telephone interview with author, June 27, 2018.

41. Mirko Arsić and Dragan R. Marković, '68. *Studentski bunt i društvo* ['68. Student uprising and society], 3rd ed. (Belgrade: Istrazivacko izdavacki centar SSO Srbije, 1988), p. 100, cited in Robert J. Donia, *Radovan Karadžić: Architect of the Bosnian Genocide* (New York: Cambridge University Press, 2015), pp. 31–32.

42. Ismet Cerić, interview in "The World's Most Wanted Man," transcript, *Frontline*, PBS, https://www.pbs.org/wgbh/pages/frontline/shows/karadzic/interviews/ceric.html.

43. Radovan Karadžić in "Interview Published in the Nedelja Magazine on July 1, 1990," *Intervjui i govori*, Vol. 5, pp. 24–25, cited in Robert J. Donia, *Radovan Karadžić: Architect of the Bosnian Genocide* (New York: Cambridge University Press, 2015), p. 62.

44. The Constitutional Court declared the Bosnian parliament's March 1990 provision banning political organization "on the basis of nationality (ethnicity)" unconstitutional. The judge who led the charge to overturn the ban, Dr. Kasim Trnka, would become an active part of the SDA leadership. Steven L. Burg and Paul S. Shoup, *The War in Bosnia-Herzegovina: Ethnic Conflict and International Intervention* (Armonk, NY: M. E. Sharpe, 1999), p. 46.

   According to Burg, the preferences of the population regarding ethnocentric political parties at that time are unclear. While some data suggests that many people supported the ban on national parties, in the end voting largely occurred across ethnic lines. Steven L. Burg, email correspondence, October 6, 2018.

45. Robert J. Donia, *Radovan Karadžić: Architect of the Bosnian Genocide* (New York: Cambridge University Press, 2015), pp. 50–51.

46. Alberto Abadie, "Poverty, Political Freedom, and the Roots of Terror-

ism," *American Economic Review*, Vol. 96, No. 2 (May 2006), pp. 50–56; James A. Piazza, "Regime Age and Terrorism: Are New Democracies Prone to Terrorism?" *International Interactions*, Vol. 39, No. 2 (2013), pp. 246–263; Jessica Stern, *Terror in the Name of God* (New York: Harper-Collins, 2003).

47. Edward D. Mansfield and Jack L. Snyder, "Democratization and the Danger of War," *International Security*, Vol. 20, No. 1 (1995), pp. 5–38.

48. Despite acknowledging that the party's newspaper, *Javnost* [Public], had taken its name from a conversation with Dobrica Ćosić, Karadžić and other leaders in the SDS rarely publicly acknowledged the role that Belgrade's Serb intellectuals played in the formation of the Bosnian SDS. Robert J. Donia, *Radovan Karadžić: Architect of the Bosnian Genocide* (New York: Cambridge University Press, 2015).

49. Dušan I. Bjelić, "Madness as a Political Factor," *Psychoanalysis, Culture & Society*, Vol. 15, No. 1 (2010), pp. 20–36.

50. The NDH (Nezavisna Drzava Hrvatska) or the Independent State of Croatia was established in parts of Axis-occupied Yugoslavia on April 10, 1941. It consisted of most of modern-day Croatia and Bosnia and Herzegovina, as well as some of modern-day Serbia and Slovenia. It was governed by the fascist Ustasha organization.

51. Dušan I. Bjelić, "Madness as a Political Factor," *Psychoanalysis, Culture & Society*, Vol. 15, No. 1 (2010), pp. 20–36.

52. Dušan I. Bjelić, "Madness as a Political Factor," *Psychoanalysis, Culture & Society*, Vol. 15, No. 1 (2010), p. 28.

Steven Burg points out that the release of traumatic memories was not as sudden as Rašković implies, but started before the elections and the war. Newspapers liberated from Communist control (e.g., *Oslobodjenje* in Sarajevo) were full of revelations of heretofore suppressed evidence of violence against civilian populations and/or vanquished enemy combatants on the part of the Communists once they secured power (including stories featuring "hidden" caves or other locations with human remains—hidden only from mass media but not local knowledge). There was indeed a deep base of "grievances," felt by individuals who had lived through World War II, and some desire for vengeance. Burg also points out that elites ("ethnic entrepreneurs") are often responsible for turning memories and structural inequalities into grievances and shaping claims for their redress. At the same time, it is obvious that appeals to memories or insecurities will be ineffective if these do not, in fact, exist. The role of ethnic entrepreneurs in legitimating these feelings, defining "remedies," and, especially, escalating emotions is central to violent ethnic conflict. Steven L. Burg, email correspondence with author, October 6, 2018.

Karadžić himself is quoted as saying, "Serbian people have suffered enough. A killing of Serbs in World War II was unpunished. We have to avenge [sic] them." M. Gabrijela Kisicek, "The Rhetoric of War— Former Yugoslavia Example," *Journal of Arts & Humanities*, Vol. 2, No. 8 (2013), pp. 75–84. Adis Maksić further quotes Karadžić as claiming that "the soul of the Serb peoples is sick from humiliations." Caric, "Moral, pa nacija," *NIN*, April 1, 1990, p. 2, cited in Adis Maksić, "Mobilizing for Ethnic Violence? Ethno-National Political Parties and the Dynamics of Ethno-Politicization," *PhD diss.* (Alexandria, VA: Virginia Polytechnic Institute and State University, 2014), p. 154.

53. Ćosić's first choice for the SDS presidency was Nenad Kecmanović, a former rector of the University of Sarajevo. Slavoljub Đukić, *Lovljenje Vetra: Politička Ispovest Dobrice Ćosića* (Belgrade: Samizdat B92, 2001), p. 172, cited in Gerard Toal and Adis Maksić, "'Serbs, You Are Allowed to Be Serbs!' Radovan Karadžić and the 1990 Election Campaign in Bosnia-Herzegovina," *Ethnopolitics*, Vol. 13, No. 3 (2014), p. 271.

Two prominent academics, Mićo Carević and Milorad Ekmečić, also both declined to lead the party, preferring academic life. Robert J. Donia, *Radovan Karadžić: Architect of the Bosnian Genocide* (New York: Cambridge University Press, 2015), p. 54; Neven Andjelic, *Bosnia-Herzegovina: The End of a Legacy* (London and Portland: Frank Cass, 2003), p. 166.

54. Gerard Toal and Adis Maksić, "'Serbs, You Are Allowed to Be Serbs!' Radovan Karadžić and the 1990 Election Campaign in Bosnia-Herzegovina," *Ethnopolitics*, Vol. 13, No. 3 (2014), pp. 267–287.

55. The founding meeting of the all-Bosnian SDS in Sarajevo occurred on July 12, 1990, Saint Peter's Day, but the party was formally registered on June 29, 1990. Alija Izetbegović and Professor Muhamed Filipović— philosopher and historian—attended and addressed the attendees.

56. While war profiteering among Bosnian Serb leaders is well documented, Karadžić never "acquired great wealth" despite drawing on party funds to allow his family to enjoy a lifestyle well above that of the average Bosnian. Robert J. Donia, *Radovan Karadžić: Architect of the Bosnian Genocide* (New York: Cambridge University Press, 2015), p. 58.

57. Semezdin Mehmedinović, *Sarajevo Blues*, trans. Ammiel Alcalay (San Francisco: City Lights Books, 1998), p. 16.

58. Semezdin Mehmedinović, *Sarajevo Blues*, trans. Ammiel Alcalay (San Francisco: City Lights Books, 1998), p. 20.

59. Adis Maksić, "Mobilizing for Ethnic Violence? Ethno-National Political Parties and the Dynamics of Ethno-Politicization," *PhD diss.* (Alexandria, VA: Virginia Polytechnic Institute and State University, 2014), p. 101.

60. Dr. Sanda Rašković-Ivić, the daughter of Jovan Rašković, did say that Karadžić was called a "peacemaker" among his psychoanalytic group because he tried to mediate conflicts within groups and did not like conflict escalation. Sanda Rašković-Ivić, email correspondence with political scientist Mladen Mrdalj, February 22, 2018.

61. Reported in Robert J. Donia, *Radovan Karadžić: Architect of the Bosnian Genocide* (New York: Cambridge University Press, 2015), p. 35.

62. Ivan Čolović, *The Politics of Symbol in Serbia*, trans. Celia Hawkesworth (London: Hurst, 2002).

63. Radovan Karadžić, Interview probably published in *Politika* on September 10, 1990, in *Intervjui i govori dr Radovana Karadžića* [Interviews and speeches of Dr. Radovan Karadžić], vol. 5 (Belgrade: International Committee for the Truth about Radovan Karadžić, 2005), p. 45, cited in Robert J. Donia, *Radovan Karadžić: Architect of the Bosnian Genocide* (New York: Cambridge University Press, 2015), p. 57.

64. Roger D. Peterson, *Understanding Ethnic Violence: Fear, Hatred, and Resentment in Twentieth-Century Eastern Europe* (New York: Cambridge University Press, 2002); Drew Westen, *The Political Brain: The Role of Emotion in Deciding the Fate of the Nation* (New York: Public Affairs, 2007); Nigel Thrift, *Non-Representational Theory: Space, Politics, Affect* (London: Routledge, 2008); Gerard Toal, "'Republika Srpska Will Have a Referendum': The Rhetorical Politics of Milorad Dodik," *Nationalities Papers*, Vol. 41, No. 1 (2013), pp. 166–204, cited in Gerard Toal and Adis Maksić, "'Serbs, You Are Allowed to Be Serbs!' Radovan Karadžić and the 1990 Election Campaign in Bosnia-Herzegovina," *Ethnopolitics*, Vol. 13, No. 3 (2014), pp. 267–287.

65. Ismet Cerić, interview in "The World's Most Wanted Man," transcript, *Frontline*, PBS, https://www.pbs.org/wgbh/pages/frontline/shows/karadzic/interviews/ceric.html.

66. Stevan M. Weine, *When History Is a Nightmare: Lives and Memories of Ethnic Cleansing in Bosnia-Herzegovina* (New Brunswick, NJ: Rutgers University Press, 1999), pp. 91–92.

67. Both Stevan Weine and the author interpret Rašković's claims as regret, but an alternative reading suggested by political scientist Mladen Mrdalj after examining the original text indicates that Rašković may have been taking credit for having a leadership role in preparing the Serbs for defense against the Croats. Jovan Rašković, interview in *Vjesnik*, January 24, 1992, cited in Stevan M. Weine, *When History Is a Nightmare: Lives and Memories of Ethnic Cleansing in Bosnia-Herzegovina* (New Brunswick, NJ: Rutgers University Press, 1999), p. 91.

Chapter Eight

MARTYRS

In *Serbian Epics*, an astonishing documentary filmed in 1992 by a then young Polish-British filmmaker, Paweł Pawlikowski, two poets are seen standing on Mount Trebević, the mountain above Sarajevo.[1] (Pawlikowski would win an Academy Award in 2015 for his film *Ida*.) The city was already under siege. The taller of the two men begins to recite a poem he wrote about the city of Sarajevo. The poem was written many years before, but its subject is Sarajevo burning.

> *Sarajevo*
>
> The city burns as an incense stick,
> In that smoke our consciousness meanders.
> Empty suits glide through town. A crimson
> Stone dies, built in houses. Plague!
> A company of armored poplars
> Marches up within. Aggressor
> Air runs through our souls
> And one moment you're a man, another an airy thing.[2]

He tells his companion that many of his poems "have something of prediction, which frightens me sometimes."

The shorter poet is the famous Russian dissident writer Eduard

Limonov. Back then, he was principally known as a poet and a memoirist, and as an international "bad boy." Limonov gazes at the taller poet admiringly, perhaps surprised to see a fellow poet, a fellow writer and intellectual, appearing so comfortable around weapons, and among military personnel who are armed to the teeth.

Limonov now looks at a large gun, palming it with a kind of reverence. "It's a mighty weapon," he purrs. We see him next, trying out a sniper rifle, shooting in the direction of the city below. The viewer is astonished. Has Limonov decided to shoot unarmed civilians—a war crime—while he's being filmed for a documentary?

It is hard to understand the meaning of Limonov's presence in Sarajevo and in this film without knowing something about him. Limonov was a Soviet poet who, after refusing to spy on fellow poets for the KGB, emigrated to New York in the mid-1970s. He mixed with a wide variety of New Yorkers, including the elite—artists, intellectuals, and politicians, as well as the merely wealthy—and those living at the bottom of society in single-room occupancy hotels. He wrote a fictional memoir, *It's Me, Eddie*, published in French as *The Russian Poet Prefers Big Blacks* (in reference to his sexual adventures) and in German as *Fuck Off, Amerika*. The book brought him international fame. He returned to Russia, shortly after the Soviet Union fell apart.[3] In 1993, he started a radical party, the National Bolshevik Party, which was eventually banned. He developed a reputation as "a poster boy of Russian fringe-politics and a vicious Kremlin detractor."[4] But once Vladimir Putin invaded and annexed Crimea, Limonov became Putin's new champion.

Back in 1992, however, he was at the very beginning of his career as a far-right Slavic nationalist.

The taller poet, now even more famous than his shorter companion, is Radovan Karadžić, my war criminal.

A poet assassin, like Gavrilo Princip in Karadžić's poem.

He was younger then, his hair just beginning to gray. When I spoke with him in prison, nearly a quarter century later, Karadžić said he did not like the film. Nor did he seem to like Limonov. "Limonov is a false homosexual, the worst kind," Karadžić said. I was not sure what to make of this assessment.

"Pawlikowski made it look as though Limonov was shooting into the city of Sarajevo, for the fun of it. That wasn't true," Karadžić told me. I assumed, as I usually did, that there was a good chance that Karadžić was lying—that Limonov had in fact been aiming at the vulnerable city spread out below him, risking indictment for war crimes. And as I generally did with the "facts" that Karadžić shared with me, I tried to find other sources. With regard to this question, I checked with Chris Landreth, a film-maker who is also an engineer. He did some careful calculations. Given the angle of the light, it is nearly impossible that Limonov was shooting at the city, he said, as the sun-lighting of the city scenes is wrong for that time of day. Landreth told me he was nearly certain that "poor Eduard is shooting at bunnies in the sur-rounding woods, and clever Paweł has framed him (so to speak) shooting at the Latin Bridge," the famous Sarajevo bridge near which Gavrilo Princip stood when he shot the archduke.[5]

Even worse, Karadžić scoffed, "Pawlikowski made it look as though I am obsessed with epic poetry."

The film includes quite a bit of haunting footage of a singer chanting epic poems while playing the *gusle,* the wooden, single-horsehair-stringed instrument. The *guslar* moans a series of bal-lads about the Battle of Kosovo and the Ottoman invasion. There is a hypnotic resonance between his voice and the instrument.

I am surprised by Karadžić's complaint that the filmmaker made it look as though he were obsessed with epic poetry, since that very topic came up in nearly every one of our conversations. We discussed Karadžić's favorite heroic ballads, the difference between men's and women's songs, the poems his mother recited to him every evening when he was a small child, the fact that he plays the *gusle*, the fact that his father played the *gusle*.[6] We talked about the epic poem that was passed down, orally, in his family but had not yet become part of any written collection (thus making it more genuine and more valuable) and about the fact that he, Karadžić, writes lyric, not epic, poetry.

I will confess that I have watched the film *Serbian Epics* a number of times and that I find the chanting of the epic poems irresistibly compelling. It is an unusual film. At the time, the siege of Sarajevo was exciting widespread horror and indignation in the West. Pawlikowski would later tell a journalist that he, like everyone else he knew, was deeply upset by what he had heard and seen on television: the terrible atrocities perpetrated by the Serbs who were said to be heirs to the Nazis. He said that for noble-minded reporters, "The choice was natural: when one side is weak and the other is stronger, even if you make it a point of honor to note that those on the weaker side aren't all angels and those on the stronger side aren't all devils, you side with the weaker. You go where the shells are falling, not where they're being fired from."[7]

Pawlikowski chose to film the side that no one else was filming: the place from which the shells were fired. He takes us behind the scenes with a group of soon-to-be indicted war criminals. The film would eventually become part of the record at the Yugoslav Tribunal—among other reasons, because it shows how the Bosnian Serbs thought about Serb ownership of parts of Bosnia.

There is of course a moment when even the noble-minded humanitarian observer, "who goes where the shells are falling, not where they're being fired from," experiences an ignoble feeling of glee, even a sense of triumph, as the perpetrator finally gets what he deserves in the form of retaliatory strikes or indictments or punishment. But the French filmmaker and writer Emmanuel Carrère says, this moment doesn't last; the wheel turns once more, and the noble-minded humanitarian might find him- or herself "denouncing the partiality of the International Tribunal in The Hague, which steadfastly prosecutes [ethnic] Serbian war criminals while leaving their Croatian and Bosnian counter-parts to the predictable leniency of their own courts."[8]

One discovers, over time, that today's evil perpetrators were yesterday's guileless victims—just as is often true in ordinary life. A victimization Olympics comes into play, and the noble-minded humanitarian observer finds herself in a moral muddle, wanting to be objective and fair to all sides.[9]

Pawlikowski clearly wants to show us the dangers of ethnic nationalism, a view with which I wholeheartedly agree. What makes the film so powerfully useful is that he exposes the viewer not only to the ugliness of Serbian war criminals plotting to "cleanse" ethnically mixed parts of Bosnia, but also to the *appeal* of the nationalists' message. The *guslar*'s slow articulation of the sad Battle of Kosovo cycle, for example, is mesmerizing. The hypnotic resonance gave the Serb nationalists' wartime propaganda a visceral power. The theme of many of these poems is Serb martyrdom—their loss of Kosovo to the Ottoman invaders, and the subsequent five-century-long occupation.

—

The Serbs see themselves as having been Yugoslavia's principal victims during the Second World War. The war was devastating in Yugoslavia, especially in Bosnia. Serbs were in fact significantly overrepresented in Yugoslavia's losses. Over a million Yugoslavians died, half of them Serbs (the Serb share of the population at that time was approximately a third).[10] The sacrifice of so many Serb lives in World War II became part of the Serb martyrology.

World War II was accompanied by a civil war in Yugoslavia. Many more citizens of Yugoslavia were murdered by fellow Yugoslavs than were killed by the Nazis and their allies. Not only did Serbs comprise the largest number of battle deaths (both in absolute terms and by percentage), they were also directly targeted by the fascist Independent State of Croatia (NDH).[11] The NDH sought to "cleanse" their territory of Serbs and other "undesirables"—including Jews and Roma—and murdered hundreds of thousands of citizens.[12]

The invading Axis powers had sought allies among the Croats, who had been chafing under Serb domination of the Kingdom of Yugoslavia (which existed between its founding in 1918 and the Communist victory in World War II). They created the NDH, comprising present-day Croatia, most of Bosnia-Herzegovina, and parts of Serbia and Montenegro. The NDH was led by the Ustasha, a violently racist terrorist organization that had been banned throughout Europe before the war. (The Ustasha terrorists had been implicated in the murder of Yugoslavia's King Alexander in 1934.) The leader of the Ustasha and the Nazi puppet state, Ante Pavelić, who had been imprisoned in Italy, returned to Croatia after the Nazi invasion to become the führer of the Independent State.[13]

The war was especially devastating to the population of Bosnia. In 1941, in Ustasha-occupied Bosnia-Herzegovina, an estimated 16.7 percent of the Serb population, 12.8 percent of the Croat population, and 8.6 percent of the Muslim population were victims of the fighting.[14] The Ustasha set up the Jasenovac extermination camp complex on the border of Bosnia and Croatia. It is not well known outside Yugoslavia that between 80,000 and 100,000 Serbs, Jews, and Roma were killed there during the war.[15] The vast majority of Bosnia's Jews were murdered.[16]

The term "ethnic cleansing" was not invented in the 1990s wars, as is commonly believed. According to political scientist Vladimir Petrović, the term "ethnic cleansing" was used during World War II by different Balkan politicians and intellectuals.[17] But the atrocities carried out by the Ustasha were so extreme that even the SS found them objectionable.[18] A February 1942 German police report stated, "The Ustasha units have carried out their atrocities not only against Orthodox males of military age, but in particular in the most bestial fashion against unarmed old men, women and children."[19] Many Bosnian Muslims joined the fascist Ustasha or were recruited into Home Guard units of the NDH.[20] Some joined the Communist Partisans (though few joined until Italy capitulated in the fall of 1943).[21] Some even joined the Serb Chetniks, the primarily Serb remnant of the Yugoslav royal army that would eventually be involved in massacring Muslims.[22] The Chetniks carried out ethnic cleansing campaigns against their ethnic and ideological enemies, and even collaborated with the Nazis when it served their interests, but not on the same scale as the fascist Ustasha.[23]

For some Serb nationalists, the 1990s war against both Muslims and Croats was partly a war of revenge for the World War II genocide against ethnic Serbs in NDH-occupied Bosnia and Croatia.[24] Serbs' share of the World War II dead was, in fact, higher than that of Croats or Muslims, according to contemporary demographers—but the official tally at the time exaggerated not only the total number of Yugoslavs killed, but also the Serbs' share.[25] According to historian Timothy Snyder, exaggerating the numbers of war dead releases "ghosts of people who never lived" into the culture. "Unfortunately, such specters have power," he writes. "What begins as competitive martyrology can end with martyrological imperialism."[26]

Still, Karadžić's form of "martyrological imperialism" was not principally motivated by the Ustasha genocide of Serbs. World War II's ethnic cleansing campaigns were downplayed under Communist rule in an effort to foster "brotherhood and unity," the guiding principle and slogan for interethnic peace in Communist Yugoslavia; other periods of Serb martyrdom may thus have loomed larger in his mind.[27] I shared with Karadžić the concept of "chosen trauma," the term that political psychiatrist Vamik Volkan used to describe the way nations so often choose a historical wrong as part of their national myth, even if the trauma occurred centuries earlier, sometimes as a way to justify attacks against an enemy as acts of revenge.[28] Karadžić told me many times that the loss of Kosovo in 1389 followed by the five-century Ottoman occupation was far more significant than the more recent traumas of World War II. "A lot of our people were stolen," he said. "They became *yanichar*, or Janissaries [elite soldiers in the Ottoman military]. It was massive—the stealing of Christian boys to serve as the sultan's elite troops." Unfortunately, the sultans found that the Bosnian Christian slaves were particularly good soldiers.[29]

Karadžić had heard about the Ottoman occupation, and the sultan's enslavement of Serbs and other Christian boys, nearly every night in the form of the epic poems his mother recited for him. "For five hundred years we were under imperial occupation," he complained, bitterly and repeatedly, as if the occupation had affected him personally, as if he wanted to imprint the memory of this pain into my mind so that I would understand the need for revenge against the "Turks," the term he used for Bosnian Muslims, who were neither Turks nor Ottoman slaveholders.

—

All sides in every war utilize propaganda. Joseph Goebbels, who served as minister for propaganda and national enlightenment for Hitler, had a great deal to say on the topic. For Goebbels, one of the most important purposes of propaganda was to "facilitate the displacement of aggression by specifying the targets for hatred." And propaganda, he said, must be presented in an intuitive and accessible way.[30]

In this war, much of the propaganda on the Serb side took the form of *gusle*-accompanied epic poetry and other forms of war-propaganda folklorism. The ballads, which tell mythologized versions of history, serve the function of emphasizing certain "self-evident and sacred tales" about the Serbian nation, especially the battles between the Serbs and the Ottoman invaders. According to Ivan Čolović, the Serb nationalists used these stories to revive old enmities from wars that ended long ago, while simultaneously putting the 1990s Bosnian War outside of historical time. The past, Čolović says, is revived into an eternal present.[31] In speaking about the Bosnian Serb military's preparation for taking over the town of Srebrenica, which ended in a genocide, General Mladić said that the time had come to take revenge on the Turks for their five-century occupation of Serb lands.[32] Frontiers, too, were altered. During the war, any place in Bosnia where Serbs were known to have lived or Serbian graves could be found might become a target for ethnic cleansing of Muslims or Croats.[33] To be clear: all sides were guilty of war crimes. According to the war-propaganda folklorism, Croats and Muslims have ersatz identities as nations, because they abandoned their true identity and adopted a foreign or invented identity. Their true identity is Serbian.[34] This idea—that Croats and Muslims are actually Serbs—was a leitmotif in my discussions with Karadžić. This kind of thinking confused me. If Croats and Muslims were really Serbs, why would Serb nationalists want to kill them? "Think of Cain and Abel," Karadžić said to me, by way of explanation.

———

"Ninety-seven thousand people died on all three sides in forty-three months of war," Karadžić said.

He said this matter-of-factly, as if it were a number of little consequence. He must have seen a look of shock on my face. He was bringing the dead into the room.

"You need to compare this with Rwanda," he said. "Up to a million people died in a very short war." The BBC reported that eight hundred thousand people were killed in Rwanda in one hundred days.[35]

Rwanda, he said, was a genocide. "Uncontrolled rage. An explosion. What happened in Yugoslavia was not a genocide but a civil war."

He had what he considered to be proof that the war in Bosnia was a civil war, not a genocide. "You need to look at the figures that Ewa Tabeau reported," he said. "She was the official demographer for the prosecution. She said that a similar percentage of Serbs and Muslims died. She calculated that 2.6 percent of Muslims died and 2.8 percent of Serbs died."

That sounded absurd to me. I was pretty sure, based on everything I heard during the war, that the percentage of Muslims and Serbs who died could not be anything close to equal. And Karadžić was claiming that an even higher percentage of the ethnic Serbs died than Muslims.

I did look up Ewa Tabeau. She is a highly respected demographer who did in fact serve as a prosecution witness for the ICTY. But Karadžić seems to have misremembered the figures she calculated. She did *not* report that a higher percentage of Serbs died than Muslims, but the opposite. What she actually calculated is that 3.1 percent of Bosnian Muslims died, and 1.4 percent of Bosnian Serbs died. According to Tabeau's figures, 89,186 Bosnians of all ethnicities died during the war, 35 percent of them civilians and 65 percent soldiers.[36] (Note: Estimates of the number of Bosnians killed and disappeared during the war went down over time. In 1996, the highest estimate was 329,000; but by 2010 the estimates hovered around 100,000. See Appendix B for a comparison of these estimates.) It is important to note that of the civilians killed during the war, the vast majority were Muslim.

"The West makes a fetish of multiethnicity," Karadžić continued. "The Hutu were deprived of their basic rights. What can you expect? They were treated like beasts. If you keep treating people like beasts, eventually they will act like beasts. If one person says you are drunk, another says you were drunk, a third says you are drunk, eventually you begin to walk like a drunk. You become stigmatized."

In other words, he wants simultaneously to argue that the Serbs were stigmatized by the United States (which is true); that this stigmatization eventually turned the Bosnian Serbs into beasts; and that the Bosnian Serbs—even despite coming to see themselves as beasts—were killed in larger numbers, at least in terms of percentages (clearly false). But it is true that the percentage of the population that died on both sides is closer than what many assumed at the time.

"The borders left after the colonial powers left are unjust and artificial." This is true all over the world, he said.

I didn't have an argument with him here.

"In some ways Yugoslavia was also artificial. There were Yugoslavist forces that held us together, but the forces that led to fissure were stronger than the forces that held us together. This was true from the very beginning of Yugoslavia's formation," he sighed. This, too, is true. A situation that ended with tragic consequences.

—

Scholars consider epic poetry to be Serbia's greatest contribution to world literature. One of the interesting, if not unique, features of Serbian epic poetry is that it does not celebrate the triumphs of Serbia's conquering heroes, but instead celebrates defeat and martyrdom. "Serbs sing of the tragic sense of life," the poet Charles Simic observes. The Turks are often portrayed as cruel conquerors, while the Serbs are either scheming slaves or wily outlaws.

Simic, a Serbian-American who served as poet laureate of the United States from 2007 to 2008, has won most of the important awards available to poets, including a Pulitzer Prize, a MacArthur

Foundation "genius grant," the International Griffin Poetry Prize, and the Wallace Stevens Award. Simic explains that despite having left Serbia as a teenager, he can still recite his favorite epic poems. "Everyone in the West who has known these poems has proclaimed them to be literature of the highest order which ought to be known better."[37]

Here is how Simic describes his first encounter with a *guslar*:

One day in school, in what must have been my fifth or sixth grade, they announced that a *guslar* would perform for us. This was unexpected. Most city people in those days had never heard a *gusle* being played, and as for us kids, brought up as we were on American popular music, the prospect meant next to nothing. In any case, at the appointed time we were herded into the gym where an old peasant, sitting stiffly in a chair and holding a one-stringed instrument, awaited us. When we had quieted down, he started to play the *gusle*.

I still remember my astonishment at what I heard. I suppose I expected the old instrument to sound beautiful, the singing to be inspiring as our history books told us was the case. *Gusle,* however, can hardly be heard in a large room. The sound of that one string is faint, rasping, screechy, tentative. The chanting that goes with it is toneless, monotonous, and unrelieved by vocal flourishes of any kind. The singer simply doesn't show off. There's nothing to do but pay close attention to the words which the *guslar* enunciates with great emphasis and clarity. We heard *The Death of the Mother of the Jugovici* that day and a couple of others. After a while, the poem and the archaic, otherworldly-sounding instrument began to get to me and everybody else. Our anonymous ancestor poet knew what he was doing. This stubborn drone combined with the sublime lyricism of the poem touched the rawest spot in our psyche. The old wounds [of oppression under the Ottomans] were reopened.[38]

A large number of Serbia's epic poems were collected and written down by Vuk Karadžić, Radovan's ancestor, who was widely recognized as a linguistic genius.[39] Vuk Karadžić's collections of epic poems were subsequently published and translated into several European languages.

In one of the most telling scenes in the Paweł Pawlikowski film *Serbian Epics*, Karadžić is seen rhapsodizing over Vuk Karadžić's portrait, describing Vuk as the most famous of his ancestors, and as the "founder of modern Serbian culture." He explains that Vuk revived Serbian medieval culture, which had been all but forgotten during the many centuries of Turkish occupation. In this way, he is also telling us that he, Radovan, the descendant of the great genius, is also reviving Serbian culture. "We have this thing in common," he says, pointing to a dimple on his chin. "My son has it also."

The Battle of Kosovo cycle, which tells the story of a decisive battle between the Serbs and the Turks in the fourteenth century, is considered by most scholars to be the most important example of Serbian folk poetry. It is also critical for us to understand, as it was of profound symbolic importance for the war. Serbs think of Kosovo as the cradle of their civilization, although it has been controlled by many different entities throughout its history, among them both Serbs and Albanians.

The historical Battle of Kosovo took place on June 28, 1389, at the Field of Blackbirds, in what is now the state of Kosovo. Prince Lazar had created the largest and most powerful state on the territory of the ruined Serbian empire, referred to as Moravian Serbia, which he ruled from 1373 until his death in the Battle of Kosovo in 1389. Kosovo was then part of the Kingdom of Serbia, and

Lazar led a pan-Christian army to defend it from the Ottoman invaders. Both sides suffered heavy casualties, but the Serbs, who were fewer in number, suffered the most. The prince is referred to as Tsar Lazar in Serbian epic poetry.[40] Lazar is venerated by the Serbian Orthodox Church as a saint and a martyr. The leader of the Ottoman invaders, Sultan Murad, is said to have been assassinated by a Serbian knight, Miloš Obilić, who purportedly snuck behind enemy lines, pretending to defect, and then killed the sultan. Despite this, the Serbian army was defeated so decisively that there were too few troops to defend the Balkan lands against the Turkish invaders. Serbia collapsed, and the crumbling Byzantine Empire was soon encircled by Turkish armies. In subsequent years, those Serbian principalities that were not already Ottoman vassals would be defeated, one by one, by the Ottomans.[41] This story—which Karadžić imparted to me many times—appears to be historically accurate, though historians claim that there are few reliable records and that parts of the history are uncertain.

According to the legend captured in the epic ballads, on the eve of the battle, Prince Lazar was offered a choice: victory if he opted for the Kingdom of Earth or defeat on the battlefield if he chose the Kingdom of Heaven. This, too, is a story that Karadžić told me many times, each time seeming to forget that he had already told me. It was another leitmotif to our long conversation. "Tsar Lazar," he would say, with reverence, as if by uttering his name he hoped to bring light into the room and into my ignorant mind, "chose to die as a Christian martyr rather than achieve victory on earth."[42] Again and again. So much so that I began to think that Karadžić saw himself as a contemporary Tsar Lazar, sacrificing himself for the Serbian people, protecting his fellow Serbs from those he refers to as "Turks," the Bosnian Muslims. And, like Tsar Lazar, he spends his time contemplating the divine, through a Byzantine mystical practice.[43]

You can't understand Serbs unless you recognize that Serbs have been repeatedly betrayed and victimized, Karadžić said. "Turks have been here as occupiers, and the Muslims are the successors of those occupiers."[44]

—

Here is what I've learned from Karadžić, and from the many years I've spent studying violence. To work up a frenzy for war or terrorism, the leader or propagandist must persuade people of this: Our people and our culture are under imminent threat. It is imperative to repel those invaders and those contaminants among us who would destroy our culture.

Fear of the invader creates anger and hatred. Fear and hatred, properly amplified, can lead to war.

In the moment before the first battle starts, war doesn't feel like offense, but defense: a response to fear of the Other. The key to distinguishing a neurotic from a realist, Karadžić keeps telling me, is to know whether the snake that he fears will bite him is real or imaginary. In the case of Bosnia, he tells me many times, the snake was real. But what does he mean? Did he really think the Muslims were about to start burning Serbs in concentration camps? I don't think so. What matters is not whether the snake is real, but whether the *fear* takes hold. How to instill a mood of fear? This is the recipe that Karadžić has taught me. Remind the public of the enemy's all-too-real past transgressions or, better yet, atrocities. People need to feel: We are the victims, you are the assailants. My people, my culture, my values are under threat. I am fully justified in protecting my people. Even if we feel required to launch a preventive attack, it is self-defense, not offense. If atrocities occur as a result of believing one is under threat, Karadžić seems to be saying, fear is the trigger.

NOTES

1. *Serbian Epics*, dir. Paweł Pawlikowski, documentary (BBC Films, 1992).
2. Robert J. Donia, *Radovan Karadžić: Architect of the Bosnian Genocide* (New York: Cambridge University Press, 2015), p. 34.
3. Marc Bennetts, "Eduard Limonov Interview: Political Rebel and Vladimir Putin's Worst Nightmare," *Guardian*, December 11, 2010, https://www.theguardian.com/world/2010/dec/12/eduard-limonov -interview-putin-nightmare; Julia Ioffe, "'Limonov,' by Emmanuel Carrère," *New York Times*, November 25, 2014, https://www.nytimes .com/2014/11/30/books/review/limonov-by-emmanuel-carrere.html ?mcubz=0&_r=0.
4. Ivan Nechepurenko, "How Nationalism Came to Dominate Russia's Political Mainstream," *Moscow Times*, August 3, 2014, https:// themoscowtimes.com/articles/how-nationalism-came-to-dominate- russias-political-mainstream-37957.
5. Chris Landreth, email correspondence with author, July 3, 2017. See also Marc Bennetts, "Eduard Limonov Interview: Political Rebel and Vladimir Putin's Worst Nightmare," *Guardian*, December 11, 2010, https://www.theguardian.com/world/2010/dec/12/eduard-limonov -interview-putin-nightmare.
6. Vuk Karadžić defined the division of ballads back in 1824. According to him, men's ballads were accompanied by *gusle*, the most important element being the moral of the stories they tell. They were most popular in Montenegro, Bosnia and Herzegovina, and southwestern Serbia. Women's ballads were focused on melodic properties and romantic motives. Mostly sung by women, they were also sung by men, mostly unmarried ones. Biljana Dojčinović-Nešić, "In Search of the Mother's Voice: The Diary of Milica Stojadinović Srpkinja," in Marcel Cornis-Pope and John Neubauer, eds., *History of the Literary Cultures of East-Central Europe*, Vol. 4, *Types and Stereotypes* (Amsterdam and Philadelphia: John Benjamins, 2010), p. 155.
7. Emmanuel Carrère, *Limonov: The Outrageous Adventures of the Radical Soviet Poet Who Became a Bum in New York, a Sensation in France, and a Political Antihero in Russia*, trans. John Lambert (New York: Farrar, Straus & Giroux, 2014), p. 217.
8. Emmanuel Carrère, *Limonov: The Outrageous Adventures of the Radical Soviet Poet Who Became a Bum in New York, a Sensation in France, and*

a Political Antihero in Russia, trans. John Lambert (New York: Farrar, Straus & Giroux, 2014), p. 217.

9. For the dangers associated with reflexively siding with the weaker side and the "responsibility to protect," see Alan J. Kuperman, "The Moral Hazard of Humanitarian Intervention: Lessons from the Balkans," *International Studies Quarterly*, Vol. 52, No. 1 (April 2008).

10. Two reliable sources, Bogoljub Kočović and Vladimir Žerjavić, put total Yugoslav deaths at 1,014,000 and 1,027,000, respectively. Of these, between 487,000 and 530,000 deaths were Serbs. Philip J. Cohen, *Serbia's Secret War: Propaganda and the Deceit of History* (College Station: Texas A&M University Press, 1996), pp. 109–110. See also: Srdjan Bogosavljević, "The Unresolved Genocide," in Nebojša Popov and Drinka Gojković, eds., *The Road to War in Serbia: Trauma and Catharsis* (Budapest, New York: Central European University Press, 1999), pp. 146–160.

   According to political scientist Vladimir Petrović, the ethnic Serb population in the Kingdom of Yugoslavia was no less than 40 percent. For more on this, see Ivo Banac, *The National Question in Yugoslavia, Origins, History, Politics* (2nd ed.). Ithaca, NY: Cornell University Press, 1992. p. 58.

11. Put another way, of the three major nationalities (Muslims, Croats, and Serbs), the Serbs sustained the most casualties compared to their total population.

12. While the exact numbers of people killed by the Ustasha are not available, Žerjavić reports that the estimated number of civilian losses in the NDH amount to 316,000 dead. This number encompasses Serb deaths (217,000), Croat deaths (62,000), and Bosnian Muslim deaths (37,000), within concentration camps and prisons, and in villages and towns. Philip J. Cohen, *Serbia's Secret War: Propaganda and the Deceit of History* (College Station: Texas A&M University Press, 1996), p. 112.

13. "The World's Most Wanted Man," script, written and directed by Kevin Sim, *Frontline*, PBS, May 26, 1998, https://www.pbs.org/wgbh/pages/frontline/shows/karadzic/etc/script.html.

14. Steven L. Burg and Paul S. Shoup, *The War in Bosnia-Herzegovina: Ethnic Conflict and International Intervention* (Armonk, NY: M. E. Sharpe, 1999), p. 38.

15. The United States Holocaust Memorial Museum reports that the Ustasha murdered "between 77,000 and 99,000 people in Jasenovac between 1941 and 1945." Of this estimate, between 12,000 and 20,000

victims were Jews and between 15,000 and 20,000 victims were Roma. Between 5,000 and 12,000 ethnic Croats and Muslims were also murdered. United States Holocaust Memorial Museum, "Jasenovac," *Holocaust Encyclopedia*, https://www.ushmm.org/wlc/en/article .php?ModuleId=10005449. Similarly, the Jasenovac Memorial Site reports 80,000–100,000 deaths. "FAQ's," Jasenovac Memorial Site, http://www.jusp-jasenovac.hr/Default.aspx?sid=7619. See also: Timothy Snyder, *Bloodlands: Europe Between Hitler and Stalin* (New York: Basic Books, 2010), p. 217.

16. According to Donia and Fine, by the end of the war, the number of Jews in Zagreb, Sarajevo, and other towns under Ustasha control "had been reduced by 90% or more." Of the 30,000 Jews living in the NDH, many were transported to Nazi concentration camps "where almost all perished." Robert J. Donia and John V. A. Fine Jr., *Bosnia and Hercegovina: A Tradition Betrayed* (New York: Columbia University Press, 1994), p. 139.

17. See Vladimir Petrović, "Ethnopolitical Temptations Reach Southeastern Europe," in Vladimir Tismaneanu and Bogdan Christian Iacob, eds., *Ideological Storms: Intellectuals, Dictators, and the Totalitarian Temptation* (Budapest: Central European University Press, 2019), pp. 317–341.

18. Alexander Korb, "Understanding Ustaša Violence," *Journal of Genocide Research*, Vol. 12, No. 1–2 (2010), pp. 1–18; Max Bergholz, "The Strange Silence: Explaining the Absence of Monuments for Muslim Civilians Killed in Bosnia During the Second World War," *East European Politics and Societies*, Vol. 24, No. 3 (August 2010), pp. 408–434. Note: Serbian masses reacted violently to Ustasha atrocities, thus stimulating more Ustasha violence as well as German concerns that the spiral of violence was contrary to their interests. Tim Judah, *The Serbs: History, Myth and the Destruction of Yugoslavia*, 3rd ed. (New Haven, London: Yale University Press, 2009).

19. Paul Roe, *Ethnic Violence and the Societal Security Dilemma* (New York: Routledge, 2004), p. 83.

20. Steven L. Burg and Paul S. Shoup, *The War in Bosnia-Herzegovina: Ethnic Conflict and International Intervention* (Armonk, NY: M. E. Sharpe, 1999), p. 38; Tomislav Dulić, "Utopias of Nation: Local Mass Killing in Bosnia and Herzegovina, 1941–42," *PhD diss.* (Uppsala: Acta Universitatis Upsaliensis, 2005), p. 231; Nevenko Bartulin, "The Ideology of Nation and Race: The Croatian Ustasha Regime and Its Policies To-

ward Minorities in the Independent State of Croatia, 1941–1945," *PhD diss.* (Sydney: University of New South Wales, 2006), p. 322.

21. For example, in the summer of 1943, Tito's 22,148-strong Main Operational Group numbered 11,851 Serbs, 5,220 Croats, 3,295 Montenegrins, and 866 Muslims. Bosnian Partisans were composed of 78 percent Serb, 9 percent Muslim, and 5 percent Croat troops. Marko Attila Hoare, "Whose Is the Partisan Movement? Serbs, Croats and the Legacy of a Shared Resistance," *Journal of Slavic Military Studies*, Vol. 15, No. 4 (2002), pp. 24–41; Marko Attila Hoare, *The Bosnian Muslims in the Second World War* (New York: Oxford University Press, 2014), pp. 35, 185; Steven L. Burg and Paul S. Shoup, *The War in Bosnia-Herzegovina: Ethnic Conflict and International Intervention* (Armonk, NY: M. E. Sharpe, 1999), p. 39.

22. Marko Attila Hoare, *The Bosnian Muslims in the Second World War* (New York: Oxford University Press, 2014), p. 49.

23. While the Chetniks did commit massacres against Muslim peasants, the Ustasha were far and away the most brutal in their atrocities. Steven L. Burg and Paul S. Shoup, *The War in Bosnia-Herzegovina: Ethnic Conflict and International Intervention* (Armonk, NY: M. E. Sharpe, 1999), p. 38.

24. While not all scholars consider the Ustasha atrocities against the Serbs to constitute a genocide, many authoritative accounts refer to the atrocities committed by the Ustasha as a genocide, or, at the very least, as genocidal. See Barry M. Lituchy, ed., *Jasenovac and the Holocaust in Yugoslavia: Analyses and Survivor Testimonies* (Brooklyn: Jasenovac Research Institute, 2006); Rory Yeomans, *Visions of Annihilation: The Ustasha Regime and the Cultural Politics of Fascism 1941–1945* (Pittsburgh: University of Pittsburgh Press, 2013); Philip J. Cohen, *Serbia's Secret War: Propaganda and the Deceit of History* (College Station: Texas A&M University Press, 1996).

   However, in 2015, the ICJ acquitted the Republic of Croatia of genocide against the Serbs in World War II based on insufficient evidence. International Court of Justice, *Application of the Convention on the Prevention and Punishment of the Crime of Genocide (Croatia v. Serbia)—Summary of the Judgment of 18 November 2008*, November 18, 2008, https:// www.icj-cij.org/files/case-related/118/14913.pdf.

25. Yugoslavia had exaggerated the figure it reported in reparations claims against Germany, claiming that 1.7 million people had died, one million of whom were Serbs (59 percent of the total number of

deaths). Tito reported these false figures publicly. According to medical doctor and historian Philip J. Cohen, the figures were generated by an undergraduate student at the Institute of Statistics in Belgrade, who had less than two weeks to complete the task. The 1.7 million figure was based on the student's estimate of demographic losses in one region, which he then extrapolated over the entire country. The figure also included projected population growth had the war not broken out, as well as losses from emigration and disease. The student understood that the Communist leaders were interested in the largest possible number of victims to report to the Allied Reparations Committee for war reparations claims against Germany. The corrected figure, as reported earlier in the text, was around 1 million war dead, 50 percent of whom were Serbs. Philip J. Cohen, *Serbia's Secret War: Propaganda and the Deceit of History* (College Station: Texas A&M University Press, 1996), pp. 108–110.

26. Timothy Snyder, *Bloodlands: Europe Between Hitler and Stalin* (New York: Basic Books, 2010), p. 406.

27. Steven L. Burg and Paul S. Shoup, *The War in Bosnia-Herzegovina: Ethnic Conflict and International Intervention* (Armonk, NY: M. E. Sharpe, 1999), p. 39.

28. Vamik Volkan, "Transgenerational Transmissions and Chosen Traumas: An Aspect of Large-Group Identity," *Group Analysis*, Vol. 34, No. 1 (March 2001), pp. 79–97.

29. The Janissaries were an elite military cadre in the Ottoman Empire, founded by Sultan Murad in 1383. They were comprised, initially, of Christian boys—particularly from the Balkans—who were converted to Islam. The Janissaries were renowned for their adherence to strict rules and principles, though these were relaxed later in the sixteenth century. The enslaving of non-Muslim boys for recruitment into the Janissaries was abolished by the early eighteenth century. The Janissaries became an influential political force in the Ottoman Empire. *Britannica Academic*, s.v. "Janissary," accessed September 14, 2018.

30. Leonard W. Doob, "Goebbels' Principles of Propaganda," *Public Opinion Quarterly*, Vol. 14, No. 3 (Autumn 1950), p. 440.

31. Ivan Čolović, *The Politics of Symbol in Serbia*, trans. Celia Hawkesworth (London: Hurst, 2002).

32. International Criminal Tribunal for the Former Yugoslavia, *Prosecution v. Radislav Krstić—Case Information Sheet*, Case No. IT-98-33,

http://www.icty.org/x/cases/krstic/cis/en/cis_krstic_en.pdf. See also Richard Holbrooke, *To End a War* (New York: The Modern Library, 1998), p. 69.

33. This point is made very strongly in the film *Serbian Epics*, and Karadžić repeatedly emphasized this point to me as well. Once it was clear that Bosnia was going to secede, the Bosnian Serbs' strategy was to create a contiguous Serb nation.

34. Ivan Čolović, *The Politics of Symbol in Serbia*, trans. Celia Hawkesworth (London: Hurst, 2002), p. 67.

35. "Rwanda Genocide: 100 Days of Slaughter," *BBC News*, April 4, 2019, https://www.bbc.com/news/world-africa-26875506.

36. For Jan Zwierzchowski and Ewa Tabeau's estimate of death tolls from the Bosnian War, please see Appendix A. For an overview of death toll estimates from the Bosnian War, please see Appendix B.

37. Charles Simic, *The Battle of Kosovo*, trans. John Matthias and Vladeta Vučković (Athens, OH: Swallow Press, 1987), pp. 7–9.

38. Charles Simic, *The Battle of Kosovo*, trans. John Matthias and Vladeta Vučković (Athens, OH: Swallow Press, 1987), pp. 7–9.

39. According to the literary historian Jovan Deretić, "During [Vuk Karadžić's] fifty years of tireless activity, he accomplished as much as an entire academy of sciences." Jovan Deretić, "Literature in the Eighteenth and Nineteenth Centuries," in Pavle Ivić, ed., *The History of Serbian Culture* (Middlesex, UK: Porthill Publishers, 1999), accessed: http://www.srpskoblago.org/serbian-history/history-of-serbian -culture/literature-in-the-eighteenth-and-nineteenth-centuries.html.

40. Tsar Lazar is venerated in the Serbian Orthodox Church as a saint and martyr. Ten cultic writings, composed in Serbia between 1389 and 1420, became the basis for spreading the cult of Saint Lazar, and became part of the liturgy on his feast day. After his death, Prince Lazar was interred in the Church of Ascension in Pristina (the capital of Kosovo), which was then the capital of Serb nobleman Vuk Branković's domain. Kosovo is Serbia's Jerusalem in the sense that it holds a kind of mystical importance for at least two peoples—Serbs and Kosovar Albanians. Kosovo has been dominated by many different entities throughout its history, among them Byzantium, the Ottoman Empire, Serbs, and Albanians. Each side points to history to "prove" that Kosovo is rightfully theirs, in the same way Jews and Palestinians claim that history proves the land of present-day Israel is each theirs. In modern times, Albanian Kosovars have vastly

outnumbered Serbs in Kosovo. Tim Judah, *Kosovo: What Everyone Needs to Know* (Oxford: Oxford University Press, 2008).

The destruction and loss in the wake of the 1389 Battle of Kosovo caused the migration of Serbs away from Kosovo, allowing for Albanians to immigrate into Kosovo instead. The Albanians largely converted to Islam upon the arrival of the Ottomans in the fifteenth century.

Albanians consider Kosovo to be the cradle of Albanian nationalism, particularly after the Balkan Wars of 1912 and 1913. Kosovo maintained four meanings for Albanians. First, they largely claim Albanians descend from the Illyrians, who were in Kosovo before the Slavs, hence enjoying a historical, legitimate right to the land. Second, Kosovo was where the first Albanian national movement was founded in 1878. Third was the claim of illegitimate inclusion into and oppression within both Yugoslav states. Fourth is the fact that Albanians make for a large majority in Kosovo. Miranda Vickers, *Between Serb and Albanian: A History of Kosovo* (New York: Columbia University Press, 1998), pp. xii–xiv.

41. *Britannica Academic*, s.v. "Battle of Kosovo," accessed September 14, 2018.

42. The epic songs offer another (contradictory) explanation for the defeat of the Serbs, which provides a different lesson, not about spiritual desire and martyrdom, but about the importance of Serb unity. This explanation involves the supposed treachery of Prince Lazar's son-in-law, Vuk Branković. Branković was a Serbian nobleman who inherited a province that included parts of present-day Serbia, North Macedonia, Montenegro, and Kosovo. His lands were known as Oblast Brankovića. Branković supplied a contingent of soldiers to Prince Lazar in the battle against the invading Ottoman army at Kosovo. Branković was said to be one of the very few Serbs who survived the war, leading to widespread suspicion about his motives. According to legend, Branković deliberately tricked his father-in-law in order to take over his father-in-law's territories. The story of Branković's betrayal is not accepted by contemporary historians, but the myth lives on, as a salutary moral tale, demonstrating the danger of Serbs fighting among themselves—as they did during World War II, when some joined the Chetniks and others the Partisans—rather than uniting to defeat a common enemy.

43. Karadžić told me many times that he is a follower of Hesychasm and Saint Gregory Palamas. He described it as a Greek form of medita-

tion. It was developed in Byzantium. Saint Gregory Palamas was born in Constantinople (now Istanbul, Turkey) in 1296 and died in 1359 in Thessalonica, Byzantine Empire (now Greece). He was an Orthodox monk, a theologian, and the intellectual leader of Hesychasm. The purpose of Hesychasm is to achieve a personal union with God. Hesychasm is similar to other spiritual exercises found in other religious traditions, such as Sufism, yoga, and Western Christian mystical asceticism. Specifically, the practitioner of Hesychasm aims at *theosis* (deification) through the assimilation of *energeiai* (divine energies). *Theosis* is possible due to the constant recitation of the Jesus Prayer ("Lord Jesus Christ, Son of God, have mercy on me, a sinner"). This process is supposed to cause the mind to descend to the heart, and leads to a personal connection to Christ. In many traditions, recitation of the Jesus Prayer is accompanied by breathing techniques and visualizations centered on the heart that are intended to increase the divine connection/identification. Marco Toti, "The Hesychast Method of Prayer: Its Anthropological and Symbolic Significance," *International Journal for the Study of the Christian Church*, Vol. 8, No. 1 (February 2008), pp. 17–32.

44. Radovan Karadžić in *Serbian Epics*, dir. Paweł Pawlikowski, documentary (BBC Films, 1992).

Chapter Nine

THE HUNT

The 1990s war in Bosnia had dragged on for over three years. The reports of concentration camps, systematic rapes, and extralethal violence (more violence than required to kill the enemy, such as dismemberment of bodies) had become a regular drumbeat on the daily news. Every Western attempt to negotiate a peace treaty had failed. But the Srebrenica genocide changed the West's attitude toward the conflict. On July 24, 1995, less than two weeks after the massacre, the ICTY issued its first indictments against Karadžić and his military commander, General Ratko Mladić.[1] The first sixteen-count indictment included charges of genocide and three counts of crimes against humanity.[2] A second twenty-count indictment was issued on November 16, 1995.[3] The charges made Karadžić the first doctor indicted for crimes against humanity and genocide since the doctors tried at Nuremberg in 1946.[4]

Although Karadžić boasted to the Bosnian Serb Assembly that he (and *not* Mladić) was responsible for initiating the Srebrenica attack, once it became clear that the attack was an indictable offense, Karadžić would claim that he was not even informed that the Muslims were being killed.[5] The relationship between Karadžić and Mladić had begun to fray several years earlier, and by mid-1995 they were in fierce competition, with Milošević taking Mladić's side.[6] Karadžić tried to demote Mladić several times. The first time was in 1993, when Karadžić tried to replace his military commander with General Manojlo Milovanović, but Milovanović was loyal to his boss and refused the promotion.[7] On August 4, 1995, eleven days after the first indictments against Karadžić and Mladić were issued, Karadžić tried, once again, to demote Mladić and replace him with another general. But the entire senior brass of the military took Mladić's side, saying that they would now obey orders issued only by Mladić, and ignore those issued by Karadžić.[8]

Two months after the Srebrenica genocide, in the immediate aftermath of a second marketplace massacre, the White House concluded that the Serbs had to be stopped with force.[9] On August 9, 1995, National Security Advisor Anthony Lake was dispatched to meet with the United States' European allies, to seek their agreement to a new, more muscular plan in the event that diplomatic efforts failed.[10] On August 30, NATO commenced Operation Deliberate Force, a massive air campaign against Bosnian Serb military targets. Although Operation Deny Flight, a 1993 operation in which NATO enforced the UN no-fly zone over Bosnia, was the first combat engagement in NATO's history, Operation Deliberate Force was NATO's first sustained air campaign.[11] Operation Deliberate Force also marked the first time that the German air force engaged in combat since 1945.[12] Three weeks after the NATO bombing began, the Serbs agreed to negotiate an end to hostilities.[13]

The Dayton Accord, which ended the war, was signed in Paris on December 14, 1995, by the presidents of Serbia, Croatia, and Bosnia.[14] With those signatures, the State of Bosnia Herzegovina was formally established to include two entities: the Federation of Bosnia and Herzegovina and Republika Srpska. Peace seemed finally to be at hand.

Six days after the Accord was signed, NATO troops began arriving in Bosnia, with a mandate to implement its terms and to deter hostilities between the formerly warring parties. The Implementation Force (IFOR), which replaced UNPROFOR, consisted of 60,000 NATO troops and 6,000 troops from twenty non-NATO countries.[15] Bosnia soon became the site of a multi-billion-dollar intelligence operation, and the largest emplacement of special forces in the world.[16]

———

Now that the Accord was signed, Karadžić was expected to resign from the presidency. The Dayton Accord required that persons indicted for war crimes relinquish their positions in government and any other public office and forbade them from running in any future elections.[17] For a few months after the Accord was signed, Karadžić disappeared from public view. But in February 1996, seven weeks after the NATO-led troops had arrived, he showed up in the Bosnian Serb city of Banja Luka, the de facto capital of Republika Srpska, where his live television appearance, "Ask the President," dominated the nightly news. Although he was explicitly forbidden to run for office, he seemed to be kicking off an election campaign. Despite the international arrest warrant that had been issued the previous July, he told the media he had no intention of turning himself in to the ICTY.[18] "It is not a court or a tribunal," he said. "It is a form of lynching for the whole nation." He brazenly defied the IFOR troops, speeding through four checkpoints manned by IFOR soldiers. No one attempted to stop or detain him.[19]

Karadžić insisted in the media that his political position was tenable despite his indictment for genocide. "I am stronger than Deng Xiaoping," he proclaimed, referring to the aging leader of China, who led the world's biggest country from behind the scenes. "My power is not informal. It is formal. All of my associates are fully loyal. All of them ask me what to do."[20]

After that, despite the Accord's requirement that he relinquish power, Karadžić remained, to use his term, "at post," as president of Republika Srpska, president of the party, and in the public eye.[21] NATO troops were visible all over Bosnia. But Karadžić asked rhetorically, "Do I look like a frightened man? They don't have any proof, not a single bit of evidence. I have done everything to prevent atrocities. We did what we had to do to defend our own people from genocide."[22]

Richard Holbrooke, who had been cochairman of the Dayton Peace Conference that led to the Accord (and whom I knew from my time at the National Security Council), wrote in his memoir that Karadžić's arrest was absolutely critical to ensuring that the warring parties remained at peace. "As we had told the President [Clinton] and his senior advisors before Dayton, Karadžić at large was certain to mean Dayton deferred or defeated," he wrote.[23]

Despite his public swaggering and claims that the Yugoslav Tribunal was set up to lynch the Serbs, I discovered in my interviews of former U.S. officials that Karadžić had actually tried to turn himself in to the Court a number of times. He was frightened that his enemies might kill him, and thought he might be safer in The Hague. On one of these occasions, he worked out a plan to make it look as though NATO had ambushed him. The reason for this ruse was that Karadžić feared that Milošević had infiltrated his guard force, and that Milošević would rather have Karadžić killed than see him testify in Court, due to the possibility that Karadžić would reveal Milošević's very substantial leadership role in all that transpired in Bosnia during the war.[24] According to William Stuebner, who had served as special advisor to the prosecutor of the ICTY, Karadžić wanted to be delivered by helicopter to a U.S. aircraft carrier stationed in the Adriatic. From there he wanted NATO to facilitate a broadcast to the Serb people, in which he planned to make clear that every action he had ever taken was done to protect the Serbs and defend their honor. Then he would submit to being transported to The Hague. But Karadžić was fantasizing that the trial was going to go like the

O. J. Simpson trial, Stuebner told me.[25] He wanted to be lionized as a hero and also to eclipse Milošević as the most important leader of the Serbs.[26]

But Karadžić did not turn himself in. Instead, seven months after the Dayton Accord was signed, he suddenly stepped down from the presidency, reportedly as a result of Richard Holbrooke's efforts.[27] Karadžić has repeatedly insisted—to family and friends, to the media, to the Tribunal, and to me—that Richard Holbrooke promised him immunity from prosecution in return for his agreement to step down from his political positions and remove himself from public life. But Holbrooke repeatedly denied that there had been any quid pro quo; he had persuaded Karadžić to comply with the terms of Dayton without any additional inducements. Holbrooke told one reporter that Karadžić's claims about a reciprocal promise of immunity was "C-R-A-P . . . crap."[28] He told another that "such a deal would have been immoral and unethical."[29]

I found the claim that Holbrooke had deceived Karadžić disturbing. Once a nation gets a reputation for this sort of manipulation of national leaders, such trickery would be unlikely to be usable again. How could one know that this was the most important time to utilize duplicity to convince a warlord to relinquish power? I went so far as to consult an ethicist about my obligation to tell this story, and whether it would have been right for Holbrooke to deceive Karadžić with a hollow promise of immunity, if he did. Together, we decided that since Holbrooke believed that Karadžić's removal was necessary to secure the peace, deception would have been warranted, even if it meant gaining a reputation for deceit.[30]

Here is what Karadžić said to me about the supposed agreement with Holbrooke: Milošević and Holbrooke had met at Milošević's house outside Belgrade, beginning on July 16, 1996. "Holbrooke said to Milošević that I had to step down. Aleksa

Buha from the philosophy faculty was there. [Aleksa Buha was a philosopher, but at that point he was serving as the RS minister of foreign affairs and was a member of the RS Senate.] If I stepped down the case against me would be dropped. The Hague would not exist for me. They sent Jovica Stanišić [chief of Serbia's state intelligence service] by helicopter to Pale. He brought me a document to sign and I signed it. Then he brought the document back to Belgrade."

He continued, "Holbrooke is a bulldozer. I said to Milošević, give this agreement to me in writing! Milošević said, 'The United States is a big power. We don't need to write down a promise from the U.S. because it is a very big power.'"

Many of the former U.S. officials with whom I spoke insisted that Karadžić's claims were true—that Holbrooke really did promise Karadžić immunity from prosecution to get him to step down from the presidency. Eighteen people signed affidavits claiming to have witnessed some aspect of the arrangement.[31] One former U.S. official told me he had a copy of the agreement in writing and promised me that he would try to locate it in his files. (He was never able to find it.) But none of the officials who were certain about Holbrooke's deception had been in the room when the negotiation took place. I tracked down every one of the still-living Americans who were with Holbrooke at Milošević's house, where the deal was allegedly negotiated. John Feeley (then serving as the director of European affairs in the National Security Council), General Doug Lute (then serving in the Directorate of Strategic Plans and Policy at the Joint Chiefs of Staff) and Ambassador Philip Goldberg (then serving as the State Department's desk officer for Bosnia and Holbrooke's special assistant) all told me that there was no deal promising Karadžić that he would be immune from prosecution or arrest.

After months of trying, I was able to acquire the document that Karadžić had referred to in his jumbled description and that the former U.S. official had told me about, but it details only Karadžić's obligations. I have the document here in front of me. It says nothing about Karadžić's immunity from prosecution. It was signed by Karadžić and several additional Serb and Bosnian Serb government personnel. It was not signed by Richard Holbrooke.[32] The former official had apparently misremembered what the written form of the agreement stipulated.

———

Whatever transpired between Holbrooke and Karadžić, Karadžić did step down from the presidency on July 19, 1996, and Biljana Plavšić took his place as RS president. But he did not step out of the public eye, at least not right away, as if he truly did feel invulnerable to arrest. He seemed to flaunt his claimed immunity. He passed freely through the IFOR checkpoints, driving back and forth from Pale several times a day. According to reporting by the *New York Times*, professor of history Charles Ingrao, who spent a lot of time in Bosnia after the war, observed Karadžić sitting in a vehicle directly across from the UN International Police Task Force station based in Pale in 1996. Surprised to see Karadžić in plain sight, he informed the UN police. But the police had no interest in arresting Karadžić, despite the international warrant for his arrest. "Why don't you arrest him?" Professor Ingrao asked an officer. The response was: "It is not in our mandate." Ingrao took the matter up with officials at IFOR. The IFOR officials explained that they had been instructed to steer clear of the war criminal. "Our guys are afraid we're going to run into Karadžić," he was told.[33]

In my interviews with former U.S. officials, they confirmed that in the beginning, when the NATO-led IFOR troops first arrived, there was a great deal of reluctance to hunt down the war criminals. U.S. commanders were worried that apprehending Karadžić, or any of the other indicted war criminals, would provoke retaliation against their troops. According to Bill Murray, the former CIA manager for field operations in the Balkans, "There was a belief in the military that President Clinton had said that any general who lost a soldier was never going to get another star."[34]

In October 1993, U.S. special forces had gone to seize two lieutenants of the Somali warlord Mohammed Farah Aidid. The operation did not succeed. Aidid's forces managed to shoot down two Black Hawk helicopters, in an incident known thereafter as Black Hawk Down. Eighteen U.S. military personnel died in the failed operation, and seventy-three were wounded. It was the most lethal U.S. military operation since the Vietnam War. The U.S. military's risk aversion, which became known as Mogadishu Syndrome, would prevail until 9/11.

For the Americans, another concern, in addition to Mogadishu Syndrome, was "mission creep"—the expansion of their peace-keeping mission to include picking up indicted war criminals, which the military considered to be a law-enforcement operation.

Determination to capture the indicted war criminals waxed and waned depending on the American election cycle and the reactions to 9/11. But NATO and the Stabilization Force (SFOR) in Bosnia and Herzegovina, which replaced IFOR, eventually became a lot more serious about rendering Karadžić and the other indicted criminals to the Tribunal. Special forces from six countries were deployed to Bosnia to search for Karadžić (and other war criminals). Bosnia became the biggest deployment of special-forces troops anywhere in the world prior to 9/11. Britain's Special Air Service forces used techniques developed in Northern Ireland. A new German special-forces unit was deployed in the Balkan manhunt, the first time Germany's ground forces had gone into action since 1945.[35] To support the mission, intelligence agencies were also deployed in the field, among them the American CIA and National Security Agency (NSA), the British MI6 and GCHQ

(Government Communications Headquarters—analogous to the NSA), and the French DGSE (the Directorate-General for External Security, the French equivalent of the CIA).[36]

But Karadžić and his protectors were adept at using disinformation to stymie the hunters.[37] Karadžić seems to have viewed the hunt as a kind of game. Still, the Americans in particular, journalist Julian Borger explains, refused to give up the pursuit. "Like a sheriff's posse unwilling to admit defeat, they were ready to try anything."[38] As NATO became more serious about capturing him, Karadžić went back into hiding. With the help of contacts in Serbian intelligence, Karadžić acquired a new identity and name—Dragan Dabić—and transformed himself into a new person: a mystic and professional new age energy healer.[39]

NOTES

1. The International Criminal Tribunal for the former Yugoslavia was created in 1993. The very first indictments were that of Radovan Karadžić and Ratko Mladić. In total, 161 people were indicted. United Nations Security Council Resolution 827, S/RES/827, May 25, 1993, accessed: http://www.un.org/ga/search/view_doc.asp?symbol=S/RES/827(1993).

   As of June 2018, 89 indictees had been sentenced and 18 had been acquitted. Four trials were ongoing (including those of Mladić and Karadžić, both of whom had appealed their sentences); 13 defendants had been referred to national jurisdictions, and 37 either had their indictments withdrawn or died before their trials began.
2. International Criminal Tribunal for the former Yugoslavia, *Prosecutor v. Radovan Karadžić and Ratko Mladić—Indictment*, Case No. IT-95-05-I, July 24, 1995, http://www.icty.org/x/cases/karadzic/ind/en/kar-ii950724e.pdf.
3. International Criminal Tribunal for the former Yugoslavia, *Prosecutor v. Radovan Karadžić and Ratko Mladić—Indictment*, Case No. IT-95-18-I,

November 14, 1995, http://www.icty.org/x/cases/karadzic/ind/en/kar
-ii951116e.pdf.

4. Robert M. Kaplan, "Dr. Radovan Karadzic: Psychiatrist, Poet, Soccer
Coach and Genocidal Leader," *Australasian Psychiatry*, Vol. 11, No. 1
(2003), p. 74.

5. On the question of whether Karadžić was telling the truth when he
took credit for initiating the attack on Srebrenica, see chapter 11. In
intercepts of FRY Supreme Defense Council (SDC) meetings cited by
Nevenka Tromp, there is evidence that Milošević was in touch with
Mladić on the occasion of the attack on Srebrenica. Nevenka Tromp,
Prosecuting Slobodan Milošević: The Unfinished Trial (London and New
York: Routledge, 2016), pp. 173, 182.

Milošević said that he had warned Mladić that while the military
price of the attack was "inexpensive . . . the political price could be
a million times higher," and said to the SDC that there had been an
unfortunate "lack of synchronization" between the military and political leadership. International Criminal Tribunal for the former Yugoslavia, "Stenographic Transcript of the 41st Session of the Supreme
Defense Council," *Prosecutor v. Momčilo Perišić*, Case No. IT-04-81, Exhibit P00797.E., August 14, 1995, p. 16, cited in Nevenka Tromp, *Prosecuting Slobodan Milošević: The Unfinished Trial* (London & New York:
Routledge, 2016), p. 182.

6. Telephone interview with former Balkans specialist for the U.S. intelligence community, March 1, 2019.

See also: DCI Interagency Balkan Task Force, "Intelligence Report: The Belgrade-Pale Relationship," (June 23, 1995, Approved for
Release October 1, 2013), https://www.cia.gov/library/readingroom
/docs/1995-06-23A.pdf; DCI Interagency Balkan Task Force, "Intelligence Report: Milosevic, Karadzic, Mladic: Serbs More United," (September 5, 1995, Approved for Release October 1, 2013), https://www
.cia.gov/library/readingroom/docs/1995-09-05B.pdf ; DCI Interagency
Balkan Task Force, "Intelligence Report: The Milosevic-Karadzic
Break: Stalemated for Now," (November 23, 1994, Approved for Release October 1, 2013), https://www.cia.gov/library/readingroom
/docs/1994-11-23.pdf; Robert Block, "The Madness of General Mladic,"
New York Review of Books, October 5, 1995.

7. "Pukovnik Milovan Milutinovic: Kako je smenjivan General Ratko
Mladic," *NIN*, February 21, 1997, http://www.nin.co.rs/arhiva/2408/1
.html.

8. Robert Block, "The Madness of General Mladic," *New York Review of Books*, October 5, 1995; Nevenka Tromp, *Prosecuting Slobodan Milošević: The Unfinished Trial* (London and New York: Routledge, 2016), pp. 167, 187.

9. The immediate trigger for NATO's air campaign against the Bosnian Serbs was the second Markale massacre in Sarajevo, which occurred on August 28, 1995. The shift from the neutral, peacekeeping approach to a more muscular approach, combining diplomacy and force, was what led the Serbs to negotiate an end to the war, according to some (but not all) analysts. Richard Holbrooke was a strong proponent of this view. In the words of the BBC's Alan Little, who was an expert on the region, "several weeks of sustained aerial bombardment in the summer and autumn of 1995 reversed many of the Serbs' territorial gains and threatened to roll them back altogether. Faced for the first time with a military opponent they could not overcome, the Serbs went to the negotiating table." Robert Mackey, "Revisiting Holbrooke's Last Remarks," *The Lede* (blog), *New York Times*, December 14, 2010, https://thelede.blogs.nytimes.com/2010/12/14/was-holbrooke-sent-to-afghanistan-too-late/.

   During the summer of 1995, the Clinton administration's Principals Committee met to discuss strategies for the end of the conflict in Bosnia. Four possible strategies were presented to President Clinton, who, on August 8, 1995, agreed to the "endgame strategy" articulated by National Security Advisor Anthony Lake. Diplomatic efforts would include engaging Milošević directly, and using a carrot-and-stick approach to get all parties involved to agree to a map largely based on the Contact Group (comprised of the United States, Russia, France, Britain, and Germany) plan. Allies mostly agreed to the endgame strategy, relieved that a concrete plan had materialized after years of "muddling through." On August 14, Holbrooke was appointed and sent to the Balkans to lead negotiations among the warring parties. Ivo H. Daalder, *Getting to Dayton: The Making of America's Bosnia Policy* (Washington, DC: Brookings Institution Press, 2000).

   American officials, including Richard Holbrooke, gave the NATO bombing campaign credit for the Serbs' new willingness to negotiate an end to the war. But a number of others disputed that interpretation. For example, Carl Bildt, who served as the European Union's special envoy for negotiating peace in the former Yugoslavia, referred to the positive role of the bombing campaign as "popular mythology." In his

view, the United States had contributed to extending the war by re-
sisting recognizing Republika Srpska, promoting an unrealistic map,
and encouraging Bosnia to refuse a number of peace agreements. Carl
Bildt, "Holbrooke's History," *Survival*, Vol. 40, No. 3 (1998), p. 187.
Carl Bildt was a Swedish diplomat who served as prime minister of
Sweden from 1991 to 1994; he was also cochairman of the Dayton
Peace Accords. He later served as the first high representative for
Bosnia and Herzegovina from December 1995 to June 1997. According to Bildt, U.S. national security advisor Anthony Lake's endgame
strategy closely followed the lines recommended by the Europeans
earlier that summer, which had been endorsed by the RS before
the NATO bombing. On Tony Lake's new strategy, see also David
Rohde, *Endgame: The Betrayal and Fall of Srebrenica, Europe's Worst Massacre Since World War II* (New York: Penguin Books, 2012) and Daaldar, *Getting to Dayton*, pp. 6–7.

Other scholars and practitioners who blamed the United States
for extending the war include Susan Woodward (personal communication, December 27, 2018); Charles G. Boyd, "Making Peace with
the Guilty: The Truth About Bosnia," *Foreign Affairs*, Vol. 74, No. 5
(September–October 1995), https://www.foreignaffairs.com/articles
/europe/1995-09-01/making-peace-guilty-truth-about-bosnia; David
Owen, *Balkan Odyssey* (New York: Harcourt Brace, 1995); and Gordon
N. Bardos (email correspondences, January 2019).

Misha Glenny, a British journalist known for his excellent reporting on the Balkans, wrote that Bosnians joked that the only difference
between the Vance-Owen Peace Plan (VOPP), which Washington opposed, and Dayton, which Washington approved, was "nothing except two years of mass graves." According to both Misha Glenny and
Lord David Owen, the VOPP, which was negotiated in the fall of 1992,
would have been better for the Muslims than the Dayton Accord, and
would have saved some two hundred thousand lives. It was the only
peace plan that would have denied the Serbs the right to secede from
Bosnia or form constitutional links with Serbia. Misha Glenny, "The
51 Percent Solution," *New York Times*, January 21, 1996, https://www
.nytimes.com/1996/01/21/books/the-51-percent-solution.html.

On this point, Glenny also cites legal journalist Anthony Lewis,
who wrote of Dayton, "The mystery is why the United States has
brought the parties to an agreement seemingly so favorable to the
Serbian leaders' ambitions. Indeed, it is more favorable than the settle-

ment crafted by Cyrus Vance and Lord Owen." Lewis noted that the VOPP would also have preserved a "genuinely sovereign Bosnia." Anthony Lewis, "Abroad at Home; What Weakness Brings," *New York Times*, September 11, 1995, https://www.nytimes.com/1995/09/11 /opinion/abroad-at-home-what-weakness-brings.html. See also: Owen, *Balkan Odyssey*.

10. See Ivo H. Daalder, *Getting to Dayton: The Making of America's Bosnia Policy* (Washington, DC: Brookings Institute Press, 2000); Richard Holbrooke, *To End a War* (New York: The Modern Library, 1998).

11. Ryan C. Hendrickson, "Crossing the Rubicon," *NATO Review* (Autumn 2005), https://www.nato.int/docu/review/2005/issue3/english /history.html.

12. Rick Atkinson, "Luftwaffe's Wings Clipped in First Action Since 1945," *Washington Post*, August 19, 1995.

13. For more discussion on whether the Bosnian War could have been ended earlier, please see note 9.

14. Holbrooke spent months conducting shuttle diplomacy in the Balkans before he was finally able to broker a cease-fire and bring Alija Izetbegović, Franjo Tudjman (the leader of Croatia), and Slobodan Milošević to the negotiating table at Dayton, Ohio. Milošević was given authority to negotiate on the Bosnian Serbs' behalf in what became known as the "Patriarch document," because it was endorsed by the Serbian Orthodox Patriarch. According to Holbrooke, "Our most important point concerned whom we would negotiate with. The United States, we said, would never again deal directly with the Bosnian Serbs who rained artillery and racist rhetoric down upon the Muslims and the Croats from their mountain capital of Pale. 'You must speak for Pale,' I said [to Milošević]. 'We won't deal with them ever again.'" Richard Holbrooke, *To End a War* (New York: The Modern Library, 1998), pp. 4–5.

In his discussions with Milošević, Holbrooke pushed for the removal of Karadžić and Mladić. He made it clear to Milošević—with whom he had cultivated a good working relationship—that without the removal of Karadžić and Mladić, there would be no trade sanctions relief for Serbia. The prospect of sanctions relief made Milošević an enthusiastic supporter of peace in the Balkans. Roger Cohen, "Taming the Bullies of Bosnia," *New York Times*, December 17, 1995, https://www.nytimes.com/1995/12/17/magazine/taming-the-bullies -of-bosnia.html?pagewanted=all.

The peace negotiations took place over three weeks, from November 1 to November 21, 1995. The Bosnian Muslim-Croat Federation received 51 percent of the territory, and the RS received 49 percent. The Agreement was comprised of a General Framework Agreement and eleven annexes. Annex 1-A established the Implementation Force, imposed the cessation of hostilities between Bosnia's two entities, and called for the withdrawal of foreign forces from Bosnia other than UNPROFOR, the UN International Police Task Force, and IFOR. Annex 1-B called for negotiations under the Organization for Security and Cooperation in Europe (OSCE) to create measures for regional stabilization (such as creating limits on the buildup of arms to avoid an arms race). Annex 2 established the boundaries between the Muslim-Croat Federation and the RS (the Inter-Entity Boundary Line). Annex 3 established guidelines for elections and voter eligibility in Bosnia, and called for an Election Commission to be created by the OSCE. It also required that the first elections in Bosnia take place six months after the Agreement entered into force, and no later than nine months if the OSCE deemed a delay necessary. Annex 4 established the Constitution of Bosnia and Herzegovina, which described the tripartite Presidency and, crucially, barred any person indicted by the ICTY from "[standing] as a candidate or [holding] any appointive, elective, or other public office" in Bosnia after the Dayton Agreement entered into force. Annex 5 obligated the Bosnian entities to implement a system for arbitrating disputes between them. Annex 6 held Bosnia to the highest standards of human rights within its territory. Annex 7 established the rights of refugees and other displaced persons, as well as conditions for their safe return. Annex 8 established a Commission to Preserve National Monuments. Annex 9 established a Commission on Public Corporations and a Transportation Corporation, and described guidelines for the creation of other public facilities. Annex 10 established the Office of the High Representative to oversee the civilian implementation of the Dayton Agreement. Finally, Annex 11 established the UN International Police Task Force for civilian law enforcement in Bosnia.

Most important, the Agreement did *not* directly mandate any arrest operations targeting the indicted war criminals. Instead, ICTY chief prosecutor Louise Arbour, sympathetic figures in the U.S. State Department such as the first U.S. ambassador-at-large for war crimes issues, David Scheffer, and the legal advisor to the German Foreign

Ministry, Hans-Peter Kaul, pieced together a legal argument for arresting Persons Indicted for War Crimes (PIFWCs). Kaul argued that Security Council Resolution 1088 gave member states the authority to "take all necessary measures" to defend SFOR in case of "attack or threat of attack." United Nations Security Council Resolution 1088, S/RES/1088 (December 12, 1996), accessed: http://unscr.com/en /resolutions/1088. Kaul argued that PIFWCs were a threat to SFOR troops, and therefore UN member states could conduct arrest operations to assist SFOR. This resolution, along with Resolution 827, and the ICTY's Rule 59 bis, which allowed "appropriate authorities" such as NATO, UN bodies, or even the ICTY prosecutor to act on an arrest warrant, empowered SFOR military personnel to detain a fugitive until the PIFWCs were rendered to the Tribunal. International Criminal Tribunal for the former Yugoslavia, *Rules of Procedure and Evidence*, IT/32/Rev.50, July 8, 2015, pp. 49–50; David Scheffer, *All the Missing Souls: A Personal History of the War Crimes Tribunals* (Princeton: Princeton University Press, 2011).

15. After he left command of UN forces in Bosnia, General Sir Michael Rose argued for a clear distinction to be drawn between peacekeeping (as in UNPROFOR) and peacemaking (as in IFOR/SFOR) missions. "A peacekeeping force designed to assist the delivery of humanitarian aid simply cannot be used to alter the military balance of force in a civil war," said General Rose. In comparison to UNPROFOR, a peacekeeping force, IFOR's mandate was to "modify political goals of one party or another." Marc Weller, "The Relativity of Humanitarian Neutrality and Impartiality," *American Society of International Law Annual Conference* (Washington, DC: 1997), accessed: https://sites .tufts.edu/jha/archives/119.

In a report on UNPROFOR operations of 1994, the UN secretary-general, Boutros Boutros-Ghali, noted that by "thwarting the military objectives" of one party, UNPROFOR was "compromising its impartiality, which remains the key to its effectiveness in fulfilling its humanitarian responsibility." United Nations Secretary-General, Report S/1994/300, March 16, 1994, cited in Weller, "The Relativity of Humanitarian Neutrality and Impartiality."

In another report, from 1995, the secretary-general argued that by "using force against only one party," UNPROFOR was altering parties' perception of its neutrality, "with the risk that its personnel and those of other United Nations agencies come to be identified with the use of force and perceived as a party of war." United Nations Secretary-General, Report S/1995/444, May 30, 1995, cited in Marc Weller, "The Relativity of Humanitarian Neutrality and Impartiality.

Professor of international law Marc Weller argued that when UNPROFOR collapsed after Srebrenica, the massive NATO air campaign that followed was unlawful, in that the legal framework had not changed. The Serbs accused UNPROFOR of having acted in violation of the principles of neutrality and impartiality. With NATO's massive air campaign, the UN's claim to be operating as an impartial and neutral entity was thus "unmasked as merely a political tactic to avoid exposing UNPROFOR to risk, at the expense of some 100,000 citizens of Bosnia and Herzegovina, who had been murdered under the very eyes of United Nations forces." Weller concludes that the confused practice of UNPROFOR damaged the faith of many in the UN as an entity that could act in accordance with the twin principles of neutrality and impartiality. Weller, "The Relativity of Humanitarian Neutrality and Impartiality."

SFOR remained in place until December 2, 2004, when it was replaced by the European Union Force in BiH (EUFOR) as part of Operation Althea. Nick Hawton, "EU Troops Prepare for Bosnia Swap," *BBC News*, October 23, 2004, http://news.bbc.co.uk/2/hi/europe/3944191.stm.

16. Julian Borger, *The Butcher's Trail: How the Search for Balkan War Criminals Became the World's Most Successful Manhunt* (New York: Other Press, 2016), p. 145.

17. Annex 4 of the Dayton Accord is the Constitution of Bosnia and Herzegovina. Article IX: General Provisions of the Constitution specifies: "No person who is serving a sentence imposed by the International Tribunal for the Former Yugoslavia, and no person who is under indictment by the Tribunal and who has failed to comply with an order to appear before the Tribunal, may stand as a candidate or hold any appointive, elective, or other public office in the territory of Bosnia and Herzegovina."

Although the wording of Article IX is unclear, a number of authorities—including the OSCE and the ICTY—have interpreted it to mean that PIFWCs holding public office at the time that Dayton entered into force had to step down from their positions, and that PIFWCs could not stand as candidates in any future elections. David Scheffer, *All the Missing Souls: A Personal History of the War Crimes Tribunals*

(Princeton: Princeton University Press, 2011); David Chandler, *Bosnia: Faking Democracy After Dayton* (London: Pluto Press, 2000). This interpretation is also reflected in a number of news articles. See: John Pomfret, "West Demands Karadzic Resign," *Washington Post*, July 2, 1996, https://www.washingtonpost.com/archive/politics /1996/07/02/west-demands-karadzic-resign/92543858-aa1e-4a02 -b5a5-080a42e7a0d0/?noredirect=on&utm_term=.d443fb90e0b2; "Karadzic Steps Down," *Irish Times*, July 20, 1996, https://www.irish-times.com/opinion/karadzic-steps-down-1.69184; Anthony Lewis, "Abroad at Home; Crime and Blunder," *New York Times*, July 8, 1996, https://www.nytimes.com/1996/07/08/opinion/abroad-at-home -crime-and-blunder.html; Christiane Amanpour, "Karadzic Reportedly May Leave Office," *CNN*, May 19, 1996, http://www.cnn.com /WORLD/Bosnia/updates/9605/19/yugo.karadzic/index.html.

18. International Criminal Tribunal for the former Yugoslavia, *Prosecutor v. Radovan Karadžić and Ratko Mladić—International Arrest Warrant and Order for Surrender*, Case No. IT-95-5-R61 and IT-95-18-R61, July 11, 1996, http://www.icty.org/x/cases/karadzic/custom4/en/960711.pdf.

19. This paragraph summarizes information contained in John Pomfret, "Bosnian Serbs' Leader Stages Show of Defiance," *Washington Post*, February 10, 1996, https://www.washingtonpost.com /archive/politics/1996/02/10/bosnian-serbs-leader-stages-show-of -defiance/54125dbc-af24-4ce3-b3b6-d625b0836aa3/?utm_term =.59a878d5ea4e1.

20. This paragraph summarizes information contained in John Pomfret, "Bosnian Serbs' Leader Stages Show of Defiance," *Washington Post*, February 10, 1996, https://www.washingtonpost.com /archive/politics/1996/02/10/bosnian-serbs-leader-stages-show-of -defiance/54125dbc-af24-4ce3-b3b6-d625b0836aa3/?utm_term =.59a878d5ea4e1.

21. "At post" is the term Karadžić used with me in describing the period after formally stepping down as leader of the RS and SDS.

22. Colin Soloway, "I Seek a New Legitimacy," *U.S. News & World Report*, May 20, 1996.

23. Richard Holbrooke, *To End a War* (New York: The Modern Library, 1998), p. 338.

24. A number of U.S. officials told me that Karadžić feared his own guard force because Milošević had inserted a plant tasked with murdering him if Milošević felt it was necessary. For example, William Stuebner,

interview with author, December 13, 2018. However, in a letter to me dated December 14, 2018, Karadžić denied that he feared Milošević or his own guard force.

25. On June 17, 1994, O. J. Simpson, suspected of murdering his wife and her friend, led police on a sixty-mile slow-speed car chase through Los Angeles and Orange Counties. An estimated 95 million viewers watched the chase on live TV. The televised trial that followed, often referred to as "the trial of the century," was the longest in California history. It lasted 133 days, generating international attention and creating Simpson-trial addicts all over the globe. A "dream team" of expensive attorneys—among them Alan Dershowitz—defended Simpson in his criminal case, and he was acquitted. An estimated 100 million people watched or listened to the verdict announcement. Afterward, family members of the victims subsequently brought a wrongful-death suit against him, and were awarded $33.5 million.

26. William Stuebner, interview with author, December 13, 2018.

Others tried to encourage Karadžić to turn himself in as well, an attempt that went on for years. NATO commander general Wesley Clark reportedly traveled to Karadžić's stronghold in Pale to directly warn him that he should turn himself in. Colin Soloway and Kevin Whitelaw, "Using Troops to Play Local Politics," *U.S. News & World Report*, September 1, 1997.

The U.S. ambassador to Bosnia at the time, John Menzies, thinks Karadžić was playing a long game. "He was constantly posturing, trying to get himself off the hook. He was playing for time. He would never really give up the reins of power." John Menzies, telephone interview with author, October 20, 2018.

27. The soldier preparing Karadžić's handover to the Tribunal said Richard Holbrooke had informed a group of IFOR personnel that Karadžić had agreed to step down from the presidency of both RS and the party, but would not be turning himself in to the Tribunal. International Criminal Tribunal for the former Yugoslavia, *Prosecutor v. Karadžić—Declaration of John Petrie*, Case No. IT-95-05/18-PT, May 16, 2011. Document provided to the author by Peter Robinson. Obrad Kesić recollected the same puzzling change in Karadžić's plans—he was no longer arranging to turn himself in, and told Kesić that he had an agreement with Holbrooke to remove himself from public life. Author interview with Obrad Kesić, November 8, 2018. Kesić is the director of the Republika Srpska Office for Cooperation, Trade, and Investment.

28. Nick Hawton, *The Quest for Radovan Karadžić* (London: Hutchinson, 2009), p. 135; Julian Borger, *The Butcher's Trail: How the Search for Balkan War Criminals Became the World's Most Successful Manhunt* (New York: Other Press, 2016), p. 267.

29. Arshad Mohammed, "U.S. Bosnia Negotiator Dismisses Karadzic Deal Claim," Reuters, July 31, 2008, https://www.reuters.com/article /us-warcrimes-karadzic-holbrooke/u-s-bosnia-negotiator-dismisses -karadzic-deal-claim-idUSN3138368720080801.

30. I thank Arthur Applbaum for being so generous with his time and for his wisdom. For more on Professor Applbaum's work, see "Arthur Applbaum," Harvard Kennedy School, https://www.hks.harvard.edu /faculty/arthur-applbaum.

31. International Criminal Tribunal for the former Yugoslavia, *Prosecutor v. Karadžić—First Supplement to Holbrooke Agreement Motion*, Case No. IT-95-5/18-PT, June 19, 2009, p. 2, accessed: http://www.peterrobinson .com/ICTY/Karadzic/Archives_Karadzic/First%20supplement --Holbrooke%20Agreement.pdf.

The Tribunal made its ambivalence toward an immunity deal for Karadžić clear, stating in its judgment of Karadžić that "the reason, or reasons, behind [Karadžić's] decision to step down and withdraw from public life are not relevant." The Tribunal did, however, consider Karadžić's withdrawal from public life to be a mitigating factor when sentencing him, writing that "his decision [to step down] had a positive influence on the establishment of peace and stability in BiH and the region in the wake of the Dayton Agreement." International Criminal Tribunal for the former Yugoslavia, *Prosecutor v. Karadžić—Judgment*, Case No. IT-95-5/18-T, March 24, 2016, http://www.icty .org/x/cases/karadzic/tjug/en/160324_judgement.pdf, p. 2533.

A 2013 book project organized by the United States Institute of Peace claimed, based on conversations with three unnamed State Department officials, that Holbrooke did in fact promise Karadžić immunity—not from prosecution, but from arrest. Matjaž Klemenčič, "The International Community and the FRY/Belligerents, 1989–1997," in Charles Ingrao and Thomas A. Emmert, eds., *Confronting the Yugoslav Controversies: A Scholar's Initiative* (West Lafayette, IN: Purdue University Press, 2013).

32. In the agreement that Karadžić alleges was arranged by Holbrooke to secure Karadžić's immunity from arrest, Karadžić committed to relinquishing his two titles, president of Republika Srpska and president

of his party. He was also required to withdraw "immediately and permanently from all political activities," and to avoid appearing in public or on television or the radio. He also pledged that he would not participate in future elections. The official who claimed to have a copy of the document confirmed that the one I found was the one he had in mind, but he had misremembered the contents. Source: http://www.peterrobinson.com/ICTY/Karadzic/Archives_Karadzic /First%20supplement--Holbrooke%20Agreement.pdf.

The agreement was signed by Karadžić, Momčilo Krajišnik, Biljana Plavšić, and Aleksa Buha; and witnessed by Slobodan Milošević and Milan Milutinović. Krajišnik, Plavšić, and Buha were all members of the Bosnian Serb leadership during the war. Krajišnik and Plavšić would both later be elected as the Bosnian Serb member of the tripartite Presidency of Bosnia and Herzegovina, and were indicted by the ICTY. Buha, a philosopher, was the minister of foreign affairs of the RS during the war. Milutinović was the Yugoslav ambassador to Greece during the war, and Yugoslav federal minister of foreign affairs at the time the agreement was signed.

The agreement established Biljana Plavšić as the "Temporary Acting President of Republika Srpska" from July 19, 1996, until the elections of September 14, 1996. Karadžić would relinquish the office of president of the RS on the same day. Aleksa Buha would carry out the powers and responsibilities of SDS president until the SDS chose a new president. International Criminal Tribunal for the former Yugoslavia, *Prosecutor v. Karadžić—Holbrooke Agreement Motion*, Case No. IT-95-05/18-PT, Annex A, May 25, 2009.

33. This paragraph summarizes an article from the *New York Times*. Anthony Lewis, "Winking At Karadzic," *New York Times*, October 28, 1996, https://www.nytimes.com/1996/10/28/opinion/winking-at-karadzic .html.

34. William Murray, telephone interview with author, August 23, 2018.

35. Julian Borger, *The Butcher's Trail: How the Search for Balkan War Criminals Became the World's Most Successful Manhunt* (New York: Other Press, 2016), p. xvi.

36. This paragraph is based largely on Julian Borger, *The Butcher's Trail: How the Search for Balkan War Criminals Became the World's Most Successful Manhunt* (New York: Other Press, 2016). After 9/11, American intelligence and special-forces resources were substantially redirected, at least for several years. But much of what the teams had learned in Bos-

nia was applicable in Afghanistan and Iraq. "Everything we learned about manhunting in Bosnia, we used again and again in Afghanistan and Iraq," a Delta force commander, Pete Blaber, said. "It was transformational." Pete Blaber, interview with Julian Borger, April 10, 2014, cited in Borger, *The Butcher's Trail*, p. 148.

Not only that, some al Qaeda members took refuge in Bosnia immediately after 9/11. Colonel Andy Milani led an operation that captured two members of al Qaida—a Jordanian and an Egyptian—at the Hotel Hollywood in a Sarajevo suburb. Sean D. Naylor, "Routing Out Terrorism in Bosnia—10th Special Forces Group Uses Sledgehammer Approach," *Army Times*, December 10, 2001. See also Borger, *The Butcher's Trail*, pp. 148–149.

Despite the increased focus on counterterrorism after 9/11, senior Bush administration officials still supported efforts to apprehend PIFWCs, not only to serve justice, but also to "hasten the day" that U.S. forces could be withdrawn from Bosnia. Greg Schulte, telephone interview with author, August 22, 2018.

It was not only American personnel who were reluctant to take on the risky mission, however. The British ambassador in Sarajevo, Charles Crawford, explained, "The rules of engagement said in effect: 'Don't pick him up unless you actually trip over him.' Anything that involved going off the road even ten yards was regarded as 'not being in the course of your normal duties.'" Borger, *The Butcher's Trail*, p. 5.

The French were also reluctant. U.S. officials I spoke to suspected that the French wanted to protect their economic relationship with Republika Srpska. Several U.S. officials mentioned the story of a French spy who was protecting Karadžić.

This hesitance to apprehend Karadžić undermined NATO's credibility around the world, and assured PIFWCs of their safety despite the presence of NATO.

37. On the topic of his protectors, Karadžić told me, "There were twelve close guards. Then the second and third circle of guards. The outer circles of guards didn't know exactly where I was."

38. Julian Borger describes many of these NATO and U.S. efforts to capture the indicted criminals, including Karadžić, in Julian Borger, *The Butcher's Trail: How the Search for Balkan War Criminals Became the World's Most Successful Manhunt* (New York: Other Press, 2016), p. 145.

The hunters commenced a psychological warfare operation in an attempt to get Karadžić's family members to reveal his location.

Helicopters were constantly buzzing over the pink house where Ljiljana, Karadzic's wife, lived. Precursors to drones were available to the task force and included intelligence, surveillance, and reconnaissance (ISR) platforms, which supplemented other means of locating Ljiljana. Colonel Andy Milani indicated that early versions of ISR systems "were frustrating to use. The ability to adjust direction on the fly was effected through chat room links to ground control stations (GCS), which controlled the UAV's movements and sensors. There was an extreme latency in this process, which made it very difficult to get adjustments in real time." Andy Milani, telephone interview with author, July 5, 2018. Karadžić's son, Saša, was brought in for questioning. Borger, *The Butcher's Trail*, pp. 271–272.

The hunters were so determined to get Karadžić to turn himself in that they even considered sending a tank to his grandson's school. Charles Allen, then the national intelligence officer for warning, said, "I remember we once asked ourselves—could we send an M1A1 tank to the grandson's school? It's hard to believe now—we were thinking of staking out a little kid, to scare his grandfather." Charlie Allen, interview with author, July 18, 2018.

39. After ICTY investigators interviewed members of Karadžić's inner circle, they concluded that he had left Bosnia for Belgrade in 1999. Julian Borger, "The Hunt for Radovan Karadžić, Ruthless Warlord Turned 'Spiritual Healer,'" *Guardian*, March 22, 2016, https://www .theguardian.com/world/2016/mar/22/the-hunt-for-radovan-karadzic -ruthless-warlord-turned-spiritual-healer. But another source says he arrived in Belgrade in 2003. Robert J. Donia, *Radovan Karadžić: Architect of the Bosnian Genocide* (New York: Cambridge University Press, 2015), p. 292.

Chapter Ten

HOUDINI

Karadžić told me that he had left Bosnia for Serbia a year before NATO understood he was gone. He had begun disguising himself as the mystic Dragan Dabić while he was still in Bosnia. When I asked him why he left for Belgrade in 1999, he said "Bosnia was too small. I was jeopardizing people. Belgrade is a jungle. You can hide there." It would be nearly thirteen years between the Tribunal's indictment of Karadžić and his transfer to The Hague.

—

Karadžić was very happy with his nom de guerre, "Dabić," because it was similar to Dajbog, the name for the lord of the underworld from Slavic mythology. Dajbog is associated with precious metals and was sometimes described as sporting a beard made of metallic silver. The god appeared in disguise when he walked among men, and thus, as historian Robert Donia points out, the name Dabić reflected Karadžić's "life-long obsession with outsmarting others with clever linguistic nuances."[1]

By sheer force of will, Karadžić transformed his appearance from the look of a president to the look of an eccentric soothsayer. He ate a special weight-reducing potion made from bee larvae called "bee power," he told me, and fasted two days a week. On this regimen he lost thirty-two kilos (seventy pounds). That bee-larva supplement was very good for his health, he said, expressing annoyance that he wasn't allowed to order it to be delivered to him in the Detention Unit. He grew his white hair very long and tied it up in a bun on top of his head with a black ribbon. He also grew a long, silver beard, the beard of Dajbog. He exchanged his tailored suits for shabby old clothing and wore unfashionable, large-framed glasses. He changed his accent and even the timbre of his voice. (Later, the police monitoring his phone calls would say that one of the reasons they had trouble recognizing his voice was that he had pitched it much higher and had acquired a Belgrade accent.)[2]

He told me, "I was worried that the Serbian secret police might find me. I started moving around, renting different apartments. The neighbors were curious about me. They would ask me questions. I told them I was an energy healer." As if he had read the expression of skepticism on my face, he added, "You have to offer them something."[3]

He was not trying to hide his glee regarding his ability to evade his pursuers.

"Once they get something about you, they are usually satisfied. But I realized that the police were sniffing around. Sometimes they are chasing a wolf and they find a fox," he said.

"I hacked into the police so I could see if they were searching for me," he said. This surprised me. How would he know how to do that? I saw no shame on his face, only pride. He suddenly looked younger, like a boy who had figured out a clever way to trick someone.

"How did you know how to do that?" I asked.

He had contacts that did this hacking for him, he said.

"The problem was that I started running out of money," he continued. This may be because Paddy Ashdown, the High Representative in Bosnia at the time, had discovered that tens of millions of dollars were missing from the accounts of several of

Republika Srpska's utilities. Ashdown suspected that the money was being diverted to Karadžić's protection force, and he shut the flow of money down.[4]

Dabić expanded his services as an energy healer in order to make more money.

He described his field as "Human Quantum Energy," advertising his services both online and in person. His business cards said that he offered "quantum-energetic support in health and in illness . . . sexual disorders, fertility disorders . . . depression, fears, tension . . . harmonization of people's vital energy, energetic harmonization of the aura."[5] He created a personal history to share with his colleagues, telling them that he had lived in the United States for ten years. He sometimes said that he had a medical degree from the United States, but that his ex-wife had refused to send him his medical documents.[6]

Dragan Dabić would become a minor celebrity in new age healing circles. He addressed alternative medical meetings with talks that sometimes drew more than a hundred people and were covered on local television.[7] He wrote articles about the kind of meditation he often spoke of with me, Hesychasm (or *tihovanje* in Serbian), practiced by Orthodox monks. The meditation involves repetitive recitation of the Jesus Prayer, accompanied by breathing techniques.[8] The purpose of this form of meditation is to assimilate divine energies. The process is said to cause the mind to descend to the heart, leading to a personal connection with God.[9] Karadžić insisted that frequent prayer of this kind made it possible for him to read people's energy and to predict the future.

He took on the air of an eccentric holy man.[10] The owner of the Madhouse (*Luda Kuća*) bar, which Dabić frequented, spoke of a time that a swarm of bees descended on the bar. They had built a hive, which had grown heavy enough to fall onto the pavement next to the bar. Someone wanted to kill the bees with insecticide. But Dabić wanted to rescue them because, he said, bees are blessed creatures. The owner of the bar called a friend who was a beekeeper to take the bees away. Dabić assisted in the rescue effort, ensuring that every bee was saved. Everyone in the bar who witnessed Dabić's care for the bees began to see him as a kind of saint.[11]

In 2005, Dabić started taking courses with Mina Minić, a famous Russian specialist whom Karadžić referred to as the "maestro of radiesthesia." The aim was to deepen his expertise. Minić taught Karadžić how to use a pendulum called a *visak*, which seers claim can help them detect or alter their clients' subtle energy.[12] From another Belgrade-based clairvoyant, Karadžić learned to use an instrument called a Multi-Zap Zapper, which is purportedly based on an invention by Nikola Tesla and is said to increase clients' health and stamina.[13] I investigated: several zappers, including the para-zapper, the ultimate zapper, and the hulda zapper can be found for sale on the internet.[14] Dabić added these modalities to his energy-healing business.

Minić would later speak with the media about his first meeting with Dabić, at which point, he said, Dabić looked "like a monk who had done something wrong with a nun."[15] Minić took him in, and even let him sleep on a cot in the basement of his home at times.[16] Dabić and Minić planned to write a book together about energy-healing modalities. Minić was so pleased with his student that he gave him the middle name David. Karadžić then began using the name Dragan David Dabić.[17] Minić recalled that there was something puzzling about his talented student: he maintained "four or five" cell phones that rang constantly. "He would always arrange to call everyone back," Minić said.[18]

Karadžić was greatly flattered when the "maestro of radiesthesia" gave him the middle name David, he told me. He explained that King David was a seer and the first bioenergetics practitioner.[19] "When he was very old, he used to recover his vital energy by laying down along with young girls, all naked. But it was completely clear and innocent," he said. He told me I would find this story in the Psalms, but I was not able to find it.

"While I was Dabić, I performed Reiki, and offered advice in doctors' offices. And I worked in a private fertility clinic. They filmed me as Dragan Dabić," Karadžić told me.

I found the film he was talking about. It was made by Russia Today. The film tells the story of a young boy named Danilo who became seriously ill when he was a year old. He was reportedly unable to communicate in any way. According to his family, Dr. Dabić healed Danilo. It was a "miracle," they said. As far as Danilo's parents were concerned, Karadžić would "forever be the good Dr. Dabić."[20]

Vladimir (Vlado) Vulović, a Serb who had emigrated to the United States to earn a PhD in physics, wrote about an encounter he had with the healer Dragan Dabić while visiting his family in Belgrade. A cousin invited him to attend a session with the energy healer. As a scientist, Vlado was extremely skeptical and at first didn't feel much when Dabić asked him to shut his eyes and silently repeat the name of a loved one, the same induction technique he had used on me. "Here and there I felt a slight push or pull, but it didn't last," he wrote. But then he felt something like a magnetic force and a lot of heat. "It was strong. It was hot. My hands trembled as I shifted them left and right in the horizontal plane. The force stayed with me. When I pushed my hands down, the force pushed them back higher. When I lifted my hands, their own weight brought them right down to the force plane," he wrote.

Vlado knew that these phenomena were not consistent with the laws of physics. He wanted to attribute the heat to the thermal radiation emitted from Dabić's warm hands. When he shared this hypothesis with Dabić, the healer plunged his own hands into cold water so that they were cool to Vlado's touch. But Dabić was nonetheless able to transmit heat from his hands to Vlado's face—

the same thing that had happened, Karadžić had told me, when he tried this technique on his wife, Ljiljana.

It was obvious to Vlado that Dabić was a trickster, but he couldn't figure out how Dabić emitted this warmth from his cold hands. His frustrated conclusion was that the phenomenon was "unbelievable, but true."[21] Vlado was even more confused when he learned that Dragan Dabić was actually Radovan Karadžić. He had trouble believing it. Not just because they looked different, and not just because Dabić's speech held no trace of Karadžić's Bosnian accent. But because he just could not accept that he had received an energy-healing treatment from the world's most wanted man and had "chortled with an alleged mass murderer."[22]

During our conversation in the prison, I asked Karadžić, "Were you lonely, trying to live as a different person?"

"I was concentrating on my task," he said. His task, he said, was very clear: "to save Republika Srpska."

Even as he was living the life of Dragan Dabić, Radovan Karadžić continued to taunt his pursuers.[23] He occasionally gave media interviews, and published a series of books in his own name. One of these books was *Under the Left Breast of the Century*, a collection of poems, one of the sections of which was entitled "I Can Look for Myself."[24] He also published a book of children's poetry titled *There Are Miracles, There Are No Miracles*, and an autobiography titled *Radovan and Serbia*.[25] He predicted to a Bosnian paper that his published memoirs would become a best seller, "and I'm sure even be proposed for the Nobel Prize."[26]

Dabić created a website. By the time I tried to find it, Dabić's website was taken down, but it was still available on the Wayback Machine.[27] It reads, "Welcome to the Official Web Site of Dr. Dragan Dabic." The title of the website is "Dr. Dragan Dabic: Healing from Within: The Ever Increasing Need for Alternative Viewpoints in the Modern World." This seems like a good way to describe his reasons for wanting to speak with me, to expose me to alternative viewpoints.

The site goes into Dr. Dabić's history. According to the site, Dr. Dragan David Dabić was born six decades earlier in the small Serbian village of Kovači. As a young boy he spent a lot of time on Kopaonik mountain, where he "tended to pick the omnipresent, natural and potent medicinal herbs that grew in those green pastures." (Kopaonik used to be called Silver Mountain on account of the silver mines located there. This may be another reference to Dajbog—the god of the underworld, with his metallic silver beard.)

The website states that as a young man Dabić had moved to Belgrade, and from there to Moscow, where he had earned an MD at Moscow State University. It further explains that Dr. Dabić had traveled in India and Japan and eventually settled in China, where he specialized in alternative medicine. His special emphasis was on "mind-body control, meditation, Yoga, spiritual cleansing, as well as Chinese herbs." He returned to "mother Serbia" for good in the mid-1990s and had emerged as "one of the most prominent experts in the field of alternative medicine . . . in the whole of the Balkans." The email address given on the website was healing-wounds@dragandabic.com.

At the bottom of the website is a list of ancient Chinese proverbs "personally selected" by Dr. Dabić. Eight are indeed Chinese proverbs. A ninth is not; it is a message from Karadžić to anyone traitorous enough to turn him in to the authorities in exchange for the five-million-dollar bounty offered by the U.S. government for information leading to his arrest.[28] The "proverb" reads: "He who turns in his own, shall dig two graves." There is an additional "proverb" on the Serbian version of the site. It reads (in translation): "A wise man thinks for himself. A stupid man follows what journalists say [both in the sense of following their advice or the news they choose to write about]."[29]

There is only one hyperlink on the site, linking a photograph to the words "young man." I followed the link. In the photograph, the young Dr. Dabić looks identical to photographs of the young Radovan Karadžić. He has the same hair—even parted the same—and the same ears. Apparently, this link was another of Karadžić's taunts.

—

By the time that Boris Tadić was elected as president of independent Serbia in 2008, Europe's most wanted man had become
a source of humiliation to the organizations trying to find him.
Tadić was strongly pro-Western and was trying to integrate Serbia into Europe.[30] But in order for Serbia to be accepted into the
European Union, Karadžić and the remaining indicted fugitives
had to be turned over to the ICTY. The problem for President
Tadić was that he did not control Serbia's Security Information
Agency (*Bezbednosno-informativna agencija*, or BIA). The BIA was
still run by people put in place by the "Euro-skeptic" prime minister Vojislav Koštunica, who had preceded Tadić. Koštunica was
opposed to turning the fugitives over to the ICTY.[31] The head of
the BIA had served as Koštunica's national security advisor.

The BIA investigators had a long list of SIM cards and phone
numbers that they routinely monitored. One day in early 2008 a
SIM card that had been used by Luka Karadžić four years earlier,
and not once since, suddenly connected with a number in Belgrade. The spies monitoring the call did not recognize the voice
on the other end of the line—it was a man with a high-pitched
voice and a Belgrade accent. The conversation was perfunctory.
Still, a couple of investigators went to check out the address
where the recipient's number was registered. They discovered
that a harmless eccentric named Dragan Dabić lived there. The
investigators were puzzled as to why the tough, hard-drinking
Luka Karadžić would be in touch with a mystic offering energy healing. So, without informing their Serb nationalist boss,
the spies continued their inquiry. They found a tomato farmer
named Dragan Dabić in Ruma, halfway to Croatia, who didn't
own a mobile phone. But the Dabić they were scrutinizing lived
in Belgrade and kept half a dozen cell phones with him at all

times. Something didn't seem right. As they dug deeper into the mystery, one of the investigators realized that without his topknot and beard, Dabić could well be Karadžić. They started monitoring him closely. By July 2008, a new coalition in Serbia's parliament favored the pro-Western bloc, which enabled Tadić to replace the head of the BIA, Rade Bulatović, with his own man. He put in place a career police officer who had worked on organized crime. These changes sealed Karadžić's fate. Now it was just a matter of time before the BIA surveillance team closed in on Dragan Dabić.

By this time, Karadžić had been informed by Serb nationalist sympathizers that his cover had been blown, and that the BIA knew who and where he was. But he hoped to slip away before they captured him. Still in the guise of Dabić, he arranged to leave his apartment, telling friends he was taking a vacation in Croatia. He took a bus at the start of his trip, carrying a white plastic bag with all the belongings he could carry, a jaunty straw hat on his head. Four police officers boarded the bus, posing as inspectors. One of them confronted Dabić, who was reading a spiritual text.

"Dr. Karadžić?" the police officer asked.

"No, it's Dragan Dabić," Dabić replied.

"No, it's Radovan Karadžić," the officer insisted.

Then Dabić asked, "Are your superiors aware of what you are doing?"

"Yes, fully," the officer responded.

The officer ordered the bus to stop and removed the old man from the bus. That was the end of Dragan David Dabić, and the beginning of the judgment of Radovan Karadžić.[32]

———

Remarkably, when Karadžić was on the lam disguised as Dabić, many of his friends refused to believe that he was really Radovan Karadžić—even after he was taken into custody by Serbian security personnel. One of these friends, editor of the magazine *Healthy Life*, said that he was deeply troubled by learning that the gentle spiritualist he had known was a war criminal. "There are two options," he said. "Either we are all a bunch of fools and madmen who believed in the existence of a nonexistent man," or Karadžić was redeemed, as Dabić, and there is the possibility of redemption for all of us. My claim, he said, is that Karadžić and Dabić represent an internal battle of a divided man. These two sides are in a life-and-death struggle, he said. "If Dabić defeats Karadžić, he has some chance not only to turn around his life but to reveal to many other people the possibility of transformation from bad to good."[33]

I want to believe in the possibility of a transformation from bad to good, for all of us.

NOTES

1. Robert J. Donia, *Radovan Karadžić: Architect of the Bosnian Genocide* (New York: Cambridge University Press, 2015), p. 294.
2. Karadžić told me, "As a child, I was speaking Ijekavski. When I was in hiding I learned to speak Ekavski, as those in Serbia do—including Croatians, Serbs, Muslims. I assumed that my voice would be easily identified as Karadžić's if I spoke Ijekavski with Bosnian idioms. It only took several months to learn to speak Ekavski."
3. "After Zoran Đinđić became prime minister in January 2001, I had to be even more careful," Karadžić said. Đinđić was strongly opposed to Serb nationalists, and there was a risk that he would have turned Karadžić over to the ICTY. Đinđić had campaigned against Milošević, and had proposed integrating Serbia into Europe. Dabić, at that time, spent most of his time inside his apartment. Two years after he became prime minister, Zoran Đinđić was assassinated by Serb national-

ists with ties to the Serbian mafia. The police started scouring the city, in search of the assassin. Karadžić realized he needed to go out and lead a normal life so as not to arouse the suspicion of his neighbors. *Belgrade Healer: The Other Life of Radovan Karadzic* (Russia Today, 2010), accessed: https://www.youtube.com/watch?v=LJ8CnasrC-c. It should be noted that Russia Today is owned by the Russian government.

4. Julian Borger, *The Butcher's Trail: How the Search for Balkan War Criminals Became the World's Most Successful Manhunt* (New York: Other Press, 2016), p. 270.

5. Robert T. Carroll, "Dr. Dragan Dabic (D. D. David)," *The Skeptic's Dictionary*, updated March 24, 2016, http://skepdic.com/dragandabic.html, accessed November 30, 2018, cited in Robert J. Donia, *Radovan Karadžić: Architect of the Bosnian Genocide* (New York: Cambridge University Press, 2015), p. 295.

6. "Karadžić radio kao lekar," *B92*, July 22, 2008, https://www.b92.net/info/vesti/index.php?yyyy=2008&mm=07&dd=22&nav_id=309674&nav_category=11; E.B., "Radovan zaljubljeni guru," *Blic*, July 23, 2008, https://www.blic.rs/vesti/tema-dana/radovan-zaljubljen i-guru/vz8bsfx, cited in Robert J. Donia, *Radovan Karadžić: Architect of the Bosnian Genocide* (New York: Cambridge University Press, 2015), p. 296.

   On his website, Dabić claimed he had a medical degree specializing in psychiatry from Moscow State University, accessed: https://web.archive.org/web/20080813005834/http://dragandabic.com/.

7. E.B., "Radovan zaljubljeni guru," *Blic*, July 23, 2008, https://www.blic.rs/vesti/tema-dana/radovan-zaljubljeni-guru/vz8bsfx, cited in Robert J. Donia, *Radovan Karadžić: Architect of the Bosnian Genocide* (New York: Cambridge University Press, 2015), p. 297.

8. The Jesus Prayer is a short prayer held in especially high esteem within the Eastern Orthodox churches, and is as follows: "Lord Jesus Christ, Son of God, have mercy on me, a sinner."

9. Marco Toti, "The Hesychast Method of Prayer: Its Anthropological and Symbolic Significance," *International Journal for the Study of the Christian Church*, Vol. 8, No. 1 (February 2008), pp. 17–32.

10. Dušan Stojaković, "Ne bi bilo rata da Alija nije mutio," *Vecernje novosti*, December 27, 2009, http://www.novosti.rs/vesti/naslovna/politika/aktuelno.289.html:260918-Ne-bi-bilo-rata-da-Alija-nije-mutio, cited in Robert J. Donia, *Radovan Karadžić: Architect of the Bosnian Genocide* (New York: Cambridge University Press, 2015), p. 293.

11. This story is recounted here: Julian Borger, "The Night Karadzic Rocked the Madhouse," *Guardian*, July 23, 2008, https://www.the-guardian.com/world/2008/jul/23/radovankaradzic.warcrimes5.

12. "English," Radionica Visak—Pendulum in Daily Life, n.d., http://radio nicavisak.blogspot.com/p/english.html.

13. For example, see: Tesla Medical Innovation, http://tmi.rs. Note that this site is based in Republika Srpska.

14. For example, see: http://www.ess-in.com.

15. Minić quoted in Jack Hitt, "Radovan Karadzic's New-Age Adventure," *New York Times Magazine*, July 22, 2009, https://www.nytimes .com/2009/07/26/magazine/26karadzic-t.html. Minić's use of the *visak* did not seem to help him identify Dabić as Karadžić. He also used it on journalist Jack Hitt, but nonetheless got Hitt's lineage and profession wrong.

16. Helen Fawkes, "Health Guru Who Says He Taught Karadzic," *BBC News*, July 26, 2008, http://news.bbc.co.uk/2/hi/europe/7526912.stm.

17. Helen Fawkes, "Health Guru Who Says He Taught Karadzic," *BBC News*, July 26, 2008, http://news.bbc.co.uk/2/hi/europe/7526912.stm.

18. Jack Hitt, "Radovan Karadzic's New-Age Adventure," *New York Times Magazine*, July 22, 2009, https://www.nytimes.com/2009/07/26 /magazine/26karadzic-t.html.

19. David is listed among the prophets in Acts 2:29–30 (from the King James Version of the Bible): "Men and brethren, let me freely speak unto you of the patriarch David . . . Therefore being a prophet, and knowing that God had sworn with an oath to him, that of the fruit of his loins, according to the flesh, he would raise up Christ to sit on his throne." Acts 2:29–30 AV, accessed: https://biblehub.com/kjv/acts/2.htm.

20. *Belgrade Healer: The Other Life of Radovan Karadzic* (Russia Today, 2010), accessed: https://www.youtube.com/watch?v=LJ8CnasrC-c.

21. Vladimir Vulović, "Healing with Dr. Radovan Karadžić," *Gettysburg Review*, Vol. 24, No. 1 (Spring 2011), pp. 55–56.

22. Vladimir Vulović, "Healing with Dr. Radovan Karadžić," *Gettysburg Review*, Vol. 24, No. 1 (Spring 2011), p. 61.

23. According to the Russia Today film, Karadžić hand-delivered letters and packages to his network in Belgrade. One of the hand-delivered packages included a CD containing a novel he had written. The recipient of the package, former information minister of Serbia Miroslav Toholj, published the novel. Toholj claimed that the novel was a best seller. *Belgrade Healer: The Other Life of Radovan*

Karadzic (Russia Today, 2010), accessed: https://www.youtube.com /watch?v=LJ8CnasrC-c.

Former U.S. Department of State advisor Andy Bair noted the similarities between Karadžić's and al Qaeda's methods of evasion. "Karadžić was very good at evasion. He would travel the back roads and stay in different places on a random basis. Like Bin Laden, Karadžić communicated using personal emissaries and nontraditional techniques." Andy Bair, interview with author, September 29, 2018.

Retired U.S. Army colonel Andy Milani said that Karadžić and his network used very old-fashioned, but very secure, methods of communication. "For them to pass messages, they had to use couriers. Their movements had to be carefully planned and masked. And they had to have absolute trust in their courier network." Andy Milani, telephone interview with author, July 5, 2018.

24. Julian Borger, "How Radovan Karadžić Embraced Evil," *Daily Beast*, March 24, 2016, https://www.thedailybeast.com/how-radovan-karadzic-embraced-evil.

25. "Radovan Karadzic," *More or Less: Heroes & Killers*, updated February 7, 2018, http://www.moreorless.net.au/killers/karadzic.html.

26. "Indicted Karadzic Dreams of Nobel Prize," *BBC News*, April 9, 2001, http://news.bbc.co.uk/2/hi/europe/1268552.stm.

27. Dr. Dragan Dabic: Healing from Within: The Ever Increasing Need for Alternative Viewpoints in the Modern World, accessed: https://web.archive.org/web/20080813005834/http://dragandabic.com/, December 20, 2018.

28. U.S. Department of State, Daily Press Briefing DPB #80, June 24, 1999, accessed: https://1997-2001.state.gov/www/briefings/9906/990624db .html.

29. Translation provided by Mladen Mrdalj.

30. Boris Tadić was elected president of Serbia in 2004 when it was part of Serbia and Montenegro (also known as the Federal Republic of Yugoslavia – FRY), and was elected for a second term in 2008 as president of independent Serbia. He resigned in 2012.

31. Vojislav Koštunica was the last president of Yugoslavia, from 2000 to 2003, and the prime minister of Serbia from 2004 to 2007, and from 2007 to 2008. He was opposed to Kosovo's independence and opposed Serbia's joining of the EU because of its position on Kosovo. Julian Borger, *The Butcher's Trail: How the Search for Balkan War Criminals Became the World's Most Successful Manhunt* (New York: Other Press, 2016), p. 248.

32. The story of Karadžić's capture has been recounted many times. The account I'm providing here is based on Borger's book, which I highly recommend. Julian Borger, *The Butcher's Trail: How the Search for Balkan War Criminals Became the World's Most Successful Manhunt* (New York: Other Press, 2016).

33. Jack Hitt, "Radovan Karadzic's New-Age Adventure," *New York Times Magazine*, July 22, 2009, https://www.nytimes.com/2009/07/26/magazine/26karadzic-t.html.

Chapter Eleven

MORAL HAZARD

Karadžić and I spoke in person only inside the Detention Unit. But we also communicated by letter and, on rare occasions, by phone. When he reached me by phone in my everyday life, I felt confused, invaded, even dizzy for a second or two. Once he called me at home while I was exercising, riding an indoor bike. Another time, I was walking with my family on the rocks in the bright sun, by a glinting sea, in Iceland. I responded, at least I think I did, as if there were nothing unusual about his calling me there. What was this darkness coming into the bright light? He had caught me unprepared—unclothed of my usual emotional armor. Until now, I hadn't realized I needed to gird myself in order to speak with him.

Gird myself against what? Against shame. But I'm not sure if the shame I needed to be protected from was his or mine or both.

While we were together in the prison, most of the time, I focused on treating him respectfully, even deferentially. I tried to keep my visceral responses to myself, not always successfully. However, for large periods of time, it felt to me as if we were a research team, working together on the project of explaining what motivated Radovan Karadžić. My impossible task involved the effort to stay open to Karadžić's explication of why he behaved as he did, rather than blindly accepting the common narrative— that the Serbs were evil genocidaires and the Muslims guileless victims. I felt committed to taking in his account, his version of history. Of course, an equally important aspect of my job was to maintain the assumption that whatever Karadžić told me would be a lie, which was why I double- and triple-checked all his claims. I have to admit I was surprised to discover that much of what he told me was true, as far as I was able to determine, or at least had some basis or kernel of truth. However, for a long time, we avoided discussing his involvement in atrocities. The incentives for him to attempt to deceive me were too high. And I told myself that there was no point in my asking Karadžić about his role in overseeing war crimes because the Tribunal, with its hundreds of trained researchers and attorneys, would do a better job at ferreting out the truth.

Let me try to restate that. The truth is, I didn't want him to lie to me. I wanted, grandiosely, to be the one person to whom he would tell the truth.

In his personal capacity, he is a likable man, and I found myself enjoying his company, at least some of the time. *How could that be?* But for the most part, that feeling did not extend beyond our meetings in the prison.

Looking back at that moment he called me in Iceland, I am bemused by my own confusion as well as by his arrogance. Of course, I had only myself to blame; I was the one who had given him my cell phone number, albeit at his request. I realize now that there were unwritten rules that I had expected him to follow (even though I was unaware of those rules until he broke them). When I was with him in The Hague, I joined him as a fellow seeker, a fellow member of a two-man team researching the topic of Radovan Karadžić. Neither of us could leave without the permission of the guards. Both of us were locked up, working together on the project of my learning about him: we were fellow prisoners. He was the more senior, older, wiser, and more learned; and I was expected to be grateful for his erudition. My challenge, over time, was to surprise him, even to surpass him; the mentee eventually transcending the mentor, perhaps with modern tricks and techniques, perhaps with her quickening intelligence.

On the surface, we were polite. But if I examine myself closely, I realize that on a deeper level, we were like two animals fighting for our lives. At the edge of my consciousness, I have an image of myself chasing him with a scythe in my hand, skirts flying. It is clear that we both wanted to win. Why did we bother? In the long run, it is obvious now who was going to triumph. I am thirteen years younger. I am the longer-lived gender. I could walk out of that prison.

When you're sitting with a bully, you can sometimes intuit the scared, bullied, little boy, and some of us can even find the bully in ourselves. But that was for when we sat together. Outside the room, he had no rights at all in regard to me. Perhaps I needed to remind him (and myself, too) that he is a despised man, a convicted criminal, found guilty of the worst imaginable crimes, even if he sees himself as Prince Lazar come back to life, even if I was willing, when sitting with him, to see him in the same way he saw himself. In prison, I was prepared to suspend judgment. Perhaps I needed to remind him that in my real life outside the little room, I'm actually not a fellow criminal: I've never been convicted of any kind of crime (even if I know in my heart of hearts that I, like the rest of us human beings, have committed countless moral and emotional transgressions). So, you see, I was not immune to feeling superior to the man, even despite his broader education, his intimidating knowledge of Greek and Roman myths, his greater manipulative skills, and my relative ignorance. What am I saying here? Between us, it was always a case of one up, one down. When he phoned me without prior notice, when he helicoptered into my life, he had the upper hand. I did not like that.

Perhaps I'm getting closer to understanding my reaction to these calls, which, in the moment I picked up the phone, took me by surprise. He was forcing two parts of myself that normally operate on separate tracks to come into contact, to scrape against one another other, to emit dangerous sparks. (Sparks of what?) I can spend an afternoon with him in his confinement. But outside of the prison, I need to breathe my own air, not his.

And what did he intend with those calls? He called to urge me to read things, to check up on whether his attorneys had sent me certain legal documents as instructed, or to inform me that his daughter was willing to meet with me in Pale. But I wonder now if what he really wanted was to show me that he (or his minions) can find me, wherever I am, anywhere in the world. Was he threatening me or warning me? He understood the power of stoking fear.

———

Toward the end of our extended conversation, on our second-to-last day together, it was Karadžić who brought up genocide. He wanted to talk about his role in the war and the Srebrenica massacre in particular.

From Karadžić's perspective, Bosnia's bid to break away from Yugoslavia was not only illegal under the Yugoslav constitution, but also a clear provocation. He is arguably correct on both counts. Yugoslavia's Constitutional Court repeatedly considered the question of individual republics' secession and determined that it was allowed only if all federal units (republics and autonomous regions) agreed to amend the constitution.[1] Some scholars argue that secession from Yugoslavia was even illegal under Bosnia's constitution.[2]

Nonetheless, on October 15, 1991, Bosnia's assembly passed a "declaration of sovereignty." By that time, Slovenia and Croatia had already declared their independence, and a full-scale war was under way in Croatia. The shaky basis on which the European Community ruled that the Yugoslav republics could legally secede raised the intriguing question as to whether other states with minority issues could face a similar threat to sovereignty.[3]

Karadžić responded with a now-infamous speech to Bosnia's multiethnic assembly, "pleading" with the Muslim members not to secede to avoid the violent fate of Croatia:

"I ask you once again, I am not threatening, I am pleading that you take seriously the political will of the Serbian people represented here today. . . . The road you are choosing for Bosnia and Hercegovina is the same highway to hell and suffering that Slovenia and Croatia have already taken," Karadžić proclaimed. "Do not think that you will not take Bosnia and Hercegovina to hell and the Muslim people maybe into extinction, because if there is a war, the Muslim people will not be able to defend themselves."[4]

Parts of this speech were repeatedly used by prosecutors and scholars to demonstrate Karadžić's malign intent, which Karadžić claims is not correct. This was a warning, not a threat, he said. In my view, it was both.

After the assembly's declaration of sovereignty, Karadžić's Serb nationalist party, the SDS, recognized that it had lost the battle to stop Bosnia's secession. From that point on, according to historian Robert Donia, Karadžić was "rapidly propelling the SDS and the various local municipal organs toward war."[5]

Four and a half months later, from February 29 to March 1, 1992, Alija Izetbegović, the Bosniak founder of the Muslim nationalist party and the president of the Presidency of Bosnia and Herzegovina, held a referendum on independence. It passed, though Serbs refused to participate. On March 3, 1992, Izetbegović announced Bosnia's independence. Fighting broke out soon thereafter.[6] Three months after the war began, the Serbs had acquired 70 percent of Bosnia's territory.

———

Izetbegović clearly knew that by demanding sovereignty for a unitary Bosnia, he was provoking the Serbs to attack. He told the Bosnian parliament on February 27, 1991, "I would sacrifice peace for a sovereign Bosnia-Herzegovina, but for that peace in Bosnia-Herzegovina, I would not sacrifice sovereignty," a statement that many Serbs understood to be a war cry.[7] He also asked rhetorically, "Will we accept peace at any price in Bosnia, bend our heads once and for all, because of peace accept an inferior position for the next 15 years, or shall we say, we want sovereignty, risking a conflict?"[8]

Why did Izetbegović take the risk of war, despite being massively outgunned? A number of Muslim leaders have said, retrospectively, that they did not want to be dominated politically by Serbs in what was left of Yugoslavia.[9] But the SDA leadership was also counting on outside powers to help defend them from Serb aggression.[10] Tragically, Izetbegović overestimated the West's support for Bosnia's independence and underestimated the Serbs' determination to stop it.

The American political scientist Alan Kuperman was able to interview President Izetbegović in 2000 on exactly this issue. Izetbegović told Kuperman, "I expected the international community would recognize our independence and then defend that state it recognized . . . politically and militarily."[11] Other SDA leaders also admitted that they had actively lobbied the West to recognize Bosnia's independence in the expectation of help. Muhamed Čengić, who had been Izetbegović's vice president, confirmed to Kuperman that the Muslim leadership assumed that the United Nations or Europe would "do anything in their power to stop or prevent war."[12] Haris Silajdžić, who had served as Bosnia's foreign minister and later prime minister, admitted that "all the [peace] negotiations were just a farce to buy legitimacy," and that his most important priority was "to get Western governments and especially the United States to get involved."[13]

While the United States and Europe recognized Bosnia's independence on April 7, 1992, NATO did not support Izetbegović militarily until 1994.[14] Not only did the West fail to support Izetbegović militarily in the way that he hoped, the UN-imposed arms embargo—intended to reduce the violence—affected only the Bosnian Muslims, since the Bosnian Serbs had access to Yugoslavia's armed forces.[15] In other words, the UN unintentionally gave the Serbs an advantage in the war.

Karadžić wanted me to understand there might be another reason that Izetbegović risked calamity. "Izetbegović saw his own people as expendable," he told me. Karadžić mentioned that he had become friends with General Slobodan Praljak, a Croatian general, who had also been detained in the UN prison.[16] "Praljak told me that he was shocked to hear from Izetbegović that 'our people must be hit hard to wake them up to Islam,'" suggesting that Izetbegović was frustrated that the vast majority of Bosnia's Muslims were secular, or certainly not fundamentalist.[17]

I must have looked skeptical when Karadžić told me this.

"He wrote these words in the Islamic Declaration!" Karadžić exclaimed.

I had not read the Islamic Declaration, a manifesto that Izetbegović had drafted in 1969 and published in 1970.[18] But I didn't believe any of what Karadžić was telling me about Izetbegović's willingness to sacrifice his own people. Consider the source. I believed that Izetbegović was a liberal democrat in favor of establishing an independent, multiethnic state, the narrative commonly accepted by Americans at the time.[19]

But later I understood that there might be some truth to Karadžić's claims regarding Izetbegović and the Islamic Declaration, and even Karadžić's claim that Izetbegović had cultivated jihadis.[20] In many places, the Islamic Declaration reads as a typical Islamist tract, in that it proposes that Islam should form the basis of all aspects of Muslims' lives. For example, Izetbegović wrote, "Announcing a revival [of Islam], we are not announcing an era of security and tranquility, but rather a period of unrest and challenge. . . . A people which is asleep can only be awakened by blows."[21] It reads, "Our goal: The Islamization of Muslims. Our motto: Believe and struggle."[22] It argues that the Islamic movement should "overturn . . . existing non-Islamic government[s]," as soon as the movement is "morally and numerically strong enough . . . to build up a new Islamic one."[23] He wrote, "There can be neither peace nor coexistence between the Islamic religion and non-Islamic social and political institutions."[24] He also promoted Pakistan as a model Islamic state. In 1983, Izetbegović, along with eleven others, was arrested for what prosecutors claimed was the promotion of an ethnically pure Bosnian state, even though there was no mention of Bosnia in the Declaration. This was the second time Izetbegović had been arrested for Islamist activities.[25] In 1946, he was arrested by the Communist Partisans for his involvement in the Young Muslims, an Islamist organization that was connected with the largely Muslim Waffen-SS Handschar Division.

However, Izetbegović's defenders claimed that the Islamic Declaration was written in a moment of youthful religious enthusiasm, and was directed to Muslims all around the world, not only in Bosnia.[26] Moreover, Izetbegović was known constantly to contradict himself, and there were many words in the Islamic Declaration that were at odds with the quotes highlighted above. For example, Izetbegović said that he did not intend for the Declaration to apply to Bosnia. "The Islamic order can only be established in countries where Muslims represent the majority of the population. If this is not the case, the Islamic order is reduced to mere power (as the other element—the Islamic society—is missing), and may turn to violence," he wrote.[27] He also wrote, "The survival, strength, or weakness of Islamic societies is subject to the same laws of work and struggle as are other communities."[28] Many scholars point out that the Islamic Declaration was selectively quoted and weaponized by Serb nationalists. There arose a parallel war among specialists about whether the manifesto should be interpreted as Islamist or as simply a theoretical assessment of how Islam and Islamic states can exist in contemporary society.[29] Western commentators seem either to have ignored the content, or assumed it was an anti-Communist tract.[30] In a book published in 2003, the last year of Izetbegović's life, Izetbegović himself would seem to have settled the question: He referred to his manifesto as "fundamentalist" in the sense that it advocated returning to Islamic sources.[31]

According to Miomir Žužul, a senior Croatian official who spent a lot of time with Izetbegović during the war, Izetbegović sometimes seemed to be deliberately speaking in a way that was hard to understand.[32] He routinely contradicted himself, Žužul said; an observation that other prominent intellectuals and officials have confirmed.[33] But it was clear, Ambassador Žužul said, that Izetbegović was prepared to sacrifice thousands of lives in order to get a state for Bosniaks. He presented himself to the West in a way he thought would appeal to Westerners. "He would say that he wanted to avoid war. But it was clear to me that he wanted to use the war to create a state for Bosnian Muslims," rather than a state for all three ethnic groups.[34]

There were many possibilities for avoiding war. Adil Zulfikarpašić, a prominent intellectual and one of the cofounders of the SDA, the Muslim nationalist party, negotiated a power-sharing agreement with the Serb leadership in mid-July 1991.[35] Within days, the two sides had agreed to the terms. But soon after an agreement had been reached, Izetbegović repudiated it.[36] "To this day I do not understand how he rejected that agreement and broke his word so easily, hurtling his people into conflict," Zulfikarpašić said after the war, accusing Izetbegović of choosing "the road to catastrophe," rather than peace.[37] Zulfikarpašić's retrospective interpretation of why Izetbegović had rejected the agreement was that he feared a loss of personal power; Milovan Djilas believed that the SDA leadership was counting on assistance from the Islamic world and (perhaps irrationally) from the United States, and that the nationalist parties—both Muslim and Serb—were "totalitarian," incapable of compromise.[38]

Djilas is right about the totalitarian bent of the nationalist parties. I can't help but wonder—could this happen to American nationalists, too?

With the failure of the Belgrade Initiative, Europe (belatedly) got involved in trying to prevent the war. The Lisbon Agreement, a plan put forward by the European Community (EC), would have created a confederation of three ethnic regions in a so-called soft partition, which the European mediators saw as the best way to avert war. Representatives of all three sides signed a Declaration of Principles on March 18, 1992, but the United States encouraged Izetbegović to reject the plan and fight for a unitary Bosnia, despite the risk of war.[39] "The policy was to encourage Izetbegović to break with the partition plan," a high-ranking State Department official admitted to the *New York Times*. "We let it be known we would support his government in the United Nations if they got into trouble."[40] In 1993, a year and a half later, with tens of thousands of lives lost, the United States reversed its policy, endorsing another partition plan similar to the Lisbon Agreement it had earlier opposed—the Owen-Stoltenberg plan. Several American officials involved at the time admitted they had made a mistake in opposing the Lisbon Agreement, which they retrospectively recognized could have averted war. Among them was U.S. ambassador Warren Zimmermann, who admitted to the *New York Times* that the United States had made a mistake in opposing the Lisbon agreement.[41] (The United States supported subsequent agreements involving partitions, including the Dayton Agreement, which finally ended the war.)

According to Miro Tudjman, who was in charge of Croatian intelligence during the war, Izetbegović signed the Declaration of Principles in order to further his goal of being seen as a representative of the state of Bosnia. But he did so cynically, Tudjman said, with no intention of coming to an agreement, since his goal was to achieve a unitary state in which Muslims outnumbered Serbs. From the beginning, Tudjman told me, Izetbegović's goal was to be seen as a victim of Serb aggression. If Bosnia were fighting to secede, it could be seen as an aggressor against Yugoslavia. If Bosnia were recognized as an independent state, the Serbs would be viewed as aggressors against Bosnia. Tudjman told me, "Ensuring that the Bosnian Serbs were viewed by the international community as the aggressors was Izetbegović's goal. And he achieved it."[42] The U.S. Department of Defense came to the same conclusion. In a document declassified in 2019, the Joint History Office argued that recognition of Bosnia "gave the Bosnian Muslims an important advantage, because it enabled them to portray the resistance of the Bosnian Serbs to the establishment of a unitary state as international aggression."[43]

—

Political scientist Alan Kuperman claims that it is rare, historically, for subnational groups significantly weaker than the state to attempt to secede or initiate an armed rebellion.[44] He views Bosnia's attempt to break away from Yugoslavia as one of these rare cases. When rebels have reason to expect outside intervention, Kuperman believes they may attempt to secede even despite knowing that their actions will provoke massive retaliation against their own civilians. In some cases, they will deliberately provoke violence against their own citizens in the hope of forcing outside powers to rescue them. This is precisely what occurred in Bosnia, Kuperman argues. The Serbs started out with the backing of Yugoslavia's military, while the Bosniaks had relatively few armaments. The brutal Serb campaign against secessionist Croatia provided a vivid preview of the likely response should Bosnia attempt to secede, but Bosnia seceded anyway. Kuperman calls this strategy of deliberately provoking aggression on the part of a significantly stronger power in the expectation of international assistance the "moral hazard of humanitarian intervention," arguing that just as people take greater risks with their health and property when they're insured, the expectation of international assistance led the Bosnian Muslims to provoke war.[45] A Department of Defense document declassified in 2019 argued that a major goal for the Bosniaks was to "secure outside intervention in [*sic*] their behalf. . . . The Serbs were hostile and antagonistic to the press, but Bosnian Muslim leaders, educated and westernized, became adept at using the media to evoke sympathy for their cause."[46]

Since 1943, in the majority of cases of genocide or mass violence, the targeted group had challenged the state's authority by acquiring arms or attempting to secede.[47] According to political scientist Ben Valentino, among others, mass violence against civilians, despite its illegality under international law, is often a "rational" policy to deter or stop a group from threatening the ascendant group's dominance.[48]

———

Karadžić insists that he tried many times to avoid war and blames the war on the Muslims. From the very beginning, he made his opposition to Bosnia's independence clear. "We would have agreed to three possibilities," he told me. The first option, he said, was for Bosnia to remain within Yugoslavia. Second, Bosnia could break away—but the areas where Serbs comprised a majority would remain within Yugoslavia. The problem with this option, from the Bosniak perspective, was the difficulty of agreeing on where Serbs comprised a majority. For example, political scientist Nevenka Tromp points out that the Republika Srpska constitution of 1992 stated that Republika Srpska territory would include areas where Serbs comprised a majority in World War II, and made Sarajevo the capital of Republika Srpska.[49] Third, Bosnia could break away, but Bosnian Serbs would also get their own fully independent state.[50]

"The Serb entity would be just like West Virginia," Karadžić said. "Virginia was the capital of the Confederacy. Slaveholding Virginia wanted to secede, just as Bosnia did. But West Virginia wanted to stay with the Union, and so it sought to become an independent state."

I looked at his face. I could see in his eyes he was pleased with himself. He was drawing a moral equivalency between Bosniaks and secessionist slaveholders, and between Serbs and abolitionists. I suspected he had made this argument before. He was guessing that as an American, I would favor states that protect minorities and civil rights, implying that this was his goal. (It was not.) He is a genius at establishing an alliance, in this case with me as an American rather than as a Jew.

"After the Civil War," he pontificated, "Virginia never united again. It was not possible to do it differently." I saw that he was implying here that Republika Srpska, the Serb entity he helped to create in Bosnia, ought to fully separate from Bosnia and remain separate.[51]

Next, Karadžić turned to the most damning case against him, the massacre at Srebrenica, where he was convicted of overseeing a genocide.

Karadžić was convicted partly on the basis of a directive (military order) issued in his name. Directive 7 reads, in part, that the Drina Corps (a part of the Bosnian Serb Army) should "create an unbearable situation of total insecurity with no hope of further survival or life for the inhabitants of Srebrenica."[52]

"I did not write or even read Directive 7," he told me. "There were at least nine directives. I often didn't write them myself, even if they were issued in my name. My title was supreme commander, but other people would copy and paste material from previous directives. Mladić wrote Directive 4 in its entirety. Directive 7 was drafted by Radivoje Miletić [deputy chief of staff of the Bosnian Serb Army]."

When he said this, I didn't believe him. But I was able to acquire a copy of the directive, given to me by the historian Robert Donia. It states very clearly that Miletić drafted it. Miletić even admitted to the Court that he drafted Directive 7.[53] But even if Karadžić didn't *author* the directive, as president he was responsible for directives issued in his name. Moreover, I see on the directive in front of me that Radovan Karadžić signed it. I even checked other documents that Karadžić had signed to make sure it was the same signature. In any case, there were many intercepts of Karadžić's conversations at the time that clearly demonstrate his knowledge of the massacre, after July 13, 1995, so his focusing on the authorship of the directive was a ruse.

Some of these intercepts were collected by historian Robert Donia. For example, on August 6, 1995, Karadžić boasted to the Bosnian Serb Assembly that as supreme commander of the VRS (Bosnian Serb Army), he, and *not* his military commander, General Mladić, was responsible for initiating orders to take the town of Srebrenica. He said to the Assembly, "All of our decisions, and I stand behind them, were recorded by the High Command and they all state that I ordered, both verbally and in writing, that we go to Žepa [another enclave that was ethnically cleansed by the Bosnian Serbs] and Srebrenica." He celebrated the military's "success in Srebrenica."[54] Later, in October 1995, he said to the Assembly, "I approved that . . . radical task and I don't regret it."[55]

Some, though surprisingly not all, of these intercepts were included in the Court's judgment against Karadžić, to prove his mens rea (intent) for genocide.[56]

Karadžić said to me, "They didn't tell me that Muslims were being killed."

I noticed that his voice had changed, as if he were now pleading with me. He could see that I didn't believe him.

—

What I believe is this: Karadžić was lying when he boasted to the Bosnian Serb Assembly in 1995 that he alone (and *not* General Mladić) was responsible for initiating the attack at Srebrenica. When speaking to the Republika Srpska Assembly, he wanted to look like

a more powerful leader than he was and to take credit for the "successful" ethnic cleansing of Srebrenica. Declassified CIA documents
make clear that Karadžić was in a fierce competition with Mladić at
that time.[57] But I also believe that Karadžić was lying during the November 2016 conversation I'm describing here, when he said to me,
"They didn't tell me that Muslims were being killed."[58] In another
intercept of his conversations soon after Srebrenica, he was critical of an officer who had allowed photographs of the massacre to
reach foreign media. The pictures, he said, "could cost [General]
Mladić his life if they were presented in The Hague," making clear
not only that he knew about the massacre—and that his claiming
"They didn't tell me that Muslims were being killed" was a lie—
but also that he understood how the genocide would be perceived
by the Yugoslav Tribunal.[59] He wanted two incompatible things:
to be applauded by the Serb nationalists for orchestrating the
Srebrenica massacre, and to be acquitted by the Tribunal.

—

Now I notice a wistful look on his face, a different kind of smile.

"I finally realized who you remind me of," he said.

I was surprised he would speak to me so directly—as if I were
a real person rather than his interviewer.

"You remind me of my wife when we were young."

I tried to brush him off with a smile. In the moment he said
this, I felt uncomfortable and wanted to move on to other topics.
Was he trying to flatter me again? I don't think so. There was a
different feeling in the room this time. Sadness.

—

I've thought about this *you remind me of my wife* proclamation
many times since then. I don't think he was flirting with me or
trying to flatter me. I believe he was momentarily (if accidentally)
sincerely expressing regret about his lost youth, and especially

about what he lost when he became president and then a war criminal. His mother had warned him not to get involved in politics.[60] Perhaps he was regretting that he hadn't listened to her. Back then, when he and his wife were young, before he pushed himself forward, before he became president, he had the potential to live as a good man and to die holding his wife's hand, with his children and grandchildren nearby. But he had a drive to be a truly *great* man. To be famous.

Dr. Angel and I spoke about this drive several times. Karadžić created a false persona, she said to me.

"People like Radovan become two people: their original personality—their true self—and the heroic personality they create."[61]

The biggest puzzle for me, I told Dr. Angel, is that I found it hard to imagine how Karadžić transformed himself into a different person and kept up the charade for years. It was not just a matter of losing a lot of weight and changing his hairstyle; he seemed to have entered the persona of a new age healer. Dragan Dabić would spend his evenings in a Serb nationalist bar in Belgrade called the Madhouse. He played the *gusle*, just as Karadžić did. He would sit in the bar, right in front of a portrait of President Karadžić, and still no one recognized the similarity between Karadžić, the president in the photograph, and Dragan Dabić, the new age energy practitioner having a drink. I went to see the bar in 2017: the picture was still there. I can't get my head around how he could keep this up for so many years.

Dr. Angel doesn't really have an answer for me.

"Did he have a heroic stance with you?" she asks. Yes, I say. Very much so.

—

In May 2015, I thought we had exhausted the visits the Court would allow. But in the end, the Court allowed three more. I remember noticing how exhausted he was when we were saying good-bye for what we thought was the last time. He must have been so tired of transforming himself into the heroic person he wanted me to see. The person he wanted to be.

"I keep expecting to get past the heroic stance," I said to Dr. Angel.

"But you won't," she said.

But I believe I did, after this conversation with Dr. Angel, especially in the moment he told me that I reminded him of his wife when they were both young. In that brief moment, I saw that he was capable of regret. Of course, as I'm writing this, I'm worried that I'm displaying naivete, that he tricked me yet again.

"Here is my take on who he was and how he became a Byronic hero, a Siegfried," Dr. Angel said to me. "When I knew him as a young doctor, he was still in the process of forming the heroic myth. He was not yet the Hero he became. He was already a poet in the public eye. But that was part of promoting the myth— but not yet being the hero of action."

To us he's a war criminal. But he views himself as a mythic hero. He feels that his trial was actually a trial of the Serbian people. He is a martyr for Serbia. Like Prince Lazar.

"He was narcissistic enough to believe that he was destined for greatness. He had a grandiose belief in his own destiny—like Jesus or a guru. And Rašković [his mentor in founding the Serb nationalist party] brainwashed him to believe in this idealized version of who he might become," Dr. Angel said. "Some narcissists use this internal drive for greatness to do good in the world. They run NGOs, they run for office, they do good works. But they're still narcissists. They're probably not good to their families but they can still make the world a better place." Dr. Angel mentioned some famous human rights activists she puts in this category.

The person she saw in the 1970s, Karadžić's real self, was "a young man with a poetic vision of life." He would have liked to be a healer, not a killer.

I heard Dr. Angel's outbreath.

"He felt obliged to be a killer because of fear."

Now Karadžić's jumbled words come back to me.

State of mind is very important. . . . If one is presuming he will be killed he will kill.

"What is the central conflict of his life?" Dr. Angel asked rhetorically. "It is the conflict between the healer and the killer. When I knew him, he was a troubadour of Serbian nationalism. Now he is Henry the Fifth."[62]

He was a poet and an assassin.

—

Karadžić wanted to be a great psychiatrist. He wanted to be a great poet. But he was too lazy to achieve those goals, his supervisor, Dr. Cerić, said.[63]

Then history offered Karadžić an opportunity to become great in a different way, though hardly as a human rights activist. As Yugoslavia was breaking up, Bosnian Serbs were frightened, Karadžić observed (or so he said to me). They were at risk of becoming a dreaded minority rather than a recognized nationality (*narod*).[64] If Bosnia became independent, Serbs would be outnumbered by Muslims and there would be no protection from "ethnic outvoting" (Yugoslavs' term for the measures put in place to prevent majoritarian rule). In that moment, Karadžić took on the mantle of a martyr for the Serb cause, even to the point of massacring Muslims. He will live out that role of martyr, imprisoned until he dies.

It's a loss of a human soul. He dug himself into a hole and he doesn't want to climb out.

—

We move on. He has more interesting things to say on the topic of genocide.

"Genocide is never useful," he sighed.

Did anyone say it was? Why does he feel the need to say this?

"Look what happened with Hitler. The genocide he perpe-trated did not work out well for Germany. The only genocide that worked out well for the perpetrator was America's geno-cide against the Native Americans," he said.

How our relationship has changed over time. We had both been so po-lite in the beginning. Now he is happy to argue with me. That was a pretty effective dig—not only at his American interlocutor but also at the Americans who helped set up the Court that convicted him.

"You can see from the Old Testament that whole peoples sometimes disappeared," he mused. "But those who initiate the disappearance of a people do not get advantages."

This talk of genocide reminds him of other examples of Western hypocrisy.

"The West is always trying to impose its version of democ-racy on others. A tribal democracy is not the same as a Western democracy. Look what happened in Libya and Iraq," he said.

I agree with him, but I don't tell him that. Americans' habit of imposing democracy on others, imagining themselves to be res-cuing people from tyranny, has not always worked out so well, especially for the countries we invade. Democracy is not a pana-cea. Electoral democracy can rapidly descend into majoritarian rule or, as political scientist Sheri Berman warns, populism.[65] The emergence of democracy in Yugoslavia is what prompted the rise of ethnonationalist parties, ultimately leading to war. It takes time for electoral democracies to develop liberal institutions. And we are discovering that liberal democracies—with equal protections under the law, separation of powers, and basic protections of civil rights and liberties—are both rare and fragile.[66]

NOTES

1. Yugoslavia's Constitutional Court considered the legality of secession several times. The Court ruled that a republic could secede legally only if *all* federal units (republics and autonomous regions) agreed to amend the constitution. Unilateral secession was deemed illegal. Serbia argued that because Croatia and Slovenia had illegally seceded, they were not entitled to any assets formerly held by the SFRY. The republics, on the other hand, argued that Yugoslavia had "disintegrated." The European Community set up an arbitration commission (commonly known as the Badinter Commission) to assess whether republics could break away under international law. The Badinter Commission, in its first opinion, ruled with the republics, claiming that Yugoslavia had dissolved on November 29, 1991 (while noting that Croatia and Slovenia had seceded earlier than that, on October 8, 1991). This ruling had international implications; Quebec later used the Badinter findings to argue the legality of its secession bid. Peter Radan, "Post-Secession International Borders: A Critical Analysis of the Opinions of the Badinter Arbitration Commission," *Melbourne University Law Review*, Vol. 24, No. 1 (2000), p. 54. Robert M. Hayden, an anthropologist of law and politics, found that the first opinion of the Badinter Commission (that the SFRY was in a process of dissolution) imparted an "extraordinary fragility" onto a "federal-type state." He wrote, "Such a state, it suddenly seems, can be 'dissolved' by a proclamation of independence by any of its components." Robert M. Hayden, *Blueprints for a House Divided: The Constitutional Logic of the Yugoslav Conflicts* (Ann Arbor, MI: University of Michigan Press, 2000), p. 88.

   Lord David Owen, the former cochairman of the International Conference on the Former Yugoslavia, opposed the Badinter Commission's finding, writing that it undermined the ability of the European Council to make peace between warring parties. David Owen, *Balkan Odyssey* (New York: Harcourt Brace, 1995), p. 33. François Miterrand, who was then the French president, also opposed the decision to recognize the breakaway republics before questions about international borders had been resolved. Walter R. Roberts, "The Tragedy in Yugoslavia Could Have Been Averted," in Raju G. C. Thomas and H. Richard Friman, eds., *The South Slav Conflict: History, Religion, Ethnicity, and Nationalism* (New York: Garland, 1996), pp. 363, 370, cited in Radan, "Post-Secession International Borders," p. 67.

2. Expert on Balkan affairs Professor Susan Woodward told me that secession was illegal not only under Yugoslav law but also under Bosnian law. Susan Woodward, interview with author, December 27, 2018. Robert M. Hayden explains that under the 1990 amendments to the Bosnian constitution, consensus (or at least lack of opposition) among constitutive peoples was critical for a republic's decision to secede. As the Bosnian Serbs boycotted the 1992 referendum on Bosnia's independence, there was no consensus among the constitutive nations (or peoples) of Bosnia. Thus, the referendum did not hold any weight under the Bosnian constitution itself. Robert M. Hayden, *Blueprints for a House Divided: The Constitutional Logic of the Yugoslav Conflicts* (Ann Arbor, MI: University of Michigan Press, 2000).

The Badinter Commission argued that Bosnia's breaking away was legal "if appropriate guarantees were provided . . . possibly by means of a referendum of all the citizens." In the February 29–March 1, 1992, referendum more than 99 percent *of those voting* approved of independence. But the Bosnian Serbs had refused to participate. The Badinter Commission was balancing two opposing colonial-era principles to justify the breakaway states' secession—the right of national self-determination for the breakaway republics, and the principle of *uti possidetis juris*, which held that when colonial states become independent, they must do so within colonial borders. "Whatever the circumstances," the commission advised, "the right to self-determination must not involve changes to existing frontiers at the time of independence (*uti possidetis juris*)." The latter principle was used against the RS during its own bid to break away from Bosnia. The decision to apply one colonial-era principle to the republics, and another to an ethnic group seeking self-determination, was arbitrary. Gale Stokes, "Independence and the Fate of Minorities (1991–1992)," in Charles Ingrao and Thomas A. Emmert, eds., *Confronting the Yugoslav Controversies:*

A Scholar's Initiative (West Lafayette, IN: Purdue University Press, 2013), pp. 100–105. See also: Anne Peters, "The Principle of *Uti Possidetis Juris*: How Relevant Is It for Issues of Secession?" in Christian Walter, Antje von Ungern-Sternberg, and Kavus Abushov, eds., *Self-Determination and Secession in International Law* (Oxford: Oxford University Press, 2014).

Moreover, Peter Radan writes that international case law only applies the principle of *uti possidetis* within the context of decolonization. Thus it cannot be said to apply to the case of the SFRY or any of the breakaway republics, as they were not colonial possessions. Peter Radan, "Post-Secession International Borders: A Critical Analysis of the Opinions of the Badinter Arbitration Commission," *Melbourne University Law Review*, Vol. 24, No. 1 (2000).

According to professor of public international law Steven Ratner, *uti possidetis* cannot be applied in cases of secession, as it reflects the imposition of a "cosmopolitan diktat" [in this context, "cosmopolitanism" refers to ethnic pluralism]. Ratner argues that while ethnic pluralism may be a laudable goal for liberal internationalists, it should not be at the expense of the human rights, dignity, and safety of minorities. In this case, the minorities were Bosnian Serbs and Croats. This is especially true where new states and new governments are concerned. Steven R. Ratner, "Drawing a Better Line: Uti Possidetis and the Borders of New States," *American Journal of International Law*, Vol. 90, No. 4 (October 1996), p. 617, cited in Radan, "Post-Secession International Borders."

3. Gale Stokes, "Independence and the Fate of Minorities (1991–1992)," in Charles Ingrao and Thomas A. Emmert, eds., *Confronting the Yugoslav Controversies: A Scholar's Initiative* (West Lafayette, IN: Purdue University Press, 2013), p. 100. In its bid for secession from Canada, the government of Quebec commissioned a report on whether Quebec's provincial borders would become international borders in the event of a successful secession. The report, prepared by five international law experts, used the Badinter Commission to justify its opinion that Quebec's provincial borders would, in fact, become international borders should Quebec secede. Canada's Supreme Court ruled that the Badinter Commission's findings could apply only in the context of the dissolution of a state, not in cases of secession. Peter Radan, "Post-Secession International Borders: A Critical Analysis of the Opinions of the Badinter Arbitration Commission," *Melbourne University Law Review*, Vol. 24, No. 1 (2000).

4. International Criminal Tribunal for the former Yugoslavia, *Prosecutor v. Karadžić—Cross-Examination of Robert Donia*, Case No. IT-95-5 /18-I, June 8, 2010, http://www.icty.org/x/cases/karadzic/trans/en /100608IT.htm.

5. International Criminal Tribunal for the former Yugoslavia, *Prosecutor v. Karadžić—Cross-Examination of Robert Donia*, Case No. IT-95-5/18-I, June 10, 2010, http://www.icty.org/x/cases/karadzic/trans/en/100610IT.htm.

6. According to Nevenka Tromp, both the prosecution and the defense in the Milošević trial thought that the aftermath of the referendum was what started the war. Nevenka Tromp, *Prosecuting Slobodan Milošević: The Unfinished Trial* (London and New York: Routledge, 2016), pp. 149–150.

7. Tracy Wilkinson, "Alija Izetbegovic, 78; Led Bosnia Through War," *Los Angeles Times*, October 20, 2003, https://www.latimes.com /archives/la-xpm-2003-oct-20-me-izetbegovic20-story.html.

8. Alija Izetbegović, interview in *Ljiljan*, July 6–13, 1994, p. 30, cited in Steven L. Burg and Paul S. Shoup, *The War in Bosnia-Herzegovina: Ethnic Conflict and International Intervention* (Armonk, NY: M. E. Sharpe, 1999), p. 77.

9. Alan J. Kuperman, "Suicidal Rebellions and the Moral Hazard of Humanitarian Intervention," *Ethnopolitics*, Vol. 4, No. 2 (2005), pp. 149–173. Muslims were 44 percent of Bosnia's population in 1992 when the war began. Izetbegović feared that Bosniaks would become "second-class citizens" in what was left of Yugoslavia after Croatia and Slovenia broke off—particularly if Milošević was a strongman in the region. Serbs would become more demographically dominant than they were in Yugoslavia. Gale Stokes, "Independence and the Fate of Minorities (1991–1992)," in Charles Ingrao and Thomas A. Emmert, eds., *Confronting the Yugoslav Controversies: A Scholars' Initiative* (West Lafayette, IN: Purdue University Press, 2013), p. 92; Alija Izetbegović, *Inescapable Questions: Autobiographical Notes* (Leicester, UK: The Islamic Foundation, 2003).

10. Bosnian ambassador to Australia Mirza Hajrić pointed out that during his campaign for president, Clinton implied that he intended to support Bosnia. Clinton's future secretary of state, Warren Christopher, promised "early concerted action to stop [the Serbs'] systematic ethnic persecution." But after the election, Christopher spoke of the conflict in terms of ancient hatreds impossible for the West to fix. Thomas L. Friedman, "Bosnia Reconsidered; Where Candidate

Clinton Saw a Challenge the President Sees an Insoluble Quagmire," *New York Times*, April 8, 1993, https://www.nytimes.com/1993/04/08/world/bosnia-reconsidered-where-candidate-clinton-saw-challenge-president-sees.html. See also: Ivo H. Daaldar, *Getting to Dayton: The Making of America's Bosnia Policy* (Washington, DC: Brookings Institute Press, 2000), pp. 6–7. During the war, Ambassador Hajrić worked in the Ministry of Foreign Affairs of Bosnia and Herzegovina.

11. Alija Izetbegović, interview with Alan J. Kuperman, 2000, cited in Alan J. Kuperman, "The Moral Hazard of Humanitarian Intervention: Lessons from the Balkans," *International Studies Quarterly*, Vol. 52, No. 1 (April 2008), p. 61.

12. Muhamed Čengić, interview with Alan J. Kuperman, 2000, cited in Alan J. Kuperman, "The Moral Hazard of Humanitarian Intervention: Lessons from the Balkans," *International Studies Quarterly*, Vol. 52, No. 1 (April 2008), p. 61.

13. Haris Silajdžić, interview with Alan J. Kuperman, 2000, cited in "Suicidal Rebellions and the Moral Hazard of Humanitarian Intervention," *Ethnopolitics*, Vol. 4, No. 2 (2005), p. 158; Alan J. Kuperman, "The Moral Hazard of Humanitarian Intervention: Lessons from the Balkans," *International Studies Quarterly*, Vol. 52, No. 1 (April 2008), p. 61.

14. The first combat engagement in NATO's history was to shoot down four Serb jets that had violated the 1993 UN-imposed no-fly zone over Bosnia in 1994. After the July 1995 Srebrenica massacre, NATO launched Operation Deliberate Force, which involved large-scale bombing of Serb targets.

15. The Serbs began to lose momentum after the US-brokered Washington Agreement of 1994, which led Croats and Bosniaks to fight together against the Serbs, and created the Federation of Bosnia and Herzegovina.

From the Serbs' and Bosnian Serbs' perspective, Bosnia was illegally seceding from Yugoslavia. From the SDA's perspective, once Bosnia was accepted into the United Nations in May 1992, the Bosnian Serbs became the rebel force (albeit extremely well armed—so that Kuperman's argument does not apply). According to Mirza Hajrić, the chief political advisor to the Bosnian foreign minister at the time, "We were expecting, as a member of the United Nations, that we would not have an arms embargo imposed on us when we were being attacked. This is the only time in history that rebels have all the weapons they need, and the UN-recognized state trying to defend itself could not get the weapons due to an arms embargo." Mirza Hajrić, telephone interview with author, October 17, 2018.

While the UN arms embargo adversely affected the Bosniaks compared to the Serbs, the Bosniaks found other sources of weapons and funding. A Dutch scholar of intelligence, Cees Wiebes, explains that Turkey and Saudi Arabia also offered military assistance, but only on the condition that Izetbegović not seek assistance from Iran. Cees Wiebes, "The Perception and Information Position of the Western Intelligence Services," in *Intelligence and the War in Bosnia 1992–1995: The Role of the Intelligence and Security Services* (Netherlands Institute for War Documentation, n.d.), p. 70, http://niod.nl/sites/niod.nl /files/C.%20Wiebes%20-%20Intelligence%20en%20de%20oorlog% 20in%20Bosnië%201992-1995.%20De%20rol%20van%20de%20 inlichtingen-%20en%20veiligheidsdiensten%20-%20Engels.pdf.

Remarkably, Izetbegović received assistance from all three countries (and more), despite Turkey and Saudi Arabia's stipulation, and Saudi Arabia's intense enmity with Iran. Bakir Izetbegović, Alija Izetbegović's son, who was elected in 2010 to serve as the Muslim member of Bosnia's tripartite presidency, confirmed this with me. At the time we spoke, he was also the head of the SDA, the party started by his father. When I visited the younger Izetbegović in the winter of 2016, he told me a surprising story. King Fahd of Saudi Arabia had given his father a plane. Bakir said he traveled with his father to visit the king in Riyadh. When father and son were taking leave of the king, he asked them where they were headed to next. Iran, explained the president. In that case, said the king to the president, I would like you to have a larger plane. And that is how President Izetbegović acquired a larger plane to use for his travels. Izetbegović was clearly a very clever politician, able to negotiate the antipathy between Saudi Arabia and Iran, presenting himself to the West as Western-oriented and, as Wiebes argues, a fundamentalist to both Iran and Saudi Arabia. Wiebes, "The Perception and Information Position of the Western Intelligence Services," pp. 155-156.

Izetbegović was able to gain the Saudis' enormous support for the Bosnian cause through various Saudi-funded humanitarian organizations, as well as pledged support of money and weapons from Iranian president Hashemi Rafsanjani. John R. Schindler, *Unholy Terror: Bosnia, Al-Qa'ida, and the Rise of Global Jihad* (St. Paul, MN: Zenith Press, 2007), pp. 54, 125. Despite the Clinton administration's public support for the arms embargo, then national security advisor Anthony Lake admitted that U.S. officials knew at the time that Iran had opened a smuggling route into Bosnia in 1992, with the assistance of Turkey. This was two years before the United States brokered a peace agreement between Croatia and Bosnia, and essentially gave a green light to the shipments. Bosnian government officials would later admit that by 1993, arms or money for arms purchases also were being supplied not only by Iran but also by Saudi Arabia, Malaysia, Brunei, Pakistan, Hungary, and Argentina. John Pomfret and David B. Ottaway, "U.S. Allies' Arms Aid to Bosnia Detailed," *Los Angeles Times*, May 12, 1996, http://articles.latimes.com/1996-05-12/news/mn-3437_1_arms-smuggling.

The CIA also knew that Iranian Revolutionary Guards were present in Bosnia, training Bosnian Army forces. Pressured by the U.S. government to force them out, Izetbegović initially denied that Iran's fighters were playing an important role. The CIA demonstrated that the fighters were closely involved with the minister of the interior. But, Wiebes reports, "a blind eye was turned to these Revolutionary Guards in the interest of what was considered to be the good cause of the struggle of the Bosnian Muslims." Wiebes, "The Perception and Information Position of the Western Intelligence Services," pp. 155–156.

According to a CIA chief of station in Sarajevo who traveled to Bosnia in mid-1995, the "Iranian influence in Sarajevo was palpable. Middle Eastern–looking 'mujaheddin' wandered the empty streets of the city between battles with the Serbs. Soviet-made vehicles bearing license plates and other symbols of Iranian private relief organizations were omnipresent, and some were involved in conducting harassing surveillance of our vehicles. The Iranians considered Bosnia to be their 'back yard' and the few Americans present were not welcome." He wrote about this experience under the pseudonym H. K. Roy. He also said that by July 1995, the Bosnian Interior Ministry was entirely under the control of the Iranian intelligence service. H. K. Roy, "Betrayal in the Balkans," *AFIO: The Intelligencer: Journal of U.S. Intelligence Studies*, Vol. 12, No. 1 (Summer 2001), pp. 48–49.

16. International Criminal Tribunal for the former Yugoslavia, *Prosecutor v. Prlić et al.—Case Information Sheet*, Case No. IT-04-74, http://www.icty.org/x/cases/prlic/cis/en/cis_prlic_al_en.pdf.

Karadžić said to me, "He told me that when they tried to reconcile with Izetbegović [presumably when the U.S. brokered a reconciliation between Bosnian Croatians and Bosniaks in the Washington Agreement] Praljak asked Izetbegović, what was the point of our fighting? All those lives lost . . . pointlessly. And Izetbegović said don't worry, our population was large, there were a lot of people. He was horrified by Izetbegović's attitude." In 2017, Praljak committed suicide by swallowing poison on live camera during his appeal.

17. Edina Bećirević, *Genocide on the Drina River* (New Haven & London: Yale University Press, 2014).

Muslim nationality [in socialist Yugoslavia] was defined—both culturally and historically—in secular rather than religious terms. Tone Bringa, *Being Muslim the Bosnian Way* (Princeton: Princeton University Press, 1995), p. 10. The majority of Bosnian Muslims were either secular or practiced a form of Islam that could be seen as "a model for an Islamic tradition that meshes well with the secular notion of separation between religion and state," political scientist Edina Bećirević explains. Edina Bećirević, *Salafism vs. Moderate Islam: A Rhetorical Fight for the Hearts and Minds of Bosnia's Muslims* (Sarajevo: Atlantic Initiative—Center for Security and Justice Research, 2016), p. 10, accessed: http://www.helsinki.org.rs/doc/Edina%20Becirevic%20-%20Salafism%20vs.%20Moderate%20Islam.pdf. The drive to recognize Muslims as a nationality was political: the aim was to satisfy growing demands among Bosnian Muslims for recognition of their status as equal to other nations.

In 1971, Bosnia's Muslims were granted a nationality status. The solution was found in capitalizing the initial letter of the word "muslim," which, according to the grammar of the then "Serbo-Croatian" language, transformed the religious meaning of the word into a national meaning. Thus, "muslims" (religious group) became "Muslims" (national group).

18. Alija Izetbegović, *Inescapable Questions: Autobiographical Notes* (Leicester, UK: The Islamic Foundation, 2003), p. 25.

According to Miroslav Tudjman, two hundred thousand copies of the Islamic Declaration were published and disseminated to the Army of the Republic of Bosnia and Herzegovina. Miroslav Tudjman, interview with author, November 22, 2018. Tudjman refered me to Jadranko Prlić's final brief, which notes that, "The *Islam Declaration* [sic] was re-printed and approximately 200,000 copies were distributed in 1990 by the Sarajevo publisher 'Bosna.' . . . It was also featured as part of the SDA's platform." Suad Arnautović, *Izbori u Bosni i Hercegovini: Analiza izbornog procesa* [Elections in Bosnia and Herzegovina:

An Analysis of the Election Process] (Sarajevo: Promocult, 1996), p. 61, cited in International Tribunal for the former Yugoslavia, *Prosecutor v. Jadranko Prlić et al.—Jadranko Prlić's Final Brief*, Case No. IT-04-74-T, March 29, 2011, p. 42. Suad Arnautović is a member of the political science faculty at the University of Sarajevo, and is the founder of the Center for Election Studies in Bosnia and Herzegovina. Miroslav Tudjman was, at the time of this writing, a professor and member of the Croatian parliament. His father, Franjo Tudjman, and Alija Izetbegović became military allies in 1994, with the signing of the Washington Agreement.

19. Western commentators considered Izetbegović to be a moderate Muslim. For example, veteran reporter John Burns refers to "the image of the quiet Mr. Izetbegović" as an Islamic fundamentalist as "incongruous, a sad misrepresentation of the leader of a cultured, almost languid Slavic people who converted to Islam under the Turkish occupation." John F. Burns, "Conversations/Radovan Karadzic; Understanding, and Letting Loose, Historic Hatreds in the Balkans," *New York Times*, May 17, 1992, https://www.nytimes.com/1992/05/17/weekinreview /conversations-radovan-karadzic-understanding-letting-loose-historic -hatreds.html.

20. A number of charitable organizations were involved in facilitating the flow of money, supplies, and personnel into Bosnia in violation of the arms embargo. For example, the Third World Relief Agency (TWRA) was established in 1987 by Elfatih al-Hassanein, a Sudanese doctor who received his medical training in Yugoslavia and became a close friend of Izetbegović. According to John Schindler, al-Hassanein (also spelled al-Hasanayn) was a "career holy warrior" whose services to "radical Islam have been underreported—precisely as he wished." John R. Schindler, *Unholy Terror: Bosnia, Al-Qa'ida, and the Rise of Global Jihad* (St. Paul, MN: Zenith Press, 2007), p. 149. Izetbegović personally vouched for his friend and for the TWRA when the agency was setting up its offices in Austria. The TWRA was originally established as a charity to promote the revival of Islam in Eastern Europe and the Soviet Union, where religion had been discouraged under Communist rule. But during the war in Bosnia, the TWRA played a new role: arranging for the transport and salaries for international jihadis traveling to Bosnia, facilitating black-market purchases of military equipment, and promoting connections between the Bosnian Muslim government and a wide variety of Islamic movements and govern-

ments. It was also involved in money laundering. This information on the TWRA summarizes an investigative report by the *Washington Post*: John Pomfret, "Bosnia's Muslims Dodged Embargo," *Washington Post*, September 22, 1996, http://www.washingtonpost.com/wp-srv /inatl/longterm/bosvote/front.htm.

The Committee that oversaw the TWRA's activities in Bosnia included not only al-Hassanein and Izetbegović, but also Hasan Čengić (a man often referred to as an "organized criminal," who was also in charge of supplying arms to the SDA's militia—the Patriotic League) and three other members of the SDA party. All of them were personally enriched as a result of their involvement in the TWRA's efforts in Bosnia. Al-Hassanein was also a close friend of the late Hassan al-Turabi (February 1932–March 5, 2016), the leader of the Islamist National Islamic Front in Sudan. When Osama bin Laden moved his al Qaeda organization to Sudan from 1991 to 1996 (and from there to Afghanistan), it was reportedly at the personal invitation of al-Turabi. Schindler, *Unholy Terror*, pp. 148, 151; Max Taylor and Mohamed E. Elbushra, "Research Note: Hassan Al-Turabi, Osama bin Laden, and Al Qaeda in Sudan," *Terrorism and Political Violence*, Vol. 18, No. 3 (2006), pp. 449–464.

The TWRA was involved in funding terrorist organizations, both inside Bosnia and beyond. In September 2005, European police, backed by antiterrorist squads, carried out a raid on TWRA headquarters in Austria. Investigators found that TWRA funding (donated mostly by Islamic organizations and governments) had enabled Bosnia to get around the United Nations–imposed arms embargo to purchase hundreds of millions of dollars' worth of weapons on the black market. The Saudi Arabian government was the biggest contributor to the TWRA, but other governments that funded the TWRA include Sudan, Iran, Pakistan, Brunei, Turkey, and Malaysia. Osama bin Laden was also a major contributor. Pomfret, "Bosnia's Muslims Dodged Embargo." See also: "Documents Back Saudi Link to Extremists," *New York Times*, June 23, 2009, https://www.nytimes. com/2009/06/24/world/middleeast/24saudi.html; Exhibit 224, "Evidence of Financial Links Between Saudi Royal Family and Al Qaeda," *New York Times*, https://www.nytimes.com/interactive/projects /documents/evidence-of-financial-links-between-saudi-royal-family -and-al-qaeda.

For information on Bosnia's continuing problem with jihadis, see Edina Bećirević, *Western Balkans Extremism Research Forum: Bosnia and Herzegovina Report* (British Council, April 2018), http://atlanticinitiative.org/wp-content/uploads/2018/10/erf_bih_report2.pdf; *Counting Violent Extremism Baseline Program: Research Findings—Bosnia & Herzegovina* (Atlantic Initiative—Center for Security and Justice Research, December 2018), http://atlanticinitiative.org/wp-content/uploads/2018/12/BiH-CVE-Survey-December-2018-Final-X-1.pdf; Vlado Azinović and Muhamed Jusić, *The New Lure of the Syrian War—The Foreign Fighters' Bosnian Contingent* (Sarajevo: Atlantic Initiative, 2016), https://www.rcc.int/p-cve/download/docs/The%20New%20Lure%20of%20the%20Syrian%20War%20%20The%20Foreign%20Fighters%20Bosnian%20Contingent.pdf/b5594b3a54e94a5f8596053b0d35db5c.pdf.

21. Alija Izetbegović, *The Islamic Declaration: A Program for Islamization of Muslims and the Muslim Peoples* (Sarajevo: Bosna, 1990), p. 5, accessed: https://www.scribd.com/document/54589375/Alija-Izetbegovic-Islamic-Declaration.

22. Alija Izetbegović, *The Islamic Declaration: A Program for Islamization of Muslims and the Muslim Peoples* (Sarajevo: Bosna, 1990), p. 3, accessed: https://www.scribd.com/document/54589375/Alija-Izetbegovic-Islamic-Declaration.

23. Alija Izetbegović, *The Islamic Declaration: A Program for Islamization of Muslims and the Muslim Peoples* (Sarajevo: Bosna, 1990), p. 56, accessed: https://www.scribd.com/document/54589375/Alija-Izetbegovic-Islamic-Declaration.

24. Alija Izetbegović, *The Islamic Declaration: A Program for Islamization of Muslims and the Muslim Peoples* (Sarajevo: Bosna, 1990), p. 30, accessed: https://www.scribd.com/document/54589375/Alija-Izetbegovic-Islamic-Declaration.

25. In 1983, Izetbegović was convicted of counterrevolutionary activities, conspiring to create a Muslim state, and spreading propaganda hostile to the Communist state. Sarajevo District Court, Case No. K212/83, August 29, 1983; Noel Malcolm, *Bosnia: A Short History* (New York: New York University Press, 1996), p. 208.

The trial, which was widely seen as a show trial, became a cause célèbre for liberals both inside and outside Yugoslavia. A report published in November 1986 by the U.S. Helsinki Watch Committee stated that "many of those arrested have neither used nor advocated the use of violence." In reference to Izetbegović, the report notes that, "Izetbegović . . . a retired lawyer . . . was given the harshest sentence of 14 years' imprisonment (reduced to 12 years) for 'associating for hostile activities' and 'counterrevolutionary endangering of the social system . . .' The work [Islamic Declaration] called for the 'Islamization' of the Muslim peoples and advised Muslims to be loyal citizens except in matters that are detrimental to Islam." United States Helsinki Watch Committee, "Violations of the Helsinki Accords: Yugoslavia," report (Vienna: Helsinki Review Conference, 1986), p. 43.

Among those who supported Izetbegović for his nationalist activities at the time was Dobrica Ćosić, the Serb nationalist political leader and celebrated novelist who would become known for his argument that Serbs were under siege in Yugoslavia. William Yardley, "Dobrica Cosic, First Friend Then Foe of Serbia's Milosevic, Dies at 92," *New York Times*, May 21, 2014, https://www.nytimes.com/2014/05/22 /world/europe/dobrica-cosic-first-friend-then-foe-of-serbias-milosevic -dies-at-92.html?_r=0.

This was Izetbegović's second conviction. His first conviction was in 1946, for his membership in the Young Muslims movement. He served a three-year sentence along with fourteen other members of the Young Muslims. Alija Izetbegović, *Inescapable Questions: Autobiographical Notes* (Leicester, UK: The Islamic Foundation, 2003); David Binder, "Alija Izetbegovic, Muslim Who Led Bosnia, Dies at 78," *New York Times*, October 20, 2003, https://www.nytimes.com/2003 /10/20/world/alija-izetbegovic-muslim-who-led-bosnia-dies-at-78.html.

26. According to Leslie S. Lebl, the Islamic Declaration became politically relevant after the fall of Yugoslavia. Leslie S. Lebl, "Islamism and Security in Bosnia-Herzegovina" (Carlisle Barracks, PA: Strategic Studies Institute and U.S. Army War College Press, May 2014), accessed: http://ssi.armywarcollege.edu/pdffiles/pub1206.pdf.

27. Alija Izetbegović, *The Islamic Declaration: A Program for Islamization of Muslims and the Muslim Peoples* (Sarajevo: Bosna, 1990), pp. 49–50, accessed: https://www.scribd.com/document/54589375/Alija-Izetbegovic -Islamic-Declaration.

28. Alija Izetbegović, *The Islamic Declaration: A Program for Islamization of Muslims and the Muslim Peoples* (Sarajevo: Bosna, 1990), p. 7, cited in Gale Stokes, "Independence and the Fate of Minorities (1991–1992)," in Charles Ingrao and Thomas A. Emmert, eds., *Confronting the Yugoslav*

Controversies: A Scholar's Initiative (West Lafayette, IN: Purdue University Press, 2013), p. 87. (Note: The copy of the Islamic Declaration used by Gale Stokes is different from that used by the author.)

29. For the claim that the Islamic Declaration was a theoretical assessment, see John V. A. Fine, "The Various Faiths in the History of Bosnia," in Maya Shatzmiller, ed., *Islam and Bosnia: Conflict Resolution and Foreign Policy in Multi-Ethnic States* (Montreal and Ithaca, NY: McGill-Queen's University Press, 2002), p. 14.

As noted in the text, there were significant differences among scholars about the extent to which Izetbegović was committed to a multi-ethnic liberal democracy, and whether he was himself an Islamist or a Muslim nationalist.

For the view that Izetbegović was a leader who thought Islam and liberal democracy were compatible, see Thomas Cushman and Stjepan G. Meštrović, eds., *This Time We Knew: Western Responses to Genocide in Bosnia* (New York: New York University Press, 1996), p. 28; Robert J. Donia and John V. A. Fine Jr., *Bosnia and Hercegovina: A Tradition Betrayed* (New York: Columbia University Press, 1994); Norman Cigar, *Genocide in Bosnia: The Policy of "Ethnic Cleansing"* (College Station: Texas A&M University Press, 1995).

In historian Gale Stokes's words, Izetbegović was "a conservative, opposed to abortion and in favor of limiting women to the home and the family," but he opposed "ideological solutions" and held that his tolerance was grounded in Islam rather than being European. Alija Izetbegović, *Izetbegovic: Odabrani govori, pisma, izjave, intervjui* (Zagreb: Prvo Muslimansko Dionic ko Drustvo, 1995), pp. 39, 89, 170, cited in Gale Stokes, "Independence and the Fate of Minorities (1991–1992)," in Charles Ingrao and Thomas A. Emmert, eds., *Confronting the Yugoslav Controversies: A Scholar's Initiative* (West Lafayette, IN: Purdue University Press, 2013), pp. 89–90.

U.S. diplomat Michael Sells acknowledged that Izetbegović's Islamic Declaration contained some "provocative" statements, but observed that it was instrumentalized by Serbian nationalists. Michael A. Sells, *The Bridge Betrayed: Religion and Genocide in Bosnia* (Berkeley: University of California Press, 1998), p. 118.

Marko Atilla Hoare found Izetbegović to have been a Muslim "nationalist," but did not see him as driven by religion. Marko Atilla Hoare, *How Bosnia Armed* (London: Saqi Books, 2004), p. 26.

Sabrina Ramet viewed Izetbegović as a leader advocating a "free civic union" who explicitly rejected "any form of Muslim exclusivism." Sabrina P. Ramet, *Balkan Babel: The Disintegration of Yugoslavia from the Death of Tito to the Fall of Milošević* (Boulder, CO: Westview Press, 2002), pp. 203–206.

Others saw Izetbegović as an Islamist. Bosniak Ahmet Alibaši viewed Izetbegović's pre-1990 circle as similar in its thinking to the Islamist intellectuals Sayyid Abul A'la Mawdudi and Sayyid Qutb, pointing out that their works were translated into Serbo-Croatian in the 1970s and 1980s. Ahmet Alibaši, "Traditional and Reformist Islam in Bosnia and Herzegovina," Cambridge Programme for Security in International Society (Sarajevo, 2003), pp. 11–13. Historian Xavier Bougarel identified a "pan-Islamic" leadership within the SDA and viewed the Declaration as an example of Islamist literature. But he did not view the political party as Islamist. Xavier Bougarel and Asma Rashid, "From Young Muslims to Party of Democratic Action: The Emergence of a Pan-Islamist Trend in Bosnia-Herzegovina," *Islamic Studies*, Vol. 36, No. 2–3, Special Issue: Islam In the Balkans (Summer–Autumn 1997), pp. 533–549; Xavier Bougarel, "Bosnian Islam Since 1990: Cultural Identity or Political Ideology?" Annual Convention of the Association for the Studies of Nationalities (New York, 1999).

Bosniak intellectual Tarik Haverić wrote that Izetbegović spoke of "ethnic people when splitting ministries and managerial positions, and civic people when expecting European protection or having a referendum [on independence]." Tarik Haverić, "Why Bosnia and Herzegovina (Unfortunately) Cannot Be a Civic Democracy: Devil Came to Take What Was His," trans., Mladen Mrdalj, *Dani*, Vol. 252 (February 2006), pp. 18–20, accessed: https://forum.klix.ba/zasto-bih-nazalost-ne-moze-biti-gradanska-demokratija-t22893.html.

In his seminal work, *Balkan Idols*, Vjekoslav Perica, a Croatian scholar of politics and religion, described Izetbegović and his associates as driven primarily by religion. Vjekoslav Perica, *Balkan Idols: Religion and Nationalism in Yugoslav States* (Oxford: Oxford University Press, 2002).

A number of Alija Izetbegović's closest colleagues identified him as an "Islamic fundamentalist." For example, Professor Halid Čaušević said that soon after joining the SDA, he realized that the party was swerving toward Islamic fundamentalism. Nerzuk Ćurak, "Halid Čaušević: Kako su Alija I SDA uništili Bosnu," *Dani*, Vol. 63 (November 1997). Adil Zulfikarpašić, who founded the SDA with Izetbegović, very clearly came to view him as an Islamist. Adil Zulfikarpašić, Milovan Djilas, and Nadežda Gaće, *The Bosniak* (London: Hurst, 1998).

Perhaps most important, in Izetbegović's published memoir, which was given to me by his son Bakir when I visited him in Sarajevo in 2016, Izetbegović referred to the Declaration as "fundamentalist." Izetbegović, *Inescapable Questions*, p. 25.

30. Leslie S. Lebl, "Islamism and Security in Bosnia-Herzegovina" (Carlisle Barracks, PA: Strategic Studies Institute and U.S. Army War College Press, May 2014), p. 22, accessed: http://ssi.armywarcollege.edu /pdffiles/pub1206.pdf.

31. Alija Izetbegović, *Inescapable Questions: Autobiographical Notes* (Leicester, UK: The Islamic Foundation, 2003), p. 25.

32. Miomir Žužul served as the Croatian ambassador to the United States (1992–1993) and the United Nations (1993–1996) and later as Croatia's foreign minister (2003–2005). Miomir Žužul, interview with author, January 30, 2018.

33. See Senad Pecanin, "Mr. President, You Are Making Stuff Up!" *Dani*, Vol. 73, (April 1998). See also: Tarik Haverić in Jens-Martin Eriksen and Frederik Stjernfelt, *Scenografija rata: Nova putovanja u Bosnu i Srbiju* (Belgrade: Helsinški odbor za ljudska prava u Srbiji, 2010), p. 221; Adil Zulfikarpašić, Milovan Djilas, and Nadežda Gaće, *The Bosniak* (London: Hurst, 1998). For an extended debate between Izetbegović and Pecanin, see Alija Izetbegović, *Inescapable Questions: Autobiographical Notes* (Leicester, UK: The Islamic Foundation, 2003), pp. 490–502.

34. Miomir Žužul, interview with author, January 30, 2018.

35. Adil Zulfikarpašić had become disillusioned by Izetbegović and the SDA. According to Burg and Shoup, the SDA contained within it two wings. The first was comprised of "the Islamic clergy and the nationalist intellectuals; the hawks within the ranks of the military; and the radical nationalists . . . notable for their antipathy toward the Serbs." The second, smaller wing—led by Zulfikarpašić—wanted to see a state that could preserve the "multi-cultural traditions of Bosnia" while constructing a modern, Western democracy. In October 1990, before the first multiparty elections in Bosnia, Zulfikarpašić removed his liberal faction from the SDA. He and Professor Muhamed Filipović, a philosopher and historian, formed their own party, called the Muslim Bosniak Organization (MBO), but that party received little support in the elections, while the populist SDA won. The MBO was in favor of reaching an agreement with the Serbs. Steven L. Burg

and Paul S. Shoup, *The War in Bosnia-Herzegovina: Ethnic Conflict and International Intervention* (Armonk, NY: M. E. Sharpe, 1999), p. 68. For more on the results of the election, see Noel Malcolm, *Bosnia: A Short History* (New York: New York University Press, 1996), p. 222.

36. Alan J. Kuperman, "The Moral Hazard of Humanitarian Intervention: Lessons from the Balkans," *International Studies Quarterly*, Vol. 52, No. 1 (April 2008), p. 56.

Zulfikarpašić says that the agreement was originally his idea. Adil Zulfikarpašić, Milovan Djilas, and Nadežda Gaće, *The Bosniak* (London: Hurst, 1998), p. 180.

37. Adil Zulfikarpašić, Milovan Djilas, and Nadežda Gaće, *The Bosniak* (London: Hurst, 1998), p. 183.

38. Adil Zulfikarpašić, Milovan Djilas, and Nadežda Gaće, *The Bosniak* (London: Hurst, 1998), pp. 185–186.

According to Vladimir Petrović, it is plausible that Izetbegović was not comfortable with a deal negotiated by his competitor, Zulfikarpašić, nor did Izetbegović trust Milošević. The proposed arrangement would have endangered the political power of both Izetbegović and Milošević. Vladimir Petrović, personal correspondence, June 2, 2019.

39. David Binder, "U.S. Policymakers on Bosnia Admit Errors in Opposing Partition in 1992," *New York Times*, August 29, 1993, https://www.nytimes.com/1993/08/29/world/us-policymakers-on-bosnia-admit-errors-in-opposing-partition-in-1992.html.

The Lisbon Agreement, also known as the Cutileiro plan, would have divided Bosnia into ethnic cantonments, leaving Muslims and Serbs with 44 percent of the territory each, and Croats with 12 percent. The Serbs believed that the Bosniaks' rejecting the deal was "their fatal mistake, not only because it led to war but because all later peace plans—with the exception of the Vance-Owen plan—proved to be more favourable for the Serbs than for the Muslims." Nevenka Tromp, *Prosecuting Slobodan Milošević: The Unfinished Trial* (London and New York: Routledge, 2016), pp. 155–157.

The Serbs themselves were emboldened by the Cutileiro plan. Karadžić said that the Cutileiro maps "legitimised Bosnian Serb demands that BiH be divided on an ethnic basis and that they be awarded 45–50 percent of Bosnian territory." Robert Donia, *The Assembly of the Republika Srpska: 1992–1995*, expert report, July 29, 2003, Exhibit P537.2a, p. 46, cited in Nevenka Tromp, *Prosecuting Slobodan*

Milošević: The Unfinished Trial (London and New York: Routledge, 2016), p. 155.

40. David Binder, "U.S. Policymakers on Bosnia Admit Errors in Opposing Partition in 1992," *New York Times*, August 29, 1993, https://www .nytimes.com/1993/08/29/world/us-policymakers-on-bosnia-admit-errors-in-opposing-partition-in-1992.html.

41. David Binder, "U.S. Policymakers on Bosnia Admit Errors in Opposing Partition in 1992," *New York Times*, August 29, 1993, https://www .nytimes.com/1993/08/29/world/us-policymakers-on-bosnia-admit -errors-in-opposing-partition-in-1992.html.

Louis Sell, a retired American Foreign Service officer who spent eight years in the Former Yugoslavia, wrote that the U.S. policy of opposing partition and promoting recognition of an independent Bosnia "did not, by itself, cause the fighting in Bosnia, [but] it helped push both the Serbs and Muslims along already existing paths toward war. . . . It also increased Sarajevo's hope, perhaps its only consistent strategy throughout the war, that someday the United States would come to its rescue. Conversely, recognition [of Bosnia's independence] increased the Serb proclivity to go for a military solution in Bosnia— an option for which they were already well prepared." Louis Sell, *Slobodan Milosevic and the Destruction of Yugoslavia* (Durham, NC: Duke University Press, 2002), p. 165.

42. Miroslav Tudjman, interview with author, November 22, 2018.

Regarding the Cutileiro plan, Jose Cutileiro wrote in a 1995 letter to the *Economist* that "after several rounds of talks our 'principles for future constitutional arrangements for Bosnia and Herzegovina' were agreed by all three parties (Muslim, Serb and Croat) in Sarajevo on March 18th 1992 as the basis for future negotiations. These continued, maps and all until the summer, when the Muslims reneged on the agreement. Had they not done so, the Bosnian question might have been settled earlier, with less loss of (mainly Muslim) life and land. To be fair, President Izetbegović and his aides were encouraged to scupper that deal and to fight for a unitary Bosnian state by well-meaning outsiders who thought they knew better." Cited in International Criminal Tribunal for the former Yugoslavia, *Witness Statement of Ambassador Jose Cutileiro*, ID70-0021. Accessed: http://www.peter robinson.com/Witness%20Lists/Week%2018%20Feb%202013_ Witness/Cutileiro%20signed%20witness%20statement.pdf.

43. Joint Chiefs of Staff, Joint History Office, "The Evolution of US Policy

Toward the Former Republic of Yugoslavia and Bosnia Since 1990," September 1997, U.S. Department of Defense, Freedom of Information Division, FOIA Ref: 16-F-0858, p. 4, declassified March 29, 2019.

44. According to Monica Duffy Toft, for a conflict to count as a civil war, it must meet certain criteria. First, it must be within the borders of an internationally recognized state. Second, there must be at least two organized combatants who can each inflict harm on the other (this excludes genocide or massacres). Third, one of the combatants must be a state (this excludes communal violence). Fourth, and finally, there must be at least one thousand "battle-related deaths per year on average" as used by the Correlates of War Data Set. Monica Duffy Toft, *Securing the Peace: The Durable Settlement of Civil Wars* (Princeton: Princeton University Press, 2009), pp. 9–10. See also: Meredith Reid Sarkees and Phil Schafer, "The Correlates of War Data on War: An Update to 1997," *Conflict Management and Peace Science*, Vol. 18, No. 1 (Fall 2000), pp. 123–144, cited in Toft, *Securing the Peace*.

Alan Kuperman does not use the Correlates of War Data Set for his studies. His data set of mass killings is based on the following definition: "a campaign that kills more than 50,000 non-combatant members of a group during a period in which at least 5,000 were killed each year." By this definition, Kuperman excludes "cases of protracted low-level killings of civilians that may stem from guerrilla or counter-insurgency campaigns," calling these "qualitatively different" from mass killings. Alan J. Kuperman, "Tragic Challenges and the Moral Hazard of Humanitarian Intervention: How and Why Ethnic Groups Provoke Genocidal Retaliation," *PhD diss.* (Cambridge, MA: Massachusetts Institute of Technology, 2002), pp. 19–20.

45. This is a summary of Alan Kuperman's arguments. For more information, see: Alan J. Kuperman, "Suicidal Rebellions and the Moral Hazard of Humanitarian Intervention," *Ethnopolitics*, Vol. 4, No. 2 (2005), pp. 149–173; Alan J. Kuperman, "The Moral Hazard of Humanitarian Intervention: Lessons from the Balkans," *International Studies Quarterly*, Vol. 52, No. 1 (April 2008), pp. 49–80; Alan J. Kuperman, "Tragic Challenges and the Moral Hazard of Humanitarian Intervention: How and Why Ethnic Groups Provoke Genocidal Retaliation," *PhD diss.* (Cambridge, MA: Massachusetts Institute of Technology, 2002).

46. Joint Chiefs of Staff, Joint History Office, "The Evolution of US Policy Toward the Former Republic of Yugoslavia and Bosnia Since 1990,"

September 1997, U.S. Department of Defense, Freedom of Information Division, FOIA Ref: 16-F-0858, p. 4, declassified March 29, 2019.
Moreover, the safe areas in particular "presented the Muslims with
opportunities to provoke incidents that might lead to international
intervention on their behalf. The Bosnian government refused to
evacuate endangered civilians, for fear of losing additional territory.
. . . The Muslims used them as bases from which to launch raids into
surrounding Serb-held territory, hoping to bring UN-authoriized
NATO air strikes down on their opponents." Joint Chiefs of Staff,
Joint History Office, "The Evolution of US Policy Toward the Former
Republic of Yugoslavia and Bosnia Since 1990," p. 7.

47. Alan J. Kuperman, "Suicidal Rebellions and the Moral Hazard of Humanitarian Intervention," *Ethnopolitics*, Vol. 4, No. 2 (2005), p. 152.

48. Benjamin A. Valentino, *Final Solutions: Mass Killing and Genocide in the
Twentieth Century* (Ithaca, NY: Cornell University Press, 2004), p. 3.
See also: V. P. Gagnon Jr., "Ethnic Nationalism and International Conflict: The Case of Serbia," *International Security*, Vol. 19, No. 3 (1994–
1995), pp, 130–166; Alexander B. Downes, *Targeting Civilians in War*
(Ithaca, NY: Cornell University Press, 2008); Scott Straus, *The Order
of Genocide: Race, Power, and War in Rwanda* (Ithaca, NY: Cornell University Press, 2006); Lee Ann Fujii, *Killing Neighbors: Webs of Violence
in Rwanda* (Ithaca, NY: Cornell University Press, 2009); John Mueller,
"The Banality of 'Ethnic War,'" *International Security*, Vol. 25, No. 1
(2000), pp, 42–70.

49. On June 19, 1992, the war in Bosnia broke out, although, according
to Tromp, "Sarajevo was under siege by Serb forces by early April
[1992]," after Bosnia and Herzegovina had declared independence.
Nevenka Tromp, *Prosecuting Slobodan Milošević: The Unfinished Trial*
(London and New York: Routledge, 2016), p. 153. Bosnia was majority Serb until 1971, but by the start of the war, Muslims had become
the dominant group in Bosnia. Robert J. Donia and John V. A. Fine,
Jr., *Bosnia and Hercegovina: A Tradition Betrayed* (New York: Columbia
University Press, 1994), p. 87.

50. For more on the legality of Bosnia's secession from Yugoslavia, see
note 2 in this chapter.

51. Peter Radan, "Post-Secession International Borders: A Critical Analysis of the Opinions of the Badinter Arbitration Commission," *Melbourne University Law* Review, Vol. 24, No. 1 (2000), p. 57.
The EC decision to recognize Croatia and Slovenia "worsened the

conflict between the principle of self determination and the idea of inviolable national borders. Treating the internal boundaries of Yugoslavia as national borders worked only in Slovenia, which was relatively homogenous. Serbs in Croatia, and Croats and Serbs in Bosnia Hezegovina, where no ethnic group enjoyed a majority, would be left stranded. In a region where no one wanted to be a minority in someone else's state, this was a recipe for violence." The EC memo goes on to say that "Croatia and Slovenia were viable entities, but the decision to recognize Bosnia Herzegovina gave international legitimacy to an entity of questionable economic, political and military viability that had never been a state in modern times." Joint Chiefs of Staff, Joint History Office, "The Evolution of US Policy Toward The Former Republic of Yugoslavia and Bosnia Since 1990," September 1997, U.S. Department of Defense, Freedom of Information Division, FOIA Ref: 16-F-0858, pp. 2, 3–4, declassified March 29, 2019.

Even today, there remains a movement among Bosnian Serbs to secede from Bosnia. Milorad Dodik, who served as the RS president from 2010 to 2018, was elected the Serb member of Bosnia's tripartite presidency in 2018. He has repeatedly expressed the view that the RS should be an independent state, and claims he is just reflecting the will of Bosnian Serbs. Barbara Surk, "Milorad Dodik Wants to Carve Up Bosnia. Peacefully, If Possible," *New York Times*, February 16, 2018, https://www.nytimes.com/2018/02/16/world/europe/dodik-republika-srpska-bosnia.html; "Milorad Dodik: Serb Nationalist Wins Bosnia Presidency Seat," *BBC News*, October 8, 2018, https://www.bbc.com/news/world-europe-45774872.

52. International Criminal Tribunal for the former Yugoslavia, *Prosecutor v. Karadžić—Judgement*, Case No. IT-95-95/18-T, March 24, 2016, para. 5681.

53. Radivoje Miletić, who was also convicted by the ICTY for committing crimes against humanity in Srebrenica, admitted that he drafted Directive 7. In its judgment of Karadžić, the Court relied on the principle of superior responsibility for crimes committed prior to his July 13 phone conversation with Miroslav Deronjić. In the phone conversation, Deronjić and Karadžić spoke in code about the killing of hundreds of Bosnian men at the Kravica Warehouse in Srebrenica. To the Yugoslav Tribunal, this proved that Karadžić knew that the VRS had killed hundreds of Bosniak detainees who had been in the VRS's custody following the fall of Srebrenica. The Karadžić judgment states

that Karadžić's conversation with Miroslav Deronjić demonstrated "beyond reasonable doubt the Accused's agreement to the expansion of the objective to encompass the killing of the Bosnian Muslim males." International Criminal Tribunal for the former Yugoslavia, *Prosecutor v. Karadžić—Judgment*, Case No. IT-95-5/18-T, March 24, 2016, para 5805. Professors of international law Kai Ambos and Marko Milanović expressed skepticism that the "only reasonable inference" that could be made from Karadžić's agreement to and knowledge of the killing of Bosniak males was that he shared a specific genocidal intent. Nonetheless, this is the assumption on which the ICTY based its judgment of Karadžić on the Srebrenica component of his trial. Kai Ambos, "Karadzic's Genocidal Intent as the 'Only Reasonable Inference'?" *EJIL: Talk! Blog of the European Journal of International Law*, April 1, 2016, https://www.ejiltalk.org/karadzics-genocidal-intent-as-the-only-reasonable-inference/; Marko Milanović, "ICTY Convicts Radovan Karadzic," *EJIL: Talk! Blog of the European Journal of International Law*, March 25, 2016, https://www.ejiltalk.org/icty-convicts-radovan-karadzic/. See also: Milena Sterio, "Radovan Karadzic Convicted by ICTY Trial Chamber," INTLAWGRRLS, March 25, 2016, https://ilg2.org/2016/03/25/radovan-karadzic-convicted-by-icty-trial-chamber/.

International Criminal Tribunal for the former Yugoslavia, *Prosecutor v. Karadžić—Decision on Accused's Motion to Subpoena Radivoje Miletic*, Case No. IT-95-5/18-T, May 9, 2013, http://www.icty.org/x/cases/karadzic/tdec/en/130509_3.pdf.

54. Robert J. Donia, *From the Republika Srpska Assembly 1991–1996* (Sarajevo and Tuzla: University Press, 2012), pp. 203, 207; Robert J. Donia, *Radovan Karadžić: Architect of the Bosnian Genocide* (New York: Cambridge University Press, 2015), p. 272.

55. Assembly of the Republika Srpska, Fifty-Fourth Session, October 15–16, 1995, cited in Robert J. Donia, *Radovan Karadžić: Architect of the Bosnian Genocide* (New York: Cambridge University Press, 2015), p. 272.

56. Interestingly, Karadžić's claim that he had approved of the "radical task" of issuing a directive to create an unbearable situation in the eastern enclaves, and that he "didn't regret it," was not used in the judgment. This is surprising, because in this intercept Karadžić not only claims that he approved of the attack but also that he recognized that it was "radical." The judgment refers only to intercepts that involve Karadžić claiming he approved of the operation to take the town, not that there was anything "radical" about how the town

was taken. When I queried Robert Donia, who was involved in the case, he said, "Both the prosecutors in the case and the judges seem to have assigned somewhat less probative value to retrospective statements than to those before the event, and even then assigned more importance the closer to the event the words were spoken. The genocide cases all came down to the question of intent, mens rea, or guilty mind, which to them meant a state of mind at the time the deed was committed, and they seemed to regard that as ephemeral, subject to being formed in the minutes or hours before the deed but altered after the deed was done. So they were content to take one or two representative retrospective comments rather than include all of them." Robert Donia, email correspondence with author, October 19, 2018.

57. Multiple sources have attested to the rift between Mladić and Karadžić. See, e.g., DCI Interagency Balkan Task Force, "Intelligence Report: The Belgrade-Pale Relationship," (June 23, 1995, Approved for Release October 1, 2013), https://www.cia.gov/library/readingroom /docs/1995-06-23A.pdf. In 1995, Mladić dramatically and publicly undermined Karadžić's authority by refusing to be removed from power as commander of the Bosnian Serb Army. Eighteen of Mladić's generals supported Mladić in this stance. Karadžić was forced to issue a public retraction. DCI Interagency Balkan Task Force, "Intelligence Report: Milosevic, Karadzic, Mladic: Serbs More United," (September 5, 1995, Approved for Release October 1, 2013), https://www.cia.gov /library/readingroom/docs/1995-09-05B.pdf.

Milošević seemed to have been weighing the benefits of replacing Karadžić with Mladić in November 1994. Central Intelligence Agency, DCI Interagency Balkan Task Force, "The Milosevic-Karadzic Break: Stalemated For Now," Intelligence Report, November 23, 1994, https://www.cia.gov/library/readingroom/docs/1994-11-23.pdf.

See also: Robert Block, "The Madness of General Mladic," *New York Review of Books*, October 5, 1995. For the view that Milošević was essentially a puppeteer manipulating Karadžić, see Nevenka Tromp, *Prosecuting Slobodan Milošević: The Unfinished Trial* (London & New York: Routledge, 2016). For example, Tromp says that Milošević at one point threatened to murder Karadžić if he didn't release the Western hostages. Nevenka Tromp, *Prosecuting Slobodan Milošević: The Unfinished Trial* (London and New York: Routledge, 2016), p. 188.

58. The Court ruled that Karadžić was in fact told that Muslims were being killed, based on an intercepted phone conversation he had with the

civilian administrator for Srebrenica, Miroslav Deronjić, on July 13, 1995. The Court noted that Karadžić was also guilty on the basis of superior responsibility, having "failed in his duty as Supreme Commander to take necessary and reasonable measures to punish the commission of genocide, murder, extermination, and killing as an underlying act of persecution." International Criminal Tribunal for the former Yugoslavia, *Prosecutor v. Karadžić—Judgment Summary*, Case No. IT-95-5/18, March 24, 2016, http://www.icty.org/x/cases /karadzic/tjug/en/160324_judgement_summary.pdf.

For more on Karadžić's knowledge of the killings at Srebrenica prior to his phone conversation with Deronjić, and his superior responsibility for the atrocities committed at Srebrenica, see International Criminal Tribunal for the former Yugoslavia, *Prosecutor v. Karadžić—Judgment*, Case No. IT-95-5/18-T, March 24, 2016, para 5833-5848. For the summary of findings on Karadžić's individual criminal responsibility for the four Joint Criminal Enterprises that the Yugoslav Tribunal accused him of being party to, see International Criminal Tribunal for the former Yugoslavia, *Prosecutor v. Karadžić—Judgment*, Case No. IT-95-5/18-T, March 24, 2016, pp. 2512-2521.

59. Karadžić justified the attack with claims that while Srebrenica was supposed to be a demilitarized zone, in fact, the Bosnian Muslim army was continually attacking Serb forces from the enclave. But at the same time, he claimed that the Bosniaks didn't care to defend the enclave. "The Muslims themselves have given up Srebrenica," said Karadžić in an interview in 1997. Rob Siebelink, "Radovan Karadzic, the Psychiatrist Who Became the Most Wanted War Criminal," *Free Republic*, August 8, 2004, http://www.freerepublic.com/focus /news/1187259/posts?page=2. There are many theories as to why the Bosniaks did not fight in Srebrenica but fled, leading some commentators to conclude that Izetbegović, recognizing the enclave's importance for the creation of a contiguous RS territory, was prepared to give up Gorazde, Žepa, and Srebrenica in a trade for three Sarajevo suburbs. See, for example, the 2015 Norwegian film *A Town Betrayed*, dirs. Ola Flyum and David Hebditch, documentary (NRK, 2011). Nevenka Tromp provides details about intercepted telephone conversations about the planned massacre between the FRY and RS military leaders as early as June 17, 1995, as well as between Milošević and Mladić from the time that the Žepa and Srebrenica enclaves fell. She also makes clear that these intercepts were known and discussed in

the United States. Nevenka Tromp, *Prosecuting Slobodan Milošević: The Unfinished Trial* (London and New York: Routledge, 2016), pp. 172–173. For details about the failure of Western powers to prevent the attack on the eastern enclaves, see David Rohde, *Endgame: The Betrayal and Fall of Srebrenica, Europe's Worst Massacre Since World War II* (New York: Penguin Books, 2012).

60. Jovanka Karadžić, interview in "The World's Most Wanted Man," script, written and directed by Kevin Sim, *Frontline*, PBS, May 26, 1998, https://www.pbs.org/wgbh/pages/frontline/shows/karadzic/etc/script.html.

61. In psychoanalysis, the "true self" and the "false self" are concepts often associated with narcissism. The true self is the more authentic personality of an individual, whereas the false self is a defensive façade behind which the true self can be protected from external threats.

62. Henry V was a fifteenth-century king of England known for his military successes in wars of conquest against France, most notably his famous victory in the 1415 Battle of Agincourt. By today's standard, Henry V was guilty of war crimes for slaughtering French prisoners of war. In 2010, a mock trial of Henry V was staged in Washington, DC, with Justices Samuel Alito and Ruth Bader Ginsburg judging. Henry V was found guilty based on "evolving standards of civil society." See: Andy Jones, "High Court Justices, Legal Luminaries Debate Shakespeare's 'Henry V,'" Law.com, March 18, 2010, https://www.law.com/almID/1202446381186/.

63. Ismet Cerić, interview in "The World's Most Wanted Man," transcript, *Frontline*, PBS, https://www.pbs.org/wgbh/pages/frontline/shows/karadzic/interviews/ceric.html.

64. As the original Yugoslav socialist framework established that no constituent peoples could be a considered a minority, regardless of actual demographics, the term "minority" "lost its neutral meaning and acquired negative—and occasionally insulting—connotations." Gale Stokes, "Independence and the Fate of Minorities (1991–1992)," in Charles Ingrao and Thomas A. Emmert, eds., *Confronting the Yugoslav Controversies: A Scholar's Initiative* (West Lafayette, IN: Purdue University Press, 2013), p. 83.

65. Sheri Berman, "The Pipe Dream of Undemocratic Liberalism," *Journal of Democracy*, Vol. 28, No. 3 (July 2017). For more on populism, see: Cas Mudde, "Europe's Populist Surge: A Long Time in the Making," *Foreign Affairs*, Vol. 95, No. 6 (November/December 2016),

https://www.foreignaffairs.com/issues/2016/95/6;   Fareed   Zakaria,
"Populism on the March: Why the West Is in Trouble," *Foreign Affairs*, Vol. 95, No. 6 (November–December 2016), https://www
.foreignaffairs.com/articles/united-states/2016-10-17/populism
-march; Cristóbal Rovira Kaltwasser, Paul Taggart, Paulina Ochoa
Espejo, and Pierre Ostiguy, "Populism: An Overview of the Concept and the State of the Art," in Cristóbal Rovira Kaltwasser, Paul
Taggart, Paulina Ochoa Espejo, and Pierre Ostiguy, eds., *The Oxford Handbook of Populism* (Oxford: Oxford University Press, 2017).

66. Many books on the topic of the fragility of liberal democracy have
been published in the last few years. Fareed Zakaria's important essay
and book from 1997 now look prescient. Fareed Zakaria, "The Rise
of Illiberal Democracy," *Foreign Affairs* Vol. 76, No. 6 (November–
December 1997), https://www.foreignaffairs.com/articles/1997-11-01
/rise-illiberal-democracy; Fareed Zakaria, *The Future of Freedom: Illiberal Democracy at Home and Abroad* (New York: W. W. Norton, 2007).

Chapter Twelve

FEAR

On my last trip to see Karadžić, I went to bed in The Hague on November 8, 2016, confident that Hillary Clinton would be elected the forty-fifth president of the United States. Trump had a 16 percent chance of winning the election, while Clinton had an 84 percent chance, according to The Upshot. FiveThirtyEight gave Clinton slightly lower odds; she had a 71.2 percent chance of winning to Trump's 28.7 percent. My husband, a former congressman, was certain Trump would win, but all the polls suggested he wouldn't. I believed the polls.

I woke up in The Hague on November 9 and saw that Trump was winning. By 9 A.M. my time in the Netherlands, Secretary Clinton had conceded defeat. I was staying with strangers in a guesthouse. The television was in the communal breakfast room. Upon hearing the news, I was shocked, undone, as if I had woken up to an unfamiliar, surreal landscape where gravity threatened to force me down, push me off my feet. I was worried that these feelings would show on my face.

I walked outside, into a world made over. The Hague is an international city, and it seemed to me that the people I saw on the street were also stunned by the election results. Or perhaps I was imagining this. . . .

Like many people who work on national-security issues, I'm

not especially partisan. I try to evaluate ideas and policies on the basis of their merit, not their political importance for one party or the other.

But I thought of my father, a refugee from Nazi Germany, who had said of Trump, "I know Nazis. That man is a Nazi." My father is not prone to emotional outbursts, especially in regard to Nazis, a subject he rarely brings up. He had uttered these words in a moment when we knew, or thought we knew, that Trump—a reality television star!—could not possibly become president of the United States. The man had dog-whistled at white supremacists! Called Mexican immigrants "rapists"!

Was Trump also an expert in metacommunication?

Nothing about him seemed presidential.

How could the polls have been so wrong?

—

Not long before the election, during a moment when the polls were predicting a Clinton victory with near 99 percent certainty, I had met with a Bosnian student at Boston University, where I now teach. She was a young woman who moved with her parents to the United States from Bosnia as a refugee. Her mother, who joined us for coffee, came from an upper-class Bosnian Muslim family. They had settled in a working-class suburb of Boston. "You look at Trump and you laugh," she said to me. "You can't take him seriously. You assume he can't possibly win."

"But that is exactly how we saw Radovan Karadžić!" she said. "We couldn't take him seriously. We laughed at his wildly exaggerated fears of Muslim 'aggression.' In the same way Trump speaks about 'Mexican rapists,' Karadžić spoke about 'Muslim killers.' We felt completely safe because we knew he was a fool."

Perhaps he seemed a fool, at least to the educated elite, before he became president. But he had an uncanny ability to read his audience—the segment of the population most frightened or triggered by societal change.

Her words came back to me that morning after the election.

—

The wars in Yugoslavia had not started with massacres. They started with someone talking about fear. Stoking fear is a powerful weapon. As Karadžić put it, if someone fears he will be killed, he may kill. Neighbors will turn against neighbors. As President Trump says, "Real power is fear."[1]

And he knew how to drum up fear. In his testimony before the ICTY, Miroslav Deronjić, the civilian administrator for Srebrenica who reported directly to Karadžić, explained how paramilitary volunteers would deliberately create a "fearful atmosphere" among both Bosniaks and Serbs. He said that the paramilitary volunteers "would start chasing around town with their cars, going into Muslim neighbourhoods, Serbian neighbourhoods, turning their sirens on, shooting into the air, so that an atmosphere was created in which Serbs and especially Muslims were extremely fearful. It was a very bad environment for all the residents. Serbs were afraid and I can imagine what the Muslims must have felt like. There was a lot of panic and fear among the population, and all of that was *created intentionally* with cars chasing noisily around town, shooting in the air, sirens and so on."[2]

An intercept of a conversation between Dobrica Ćosić and Karadžić caught the two men seemingly discussing the importance of spreading fear among Serbs in particular. Ćosić said to Karadžić, "A man who is not afraid and does not know the fear can not be smart."

Karadžić responded, "He can not, he can not be smart and responsible for, for . . ."

Ćosić said, "Such a man can be neither smart nor moral."[3]

—

I took a taxi to the prison, feeling too unstable to bike, annoyed by my shakiness, but also puzzled by it. It seemed to me I was having a hysterical reaction. As the guard accompanied me from the Dutch prison to the Detention Unit, I was concerned that in my strange mood I might do something stupid. In my mind's eye, I saw myself fainting and falling onto the paved walkway between the two prison buildings, bruising myself. I saw my ill-behaved blood leaking, not staying inside my body as it should. My country had just elected a president who doesn't like women who leak blood from their "wherevers," who had referred to women he doesn't like as "fat pigs," "dogs," "slobs," and "disgusting animals."[4] Even Republicans had accused him of "trickle-down racism" and misogyny.[5]

I didn't fall. I made it back to the little room with the little table and little chairs and the fluorescent tubes overhead.

—

My war criminal was waiting for me this time. He was in a celebratory mood. "I knew Trump would win," he said. "I predicted it. I performed a kind of divination," based on practices from the Kabbalah. (I have investigated his mystical practices and they are not based on the Kabbalah, but I understood that he wanted, as usual, to claim some kind of mystical link to his Jewish interviewer.) Karadžić was so proud of his prognostication (and maybe he wondered if I'd believe him) that he insisted I talk to his lawyer, Peter Robinson, who could confirm that he, Karadžić, had foreseen Trump's victory.

(In a small act of rebellion against my war criminal, I never bothered to contact Peter about Karadžić's alleged prophecy.)

"This type of divination only works when it's something not personal to me. Something I don't care about too much," he explained. I took these words to be his concession, perhaps to him-self and perhaps to me, that he could not predict—much less influence, despite having spent so much time in meditation and prayer—the outcome of his trial and upcoming appeal.

"I understand why so many Americans voted for Trump," Karadžić said, bringing me back into the room. "They are fed up with globalization. It leaves too many people behind. Fed up with jihadis. People all over the world are realizing that multi-culturalism is a threat to what people value most—their *own* cultures."

"Globalization is about melding of cultures," he said. "What does it do for us? There is nothing about maintaining tradition. Globalization is just deculturation! We are removing cultural content of people. Culture comes from God and the mother's milk."

It would be some time before I recognized that Karadžić had a better handle on what motivated Trump's supporters than many American pollsters and experts prior to the election. It now seems to me that Karadžić intuited what was motivating the rise of right-wing populism all over the world.

In a conversation he had with Ćosić, Karadžić prophesied: "European nationalisms are yet to flame up. They think that the time for nationalism has passed."[6]

It turns out that Trump's explicitly racist and sexist remarks helped him win the election. According to political scientists Brian Schaffner, Matthew MacWilliams, and Tatishe Nteta, the gap be-tween college-educated and non-college-educated whites was the most important divide documented in 2016. Making use of two large national-level surveys, the authors found that "while eco-nomic considerations were an important part of the story, racial attitudes and sexism were much more strongly related to support for Trump; these attitudes explain at least two-thirds of the educa-tion gap among white voters in the 2016 presidential election."[7] It's not so much about economic issues, but about a presumed threat to "our" culture, caused in part by migration, globalization, and a trend toward multiculturalism.

—

I had never seen Karadžić the way he was the day we learned of Trump's victory. He was jubilant, effervescent, overflowing with excitement. He couldn't hold back his delight. He was, unusually for him, not reading my mood at all.

The door to our little room opened, and a guard entered. I'd not seen this guard before. Maybe he was new. "Everything okay in here?" he asked. Perhaps the guard had heard Karadžić's loud voice. Karadžić didn't seem bothered by the sudden intrusion. On the contrary, he wanted to share his good humor with the guard. With the world!

"We're both in happy marriages, so you don't have to watch over us," he said. He was flirting with me, just a little bit, in front of the guard, the only time I ever saw this side of him. The guard smiled and turned to go, leaving me alone with Karadžić's excessively high spirits.

—

I don't usually share my views with interviewees. I consider it a waste of time. Still, on the topic of Trump's victory, I was pretty certain that the anxiety I was feeling that morning was visible on my face. He finally noticed I wasn't as ecstatic as he was about the topic of our conversation.

"What do you *like* about globalization?" he challenged, not quite catching the source of my discomfort.

"I like being exposed to different cultures," I said, feeling defensive, a bit childish. He definitely had the upper hand today, but he was in such a generous mood, he didn't seem to notice.

"Travel," I continued, answering a slightly different question from the one he had posed. "I like that there are people from so many different countries living in the United States."

"Would you like it if you traveled to China and you saw people looking just like they look in the United States?" he asked.

"I would not," I conceded, thinking about how young people everywhere I've been lately seemed to look alike: iPhones on their ears, Zara or H&M clothing, Nike shoes or shoes that look like Nike shoes.

"People long for their own cultures," he said. "Culture helps people feel secure in their own identities."

I saw the logic of much of what he was saying. Mixing of cultures to create new hybrids does entail loss. Grave loss. In my country and in much of Europe, what "white advocate" Jared Taylor refers to as "white European culture" could indeed be eclipsed due to immigration and cultural mixing.[8] Taylor refers to immigration as the biggest threat to whites today.[9] And multiculturalism is not always working as well as many of us might wish. Some immigrants have very different values from Western ones; they are intolerant of homosexuality, of Western views about women's rights, even of minority rights. Sometimes lack of integration leads to ethnic ghettos. But I have a bias against sameness and a prejudice against nationalism. Nationalism, I think to myself, starts wars.

———

"Civilization is founded on banks, receipts, orders, all external things," Karadžić tells me, echoing Freud. "But culture is the way we reconcile our own being."

He continued his rant against globalization.

"Global companies want to create a new form of man," he said to me, "a pure consumer, shorn of culture. This doesn't work. The Communists tried engineering human souls to make a new man. They wanted to make all the flowers look and smell the same. It didn't work at all."[10]

Even proglobalization economists concede that some companies and some people will not be able to compete in global markets. But the claim is that in this "pareto-optimal" arrangement, even if the winners compensate the losers for whatever they lose many times over, everyone would still be better off. There are a number of problems with this argument.[11] The winners are not actually paying off the losers—for example, the coal miners. And even if they did, the losers' economic losses pale in comparison with their perceived loss of status, and the erosion of local norms and culture.

Even worse than economic losses for the people left behind by globalization are their losses in status and dignity. A study by Diana C. Mutz, published by the National Academy of Sciences, found that perceived status threat among high-status groups, whom she identifies as whites, Christians, and men, was the most important motivation underlying support for Trump. She identifies the declining numerical dominance of white Americans, the rising status of African Americans, and insecurity about whether the United States still dominates the global economy, as the specific anxieties plaguing whites, Christians, and men.[12] "Growing domestic racial diversity and globalization contributed to a sense that white Americans are under siege by these engines of change," she wrote.[13]

Karadžić continued, "When I meet a French guy, I want him to be French! If I pick up a pear, I don't want it to taste like a potato." He looked pleased with himself, as if it were obvious what he meant with this vegetational metaphor.

NOTES

1. Donald Trump, as quoted in Bob Woodward, *Fear: Trump in the White House* (New York: Simon and Schuster, 2018), p. 175.

2. International Criminal Tribunal for the former Yugoslavia, *Prosecutor v. Milošević—Statement for Witness Miroslav Deronjić*, Case no. IT-02-54, November 26, 2003, p. 25. Accessed through a special database for the ICTY: http://icr.icty.org/LegalRef/CMSDocStore/Public/English/Exhibit/NotIndexable/IT-02-54/ACE17806R0000098758.TIF.

    Deronjić had been appointed the civilian commissioner for Srebrenica Municipality on July 11, 1995. On July 13, he spoke with Karadžić through an intermediary. In the conversation, Karadžić and Deronjić spoke in code about the fates of the Bosnian Muslim men detained by the Serbs. They also met in person the following day, when Deronjić reported on the situation in Srebrenica to Karadžić. The Tribunal also received evidence that Karadžić and Deronjić spoke frequently on the phone or in person during the Srebrenica operation. These points were used as evidence by the Tribunal that Karadžić knew about the killings in Srebrenica in advance. International Criminal Tribunal for the former Yugoslavia, *Prosecutor v. Karadžić—Judgement*, Case No. IT-95-5/18, March 24, 2016, para 5805, 5807–5811. For more on this, see Marko Milanovic, "ICTY Convicts Radovan Karadzic," *EJIL: Talk! Blog of the European Journal of International Law*, March 25, 2016, https://www.ejiltalk.org/icty-convicts-radovan-karadzic/.

    As discussed earlier, Directive 7, issued under Karadžić's name, essentially commanded the Drina Corps to terrify people. It ordered the Corps to "create an unbearable situation of *total insecurity with no hope of further survival or life* for the inhabitants of Srebrenica and Žepa." Supreme Command of the Armed Forces of Republika Srpska, "Directive for Further Operations Op. No. 7," March 8, 1995 (author's emphasis), accessed: https://www.documentcloud.org/documents/251259-950308-directive-7.html.

3. Conversation between Dobrica Ćosić and Radovan Karadžić, International Criminal Tribunal for the former Yugoslavia, *Prosecutor v. Momčilo Krajišnik*, Case No. IT-00-39, Exhibit P64A.185.1, cited in Emir Suljagic, "Targeting 'Turks': How Karadzic Laid the Foundations for Genocide," Balkan Transitional Justice, April 15, 2019, https://balkaninsight.com/2019/04/15/targeting-turks-how-karadzic-laid-the-foundations-for-genocide/.

4. Robert Farley, "Fact Check: Trump's Comments on Women," *USA Today*, August 12, 2015, https://www.usatoday.com/story/news/politics/elections/2015/08/12/fact-check-trump-comments-women-megyn-kelly/31525419/; Samantha Cooney, "Why Is the President So

Disgusted By Women and Our Blood?" *Time*, June 29, 2017, http://time.com/4839415/donald-trump-mika-brzezinski-women-blood/.

5. In an interview on CNN, former presidential candidate Mitt Romney used the term "trickle-down racism" in reference to how Trump would change the character of America. Theodore Schleifer, "Mitt Romney Says Donald Trump Will Change America with 'Trickle-Down Racism,'" *CNN*, June 11, 2016, https://www.cnn.com/2016/06/10/politics/mitt-romney-donald-trump-racism/index.html.

Former Republican Speaker of the House Paul Ryan chided Trump over Trump's claim that a Mexican American judge presiding over the Trump University case would have "an absolute conflict" due to his Mexican heritage. Ryan called Trump's statement "the textbook definition of a racist comment" and said that those comments should be "absolutely disavowed. It's absolutely unacceptable." Tom Kertscher, "Donald Trump's Racial Comments About Hispanic Judge in Trump University Case," *PolitiFact*, June 8, 2016, https://www.politifact.com/wisconsin/article/2016/jun/08/donald-trumps-racial-comments-about-judge-trump-un/.

6. Conversation between Dobrica Ćosić and Radovan Karadžić, International Criminal Tribunal for the former Yugoslavia, *Prosecutor v. Momčilo Krajišnik*, Case No. IT-00-39, Exhibit P64A.185.1, cited in Emir Sujagic, "Targeting 'Turks': How Karadzic Laid the Foundations for Genocide," *Balkan Transnational Justice*, April 15, 2019, https://balkaninsight.com/2019/04/15/targeting-turks-how-karadzic-laid-the-foundations-for-genocide/.

7. Brian F. Schaffner, Matthew MacWilliams, and Tatishe Nteta, "Understanding White Polarization in the 2016 Vote for President: The Sobering Role of Racism and Sexism," *Political Science Quarterly*, Vol. 133, No. 1 (March 2018).

8. The United States, a very young country, has always been a country of immigrants, starting with the Pilgrims. But that is not true in Europe. Jared Taylor objects to being referred to as a white supremacist, insisting he is a "white advocate." Amna Nawaz, "'People Like You': White Nationalist Jared Taylor to Muslim-American Journalist," *ABC News*, March 21, 2017, https://abcnews.go.com/Politics/people-white-nationalist-jared-taylor-muslim-american-journalist/story?id=46211947. For more by Jared Taylor, see "Archive: Jared Taylor," *American Renaissance*, https://www.amren.com/author/jartaylor/.

9. Jared Taylor, "Arguments for Our Side," *American Renaissance*, June 2001, https://www.amren.com/news/2011/03/the_revolution_2/.

10. He wanted me to understand the absurdity of trying to create a "new Communist man" and, by analogy, the new multicultural man, a product of out-of-control ethnic mixing brought about by globalization and weak national borders. What about globalization's new man? In this fantasy, cultural identity begins to erode in favor of consumerism. The influence of individual cultures begins to weaken, as the influence of global trends and brands rises. The upside to this is that access to cultural products—such as art, ideas, and entertainment—increases. The downside is that the dominant (American) consumerist ethos could eclipse indigenous cultures and values, in a form of cultural imperialism.

    I didn't tell him, but I already knew all about this. I lived in Soviet Russia in the 1980s.

    The Communist "new man" was expected to be selfless in his efforts on behalf of the state and of fellow Communists. Rather than furthering his own interests the way selfish capitalists do, he would work for the betterment of society. Most relevant here, he would also have no nationalist feeling—he would be Soviet rather than Russian or Chechen or Ukrainian; Yugoslav rather than Serbian or Slovenian or Montenegrin. Serge Schmemann, "In Soviet, Eager Beaver's Legend Works Overtime," *New York Times*, August 31, 1985, https://www.nytimes.com/1985/08/31/world/in-soviet-eager-beaver-s-legend-works-overtime.html; Yinghong Cheng, *Creating the "New Man": From Enlightenment Ideals to Socialist Realities* (Honolulu: University of Hawai'i Press, 2009), pp. 33–34.

    What I learned living in Soviet Russia was that the attempt to eradicate human nature seemed to have a perverse effect, making people even more acquisitive, selfish, and nationalistic. The privileged elite—the people imposing this fantasy on others—lived in a world that was unimaginably lavish in comparison with the world of ordinary workers. The new man that Communism bred was in fact a liar and a thief who stole from the state to protect his family. The denial of human nature didn't seem to work for the Communists, but that doesn't mean that people won't keep trying to fashion societies that they hope will force the emergence of more ideal humans. Other examples of the "New Man" include the Nietzschean Übermensch and the Transhumanist New Man, who will be cybernetically enhanced. The latter is a contemporary and more literal take on the concept.

Most relevant to us, the denial of nationalism did not work very well, either, neither in the Soviet Union nor in Yugoslavia. After the end of Communist rule, nationalism, occasionally violent, burst forth. To be human is to be selfish, self-aggrandizing, and self-promoting. It is also to be tribal, violent, and cruel. Stevan E. Hobfoll, *Tribalism: The Evolutionary Origins of Fear Politics* (New York: Palgrave Macmillan, 2018).

If we recognize these dangerous tendencies, might we be able to keep them in check? See Jessica Benjamin's essay on this topic: Jessica Benjamin, "Non-violence as Respect for All Suffering: Thoughts Inspired by Eyad El Sarraj," *Psychoanalysis, Culture & Society*, Vol. 21, No. 1 (2016), pp. 5–20.

11. Economist Dani Rodrik has been predicting a backlash against globalization for many years. See, e.g., Dani Rodrik, *Has Globalization Gone Too Far?* (Washington, DC: Institute for International Economics, 1997); and Asher Schechter, "Globalization Has Contributed to Tearing Socities Apart," *ProMarket* (blog), University of Chicago Booth School of Business, Stigler Center, March 29, 2018, https://promarket .org/globalization-contributed-tearing-societies-apart/.

12. Diana C. Mutz, "Status Threat, Not Economic Hardship, Explains the 2016 Presidential Vote," *Proceedings of the National Academy of Sciences*, Vol. 115, No. 19 (May 8, 2018), http://www.pnas.org/content/115/19 /E4330.

13. Diana C. Mutz, "Status Threat, Not Economic Hardship, Explains the 2016 Presidential Vote," *Proceedings of the National Academy of Sciences*, Vol. 115, No. 19 (May 8, 2018), http://www.pnas.org/content/115/19 /E4330.

Chapter Thirteen

THE RETURN OF NATIONALISM

During the war, Karadžić compared Serbs and Muslims to "dogs and cats" who lose their "natural characteristics" if they remain together.[1] He believed that Muslims and Serbs could not and should not be living together. "It's only in America that a melting pot works," he said.

Clearly, things have changed since Karadžić spent that year in America, in 1974–1975. There seem to be a lot more people who grieve the loss of "white European culture" now. As George Packer explains:

> After the Cold War, grand strategists proposed various scenarios for the future of the world: liberal capitalist triumph, the clash of civilizations, great-power rivalry, borderless anarchy. Nationalism didn't make the short list. The squalid, murderous politics of dying Yugoslavia was an atavistic embarrassment, a throwback to what Bismarck, in a fit of irritable prescience, called "some damned foolish thing in the Balkans." The fratricidal wars of the 1990s had nothing to do with the age of high-speed globalization that would soon erase national identities and make us all networked cosmopolitans. The [Balkan] warlords turned out to be ahead of their time. Kurt Bassuener, an

American expert on Bosnia, calls Trump "America's first Balkan president."[2]

By early in the twenty-first century, nationalisms had returned with a vengeance.

—

At the end of Communism in Yugoslavia, there was a threat to group identity; the state was falling apart. Values were in flux. The Communist party's political monopoly was eroding, and there was a possibility that democracy would emerge. As Steven Burg and Paul Shoup point out, "It was a tragedy of the first order that the first truly free elections in Bosnia-Herzegovina should have delivered power to three nationalist parties claiming to represent the three ethnic communities, rather than to either of the non-nationalist forces, democratic or former communist."[3] When the two richest republics demanded independence, there was a sense that the country was dissolving.

According to political scientists Gerard Toal and Adis Maksić, in Tito's Yugoslavia, Bosnia was considered to be the most orthodox republic—the one with the most ardent supporters of Communism. Public opinion polls before the 1990 election suggested that the Communist party would do well in Bosnia. But the polls were wrong: the election was a triumph for the SDS and its Serb nationalist leader, Radovan Karadžić. The ethnonationalist parties, in general, did far better than the Communists, in what has been called the "ethnification of politics."[4] Many people, though certainly not all, began shifting their allegiance from multiethnic Yugoslavia, whose institutions were crumbling, to their own ethnic groups.[5] Why? Political psychologists who study people's responses to threats to group identity have put forward some possible explanations.

Experts on identity, prejudice, and authoritarianism agree with my war criminal's argument that demographic shifts can be threatening to some people. Numerous experiments carried out by social psychologist Susan Fiske and her team have shown that people have an innate bias in favor of others like themselves and against those who are different. When they are put under stress (for example, by societal changes that threaten their job security, or demographic shifts), or are pressured by their peers, or receive approval from their leaders, they may nurture and act on their innate biases against the Other in the worst ways, including violently. Prejudice is associated with a variety of emotions—among them disgust, fear, pity, or envy. It turns out that prejudice that involves envy is the most dangerous. It can ignite violence when people feel especially threatened.[6]

According to political psychologist Karen Stenner, about a third of the population has an innate preference, which is about 50 percent heritable, for "oneness" (the acceptance of a common authority) and "sameness" (shared values) over freedom and diversity.[7] People range in this innate tendency from very low to very high authoritarianism.[8] It is a latent tendency; it can sit dormant when authoritarians don't perceive a threat. But when there is a threat to "who we are" and "our way of life," or a threat to racial, cultural, or group identity, authoritarians are triggered.[9] Thus, according to Stenner and Jonathan Haidt, multiculturalism and globalization are triggers for the 30 percent of society that is innately authoritarian.[10] When they are triggered, they will strongly oppose groups and individuals different from themselves.

To succeed in a moment of ethnic arousal and threats to ethnic groups' status, the leader needs to satisfy people's need for oneness and sameness. This could be accomplished by building a wall to keep out immigrants; creating an all-white ethnostate, as advocated by Richard Spencer and other American members of the alt-right; or, in the context of Bosnia, splitting off a state for Bosnian Serbs.[11]

The social psychologist Michael Hogg, who studies leadership in times of identity confusion, explained to me, "Social disruption and fast and dramatic social change can often create uncertainty among people about who they are in society—what their identity is, who they are, how they should act. This uncertainty can be very aversive and cause people to seek out and identify with distinctive groups that are clearly and consensually defined and have sharp boundaries. They yearn for leaders who deliver a simple, unambiguous, and authoritative message about identity—a message that is often ethnocentric, and is intolerant of disagreement and divergence."[12] According to the social-identity theory of leadership, when their identity is most threatened or confused, followers yearn for leadership per se, and may even yearn for strong or authoritarian or even "nasty leadership."[13]

But how do these leaders suddenly appear?

Perhaps such leaders just need to be able to intuit what people need to hear when they fear a loss in status. I recall Karadžić's words:

> I tried to make my speeches interactive. I would wait
> to see who was in the room. I would try to please them,
> to meet their expectations and desires. Many mobs have
> been transformed before my eyes.

He intuited that Serbs were frightened, he said, both before and during the war. "The Muslims wanted to control Bosnia."

Leaders play an important role in arousing as well as strengthening ethnic fears. They will often exaggerate threats to "our group"—whether that group is a nation-state or a single ethnic group within a state—and then claim to have the solution to the threat. They simultaneously strengthen "ethnic panic" by calling attention to threats such as "white al Qaeda" (in the case of Bosnian Serbs) or "white genocide" (in the case of American white supremacists) while endorsing policies that would seem to protect "us," the supposedly threatened group, while endorsing policies that actually threaten the Other.[14]

In Yugoslavia, leaders deliberately inflamed ethnic hatred. Warren Zimmermann, who was ambassador to Yugoslavia as it was
beginning to fall apart, wrote in his memoir, "Those who argue
that 'ancient Balkan hostilities' account for the violence that over-
took and destroyed Yugoslavia forget the power of television in the
hands of officially provoked racism. While history, particularly the
carnage of World War Two, provided plenty of tinder for ethnic
hatred in Yugoslavia . . . what we witnessed was violence-provoking
nationalism from the top down, inculcated primarily through the
medium of television. . . . An entire generation of Serbs, Croats,
and Muslims were aroused by television images to hate their neighbors."[15] Social psychologists have run experiments demonstrating
that hate speech is effective at increasing prejudice.[16]

Karadžić himself had an explanation for why he suddenly
found himself elected to lead the Serb nationalist party. He told a
newspaper interviewer that a simple sentence brought him to the
fore of the Serbian Democratic Party. It was this: "Serbs, you still
exist and are allowed to be Serbs, despite the persecutions, slaugh-
ters, pressures and suffering."[17] He was talking about Serbs the way
"white identitarians" speak about whites and the threat of "white
genocide." I believe he meant that ethnic Serbs could take on a Serb
identity, distinct from their identity as citizens of a multiethnic
state. "No [other] nation in the world would feel joy upon hearing
such a sentence," he said, "but for Serbs it was magical."[18]

Karadžić was wrong in arguing that no other nation would
take joy in being told it's okay to identify itself as a member of an
ethnic group in a multiethnic state. I see this today among "white
identitarians," who claim to be promoting the interests of white
people, whom they see as under threat. Jason Kessler, who organized the August 2017 white nationalist "Unite the Right" rally in
Charlottesville, Virginia, has written about "white genocide." He
asks rhetorically: why can't there be a National Association for the
Advancement of White People, given the demographic shifts in

the United States, and declining life expectancy for working-class whites?[19]

—

Nearly a quarter century after the end of the Bosnian War, on March 15, 2019, a white supremacist went on a mass-shooting spree in Christchurch, New Zealand, killing fifty-one Muslim worshippers during Friday prayers. The killer attached a GoPro camera to his head to film his attack and live-streamed it on his Facebook page. It took Facebook seventeen minutes to remove the extremely disturbing video and shut down the killer's account. But by then, many people had re-uploaded the film and were spreading it still further. In the following twenty-four hours, Facebook removed 1.5 million copies of the film.[20] One expert on the alt-right compared the attack to 9/11. "We'll be seeing Christchurch as the wake-up call to understanding how extreme far-righters organize themselves online," he said.[21] It was also a wake-up call that anti-Muslim sentiment among a white population frightened of being "replaced" by immigrants had reached a dangerous level. The historian Niall Ferguson asked, "Is the world turning into a giant Bosnia?"[22]

The killer's Twitter account posted images of the weapons he used. The rifles were covered with white writing. Some of the names were of legendary Serbian knights known for their involvement in anti-Ottoman campaigns, including Prince Lazar and Miloš Obilić, who tried but failed to fight back the Ottoman invasion of Kosovo in 1389. Others were historical figures involved in fighting the Ottoman rulers, who occupied the Balkans for five hundred years.[23]

As he drove to the mosque where his killing spree began, the killer played a song that glorified Radovan Karadžić. The song's video shows three men in ethnic Serbian paramilitary uniforms performing on a field. The face of the accordionist, Novislav

Djajić, had already become a meme in white nationalist circles. It is called "Dat Face Soldier."[24]

The lyrics include the words "The wolves are coming, beware, Ustashi and Turks," the terms used during the Yugoslav wars to refer to Croatian nationalist fighters and Bosnian Muslims. "Karadžić, lead your Serbs," the lyrics continue.[25] The lyrics had been rewritten in many languages and had become the premise for a meme popular with white supremacists around the world. It became known as "remove kebab" or "Serbia strong."[26]

Like Anders Breivik, the far-right Norwegian terrorist who murdered seventy-seven people, most of them teenagers, in 2011, the Christchurch terrorist wrote a manifesto, which he disseminated prior to his attack. He dubbed his manifesto "The Great Replacement," after French writer Renaud Camus's 2012 book *Le Grand Remplacement*. The "great replacement" is a conspiracy theory that claims that whites are being replaced by nonwhites all over the Western world, due to immigration of nonwhites and a secret Muslim plot to "outbreed" white Christians. The shooter arrived at these beliefs through a "specific ideological prism—his familiarity with and interest in Serbian ultra-nationalism."[27] The Christchurch killer had visited Serbia, Croatia, and Bosnia in 2016–2017.[28]

During his trial in April 2012, Breivik explained why he turned to Serb nationalism. One had to "distance oneself sufficiently from national socialism because it was quite blood-stained," he said. "We felt it completely essential to do so. For the extreme right to be ever be able [sic] to prevail in Europe in the future, one had to distance oneself from the old school ideology. One would choose a new identity." That identity, he said, "was, in a way, imported from Serbia." Norway's involvement in NATO's attacks on Serbia during the Kosovo War was what had motivated Breivik's terrorist attack, he said.[29] Breivik lionized Karadžić, who he said was an "honourable crusader" and a "European war hero" for his efforts to "rid Serbia of Islam." He identified Karadžić as one of the people in the world he would most like to meet.[30] NATO forces' involvement in the war to stop the Serbs' ethnic-cleansing campaigns amounted to war crimes, he said. Breivik mentioned the Balkans at least one thousand times in his manuscript, though he doesn't mention Srebrenica even once ("Kosovo" comes up with 143 matches, "Serb" yields 341 matches, and "Bosnia" yields 343 matches).[31] He discussed a plan for deporting all Muslims from Europe and endorsed killing any Albanians and Bosniaks that resisted deportation.[32]

It's hard to pinpoint exactly when white extremism began to fuse Serbian and white nationalist tropes.[33] But Anders Breivik's manifesto was an important contribution. According to Tony McAleer, a former member of the neo-Nazi group White Aryan Resistance, the Christchurch killer's focus on Serbia is not uncommon among white extremists. "In the 1990s, at the height of the Balkan crisis, I knew a lot of people who went over there to fight," McAleer told a reporter. "Someone like him [the Christchurch terrorist] might look to Serbia as they took whatever steps they thought were necessary to deal with Muslims in their backyard."[34]

—

I have been writing about terrorism across ideologies for several decades, and for that reason, I've periodically been monitoring the white nationalist website Stormfront since it first appeared in 1996. Stormfront, which is the oldest white nationalist site, refers to itself as the "voice of the new, embattled white minority." It contains a section for Serbs called "Stormfront Srbija," which was where I found a posting of a translation of Karadžić's mother's letter to her son, urging him to commit suicide rather than turn himself over to the Yugoslav Tribunal.[35] I've been watching the international section of Stormfront grow over the years.

Many of us in the West hoped that after the horrors of the First and Second World Wars, virulent ethnonationalism was on its way out, never to return. But it turns out that the ugly war in Bosnia may have been a portent of nationalisms to come. Karadžić may have been the vanguard. Bosnian-style nationalism is based on fear of demographic shifts, of being outnumbered by a hated minority. As horrific as the New Zealand attack was, it may well be just the beginning.

———

The United States is increasingly riven by ethnic divisions, and hate crimes are on the rise. According to Kevin E. Grisham of the Center for the Study of Hate and Extremism at California State University, San Bernardino, since the election of Donald Trump, "hate has become more mainstream and increasingly normalized."[36] A number of surveys suggest that since Trump was elected, America is more divided than at any point since the Civil War.[37] Given these trends, could another civil war come to America? I fervently hope not.

There is in fact a deep state in the United States. Not the deep state of President Trump's fantasies, but the institutions that protect the liberal democracy. Are they strong enough to hold?

NOTES

1. The prosecutor for Karadžić's trial quoted Karadžić as saying, "It all reminds me of the experiment in which a dog and a cat are held in a box together against their will or a bad marriage maintained by all sorts of forceful means. It transpired that a dog and a cat can remain in the box together only under one condition, namely, that they lose their natural characteristics and cease being a dog and a cat. We will remember that we could not be Serbs and live in such a box." International Criminal Tribunal for the Former Yugoslavia, *Prosecutor v. Karadžić—Opening Statements*, Case No. IT-95-5/18-T, October 27, 2009, p. 546.

2. George Packer, "The End of the American Century," *Atlantic*, May 2019, https://www.theatlantic.com/magazine/archive/2019/05/george -packer-pax-americana-richard-holbrooke/586042/.

3. Steven L. Burg and Paul S. Shoup, *The War in Bosnia-Herzegovina: Ethnic Conflict and International Intervention* (Armonk, NY: M. E. Sharpe, 1999), p. 56.

4. For details, see Gerard Toal and Adis Maksić, "'Serbs, You Are Allowed to Be Serbs!' Radovan Karadžić and the 1990 Election Campaign in Bosnia-Herzegovina," *Ethnopolitics*, Vol. 13, No. 3 (2014), pp. 267–287.

   According to Burg and Shoup, despite the fact that the League of Communists–Social Democratic Party would receive the greatest amount of support among Bosnians, the party turned out to be "politically the weakest of all the former communist regional parties." This failure to capture the popular vote reflected the wide appeal of ethnonationalist parties among anti-Communists in addition to nationalists. Steven L. Burg and Paul S. Shoup, *The War in Bosnia-Herzegovina: Ethnic Conflict and International Intervention* (Armonk, NY: M. E. Sharpe, 1999), p. 48.

   Robert Donia suggests that SDS's uncompromising stance on the question of constitutional changes from the other parties was the "kernel of contention" that would later result in war. Robert J. Donia, *Radovan Karadžić: Architect of the Bosnian Genocide* (New York: Cambridge University Press, 2015), p. 65. Burg and Shoup agree, saying that the outcome of the 1990 elections was "crucial" among the many causes for the war in Bosnia. Burg and Shoup, *The War in Bosnia-Herzegovina*, p. 56.

   Toal and Maksić assess the two main arguments about whether ethnic radicalization in Bosnia occurred before or after the war and posit a third argument of their own. The first thesis, put forth by V. P. Gagnon, is that the parties in Bosnia attempted to appear more moderate and less nationalistic than they actually were. Gagnon claims that ethnic radicalization occurred after the 1990 election. V. P. Gagnon, *The Myth of Ethnic War: Serbia and Croatia in the 1990s* (Ithaca, NY: Cornell University Press, 2004), pp. 46, 50. The second thesis, furthered by Nina Caspersen, argues that ethnic radicalization had already been realized by the late 1990s. According to Caspersen, while Gagnon and John Mueller hold that ethnic radicalization was a consequence of violence, it is the opposite; violence broke out as a consequence of ethnic radicalization. See: John Mueller, "The Banality of

'Ethnic War,'" *International Security*, Vol. 25, No. 1 (2000), pp. 42–70. Caspersen claims that instead of attempting to appear more moderate and less nationalistic than they actually were, the SDS used vague rhetoric to bill itself as a "catch-all" Serb party, thus amassing a "near monopoly among self-identifying Serbs" in Bosnia. Nina Caspersen, *Contested Nationalism: Serb Elite Rivalry in Croatia and Bosnia in the 1990s* (New York: Berghahn Books, 2010), p. 96.

Toal and Maksić disagree with both these theses. They argue, instead, that Karadžić hid his commitments "in plain sight." While the debates over the future of Bosnia were all "still hypothetical and conjecture," Karadžić's hostility "towards an independent Bosnia was manifest from the outset," Toal and Maksić say. Gerard Toal and Adis Maksić, "'Serbs, You Are Allowed to Be Serbs!'" pp. 270, 283–284.

5. As one Serb put it to me, "I personally was a Yugoslav until the breakup. My Yugoslav way of life was attacked. The attack came in the form of demands for separation, we were supposed to end Yugoslav common state and erect borders among us, Yugoslavs. That left me no option. I, personally, was marooned into my Serbian identity." Mladen Mrdalj, email correspondence, February 1, 2019.

6. Susan Fiske, "How Ordinary People Become Violent: Frustration and Dehumanization," The Brains That Pull the Triggers—3rd Paris Conference on Syndrome E (Paris: Institut d'etudes avancees de Paris, 2017). See also Susan T. Fiske, "Look Twice," *Greater Good Magazine*, June 1, 2008, https://greatergood.berkeley.edu/article/item /look_twice; Amy Cuddy, "The Psychology of Anti-Semitism," *New York Times*, November 3, 2018, https://www.nytimes.com/2018/11/03 /opinion/sunday/psychology-anti-semitism.html.

7. Karen Stenner, *The Authoritarian Dynamic* (New York: Cambridge University Press, 2005).

8. Karen Stenner, *The Authoritarian Dynamic* (New York: Cambridge University Press, 2005).

9. Tom Jacobs, "Authoritarianism: The Terrifying Trait That Trump Triggers," *Pacific Standard*, March 26, 2018, https://psmag.com/news /authoritarianism-the-terrifying-trait-that-trump-triggers; Karen Stenner and Jonathan Haidt, "Authoritarianism Is Not a Momentary Madness, but an Eternal Dynamic Within Liberal Democracies," in Cass R. Sunstein, ed., *Can It Happen Here? Authoritarianism in America* (New York: Dey Street Books, 2018), p. 180.

10. Karen Stenner and Jonathan Haidt, "Authoritarianism Is Not a

Momentary Madness, but an Eternal Dynamic Within Liberal Democracies" in Cass R. Sunstein, ed., *Can It Happen Here? Authoritarianism in America* (New York: Dey Street Books, 2018), p. 183; Karen Stenner, *The Authoritarian Dynamic* (New York: Cambridge University Press, 2005); Jonathan Haidt, "When and Why Nationalism Beats Globalism," *American Interest*, July 10, 2016, https://www.the-american -interest.com/2016/07/10/when-and-why-nationalism-beats-globalism/.

11. "Richard Bertrand Spencer," Southern Poverty Law Center, https:// www.splcenter.org/fighting-hate/extremist-files/individual/richard -bertrand-spencer-0, accessed: March 7, 2019.

12. Michael Hogg, email correspondence with author, January 19, 2018.

13. David Rast and Michael Hogg, "Leadership in the Face of Crisis and Uncertainty," in John Storey et al., eds., *The Routledge Companion to Leadership* (New York: Routledge, 2017), p. 55.

14. The phrase "ethnic panic" was coined by Vladimir Petrović. See Vladimir Petrović, "Ethnopolitical Temptations Reach Southeastern Europe," in Vladimir Tismaneanu and Bogdan Christian Iacob, eds., *Ideological Storms: Intellectuals, Dictators, and the Totalitarian Temptation* (Budapest: Central European University Press, 2019), pp. 317–341.

15. Warren Zimmerman, *Origins of a Catastrophe: Yugoslavia and Its Destroyers* (New York: Times Books, 1996), pp. 151-153, cited in Richard Holbrooke, *To End a War* (New York: The Modern Library, 1998), p. 24.

16. See, for example, Wiktor Soral, Michał Bilewicz, and Mikołaj Winiewski, "Exposure to Hate Speech Increases Prejudice Through Desensitization," *Aggressive Behavior*, Vol. 44, No. 2 (2017), pp. 136–146.

17. Radovan Karadžić quoted in Aleksandar Tijanić, "We Are Teaching Serbs to Be Serbs," *Oslobodjenje*, October 2, 1990, cited in Gerard Toal and Adis Maksić, "'Serbs, You Are Allowed to Be Serbs!' Radovan Karadžić and the 1990 Election Campaign in Bosnia-Herzegovina," *Ethnopolitics*, Vol. 13, No. 3 (2014), pp. 267–287.

18. Radovan Karadžić quoted in Aleksandar Tijanić, "We Are Teaching Serbs to Be Serbs," *Oslobodjenje*, October 2, 1990, cited in Gerard Toal and Adis Maksić, "'Serbs, You Are Allowed to Be Serbs!' Radovan Karadžić and the 1990 Election Campaign in Bosnia-Herzegovina," *Ethnopolitics*, Vol. 13, No. 3 (2014), pp. 267–287.

19. In an interview with NPR's Noel King, Jason Kessler, in response to a question about the ways in which white people in America are under-represented, said, "Well, because [white people are] the only group that is not allowed to organize into political organizations and lobbies

and talk explicitly about what interests are important to them as a people. You have blacks, who are able to organize with Black Lives Matter or the NAACP. You have Jews, who have the ADL. Muslims have CAIR." He further said, "It's not that there are laws specifically prohibiting white people from organizing as a lobby. But there is such a stigma around it where white people can do the exact same thing that another group of people do, and it's called supremacy, but if the other group does it, it's called civil rights." Noel King, "Jason Kessler on His 'Unite the Right' Rally Move to D.C.," transcript, NPR, August 10, 2018, https://www.npr.org/2018/08/10/637390626/a-year-after-charlottesville-unite-the-right-rally-will-be-held-in-d-c.

20. Jim Waterson, "Facebook Removed 1.5m Videos of New Zealand Terror Attack in First 24 Hours," *Guardian*, March 17, 2019, https://www.theguardian.com/world/2019/mar/17/facebook-removed-15m-videos-new-zealand-terror-attack; Shibani Mahtani, "Facebook Removed 1.5 Million Videos of the Christchurch Attacks Within 24 Hours—And There Were Still Many More," *Washington Post*, March 17, 2019, https://www.washingtonpost.com/world/facebook-removed-15-million-videos-of-the-christchurch-attacks-within-24-hours--and-there-were-still-many-more/2019/03/17/fe3124b2-4898-11e9-b871-978e5c757325_story.html?utm_term=.02b0051a2806.

21. Mike Wendling, interview with Dominic Casciani, *Beyond Today*, podcast audio, March 18, 2019, BBC Radio 4, https://www.bbc.co.uk/programmes/p073xh36.

22. Niall Ferguson, "Bosnia Is Everywhere—Even in Christchurch," *Boston Globe*, March 25, 2019.

23. In addition to Prince Lazar and Miloš Obilić, the guns also referenced Marko Miljanov Popović (a nineteenth-century Montenegrin Serb general and writer who led Montenegrins against the Ottomans in several raids), Bajo Pivljanin (a seventeenth-century *hajduk*—peasant irregular infantry—commander who is widely praised in Serbian epic poetry, notably by Vuk Karadžić), and Novak Vujošević (a Montenegrin from the Kuci tribe who killed twenty-eight Ottoman soldiers in the 1876 Battle of Fundina). Jasmin Mujanović, "Why Serb Nationalism Still Inspires Europe's Far Right," *Balkan Insight*, March 22, 2019, https://balkaninsight.com/2019/03/22/why-serb-nationalism-still-inspires-europes-far-right/; Gillian Brockell, "The Accused New Zealand Shooter and an All-White Europe That Never Existed," *Washington Post*, March 16, 2019, https://www.washington

post.com/history/2019/03/16/accused-new-zealand-shooter-an-all-white
-europe-that-never-existed/?noredirect=on&utm_term=.d2c1765001d1.

24. Robert Coalson, "Christchurch Attacks: Suspect Took Inspiration from Former Yugoslavia's Ethnically Fueled Wars," RadioFreeEurope RadioLiberty, March 15, 2019, https://www.rferl.org/a/christchurch -attacks-yugoslavia-tarrant-inspiration-suspect-new-zealand/29823655 .html. See also: sergej [pseud.], last updated by Matt Schimkowitz, "Serbia Strong/Remove Kebab," Know Your Meme, June 21, 2010, last updated March 28, 2019, https://knowyourmeme.com/memes/serbia -strong-remove-kebab.

25. Robert Coalson, "Christchurch Attacks: Suspect Took Inspiration from Former Yugoslavia's Ethnically Fueled Wars," RadioFreeEurope RadioLiberty, March 15, 2019, https://www.rferl.org/a/christchurch -attacks-yugoslavia-tarrant-inspiration-suspect-new-zealand /29823655.html.

26. sergej [pseud.], last updated by Matt Schimkowitz, "Serbia Strong/ Remove Kebab," Know Your Meme, June 21, 2010, last updated March 28, 2019, https://knowyourmeme.com/memes/serbia-strong -remove-kebab.

27. Jasmin Mujanović, "Why Serb Nationalism Still Inspires Europe's Far Right," *Balkan Insight*, March 22, 2019, https://balkaninsight .com/2019/03/22/why-serb-nationalism-still-inspires-europes-fa -right/.

28. Hina, "Christchurch Gunman Visited Croatia, Serbia, Bosnia in Late 2016, Early 2017," *N1 Zagreb*, March 16, 2019, https://ba.n1info .com/English/NEWS/a322274/Christchurch-gunman-visited-Croatia -Serbia-Bosnia-in-late-2016-early-2017.html.

29. In his hearing, Breivik said that he was inspired by Serbs who had fought and died during the NATO bombing of Kosovo, as they had a "crusader" mentality. As quoted in Helen Pidd, "Anders Behring Breivik Attacks Inspired by Serbian Nationalists, Court Hears," *Guardian*, April 18, 2012, https://www.theguardian.com/world/2012/ apr/18/anders-behring-breivik-serb-nationalists.

Questioned about his path to radicalization, Breivik said the bomb-ing of Serbs was "the straw that broke the camel's back" for militant nationalists like himself. Pidd, "Anders Behring Breivik Attacks"; Robert Coalson, "Christchurch Attacks: Suspect Took Inspiration from Former Yugoslavia's Ethnically Fueled Wars," RadioFreeEurope

RadioLiberty, March 15, 2019, https://www.rferl.org/a/christchurch
-attacks-yugoslavia-tarrant-inspiration-suspect-new-zealand
/29823655.html.

30. The following is reproduced from Anders Breivik's manifesto.

Q: Other people you would want to meet?

A: The following people have to condemn us at this point
which is fine. It is after all essential that they protect their repu-
tational shields. Anders Fogh Rasmussen, Geert Wilders, Radovan Karadzic, Lee Myung-bak and Taro Aso.

Q: But isn't Radovan Karadzic a mass murderer and a racist?!

A: As far as my studies show he is neither. The Muslims in Bosnian Serbia; the so called Bosniaks and Albanians had waged
deliberate demographic warfare (indirect genocide) against
Serbs for decades. This type of warfare is one of the most de-
structive forms of Jihad and is quite similar to what we are experiencing now in Western Europe. He offered the Muslims
in Bosnian Serbia the chance to convert or leave the country
(the same standard deal Christians are offered in many Muslim countries), he even went as far as offering the Muslims certain enclaves. When they refused he wanted to deport them
by force. When this was made impossible by NATO he gave
the order to fight the people who refused which was his sovereign right and responsibility as one of the primary leaders of
Serb forces. This was never about ethnicity but about ridding
the country of the genocidal hate ideology known as Islam. I
do condemn any atrocities committed against Croats and vice
versa but for his efforts to rid Serbia of Islam he will always be
considered and remembered as an honourable Crusader and a
European war hero. As for the NATO war criminals, the Western European category A traitors who gave the green light,
they are nothing less than war criminals.

Andrew Berwick (pseud.), *2083—European Declaration of Independence*, manifesto (London, 2011), p. 1408.

31. T.J., "Breivik's Balkan Obsession: The Norway Killings," *Economist*,
July 25, 2011.

32. Reproduced from Anders Breivik's manifesto.

The new "conservative order" should (once consolidations
of Western and/or Eastern European cultural conservative

military tribunals have been established) prepare for mass deportations of all Muslims living in Europe. The first step will be the construction of huge transit zones.

Deportation should be completed in two stages

1. Deportation of all Western European Muslims.

2. Deportation of all Eastern European Muslims.

It's important to create a different strategy for both stages as most Muslims in Eastern Europe have lived there for several centuries (a majority who are even ethnic European—Bosniaks and Albanians). As such, they will not accept being deported from Europe and will fight for their survival. A more long term and brutal military strategy must therefore be applied.

Andrew Berwick (pseud.), *2083—European Declaration of Independence*, manifesto (London, 2011), p. 1316.

33. Historian of modern Europe Edin Hajdarpašić believes that nationalist, fascist, and far-right politicians across the world have been learning from each other since the 1930s. Edin Hajdarpašić, "How a Serbian War Criminal Became an Icon of White Nationalism," *Washington Post*, March 20, 2019, https://www.washingtonpost.com /outlook/2019/03/20/how-serbian-war-criminal-became-an-icon -white-nationalism/?utm_term=.aec916702696.

In a review of James Q. Whitman's *Hitler's American Model: The United States and the Making of Nazi Race Law*, writer Omer Aziz notes that Nazi lawyers, jurists, and medical doctors were expressly inspired by American jurisprudence. The Prussian Memorandum—a policy paper that served as the foundation of Nazi legal thought and, later, the Nuremberg Laws—adapted its most racist policies from U.S. law, particularly the immigration law of the early twentieth century that outright banned Asians and many Arabs from entering the United States. The Nazis were also inspired by eugenicist and prosegregation movements and laws in the United States, some of which would not be overturned until much later in the twentieth century. In *Mein Kampf*, Adolf Hitler wrote admiringly of the dominance of "the racially pure and still unmixed German" over the American continent. Omer Aziz, "America Through Nazi Eyes," *Dissent*, Winter 2019, https://www .dissentmagazine.org/article/america-through-the-nazi-eyes.

34. "Why the Accused New Zealand Killer was Fascinated with Serbia, Ottoman Empire," *VTN News Network*, March 20, 2019, https://vtn

.co/2019/03/20/why-the-accused-new-zealand-killer-was-fascinated
-with-serbia-ottoman-empire/.

35. ktvrdi [pseud.], "Karadzic's Mother—Do Not Surrender, My Son,"
Stormfront (forum), September 19, 2003, https://www.stormfront
.org/forum/t54165/.

36. For the FBI's hate crimes statistics, which show a 17 percent increase in
2017 over the previous year, see https://ucr.fbi.gov/hate-crime/2017.
According to Kevin E. Grisham of the Center for the Study of Hate
and Extremism at California State University, San Bernardino, two
distinct trends are visible in the data. First, after a general trend down-
ward in the number of hate crimes in the United States, a marked
increase began in 2017. "These type of increases have not been seen
since right after the terrorist attack of September 11, 2001," he wrote
me. Second, he said, those committing hate-related crimes seem to
be emboldened to act out in a more visible and public manner. "Hate
has become more mainstream and increasingly normalized." Kevin
E. Grisham, email correspondence, December 18, 2018.

The Anti-Defamation League's "Murder and Extremism in the
United States" report for 2018 showed a sharp increase in the number of people killed by domestic extremists as compared to 2017, with
an increase from 37 killed in 2017 to 50 people killed in 2018. Almost
every instance of domestic extremist violence in the United States in
2018 had ties to at least one right-wing extremist movement, with the
majority of the perpetrators being white supremacists. "Murder and
Extremism in the United States in 2018," Anti-Defamation League,
https://www.adl.org/murder-and-extremism-2018.

37. Conor Lynch, "America May Be More Divided Now Than at Any
Time Since the Civil War," Salon, October 14, 2017, https://www
.salon.com/2017/10/14/america-may-be-more-divided-now-than-at
-any-time-since-the-civil-war/; Livia Gershon, "Just How Divided
Are Americans Since Trump's Election?" History, November 8, 2017,
https://www.history.com/news/just-how-divided-are-americans
-since-trumps-election; John R. Schindler, "A Divided America
Does Not Mean Civil War," Observer, July 4, 2018, https://observer
.com/2018/07/second-civil-war-in-trumps-divided-america/.

Chapter Fourteen

THE PROBLEM OF EVIL

Karadžić tried to intimidate me once, but only once, when we were together.

"The most important thing is to tell the truth," he declared. "At one time it was politically correct to dislike me," he continued, "but times are changing. The number of people who dislike me is decreasing by the minute."

It was not so much his words that set off my alarm. His tone was quite different from what I was used to. Not avuncular. Not kind. He had switched from the role of patient professor, explaining the ways of the world to his sadly ignorant student, to a bossy and snappish old man.

"I see there is a new generation coming in . . . they are not so anti-Serb. Holbrooke and [Madeleine] Albright were anti-Serb. This Tribunal is Albright's child. This coming new generation is different. The anti-Serb tide is turning."

Then he said, incongruously, "If you can't say something good, don't say it at all. The Bible says it is a sin to testify falsely against someone. If you write a good book that tells the truth, I can promise you it will be a best seller. I have many supporters all over the world. They will buy your book."

He didn't say what would happen if I wrote a "bad" book. He just hinted that God would be unhappy with me. As with his infamous highway-to-hell speech, he wasn't exactly "threatening." He was issuing a "warning" to me about the spiritually bereft future that would befall me if I were not a good person, if I failed to tell the truth about Radovan Karadžić. At the same time, he was enticing me with the prospect that my book would be a best seller if I behaved. (He continued along the same lines in a letter that he sent me after our final in-person meeting, which I have included in Appendix C.)

—

Karadžić has shown me sides of himself that he correctly perceives are interesting to me. He knows that I am moved and confused by his love of poetry and culture. That I am charmed by his admiration for Albert Lord. That I seem to like epic poems, in the same way he does. He hopes that I will not want to sin by testifying "falsely," which would be to concur with the Court about his responsibility for war crimes. He wants and expects a "good book."

He was lying to me when he said that he hadn't been informed that Muslims had been killed in Srebrenica. But he has been completely transparent in his attempts to manipulate me. I am simultaneously impressed and nauseated.

—

I learned a great deal about Karadžić and how he rose to prominence. His psychiatric supervisor reported that Karadžić referred to himself as an "excellent psychiatrist," but in fact he was not excellent, his supervisor said, on account of his laziness and entitled attitude. However, Karadžić wasn't really that interested in professional success as a mere doctor. He wanted to be a great man, to wield great power as a poet or a prophet. He referred to himself as "the third best poet in Serbian history," and predicted that one of his books would win him a Nobel Prize. I wonder if he allows himself to realize that he fell short of his own expectations.

Nevertheless, he has a skill—"I can control a mob with my eyes," he told me. He knows how to read a crowd, he said. He boasted to me that he never wrote out his speeches. He changed his story depending on what the people listening wanted or needed to hear. And then there was a political crisis in Yugoslavia. People were afraid. He intuited his way to an approach that involved heightening their fear even more, while presenting himself as the only person who understood the seriousness of the threat. How does one get neighbor to kill neighbor? I asked.

The answer, he said, is fear.

—

People are constantly asking me: How evil was he? Was he a psychopath?

I'm slightly uncomfortable with these questions. I am neither philosopher nor priest, trained to hold forth on evil, nor a psychiatrist trained to diagnose personality disorders. Nonetheless, I've spent my career studying violent men. Not just violent men, but men who target civilians in violation of both ethical norms and law.

It's slightly embarrassing to have carved out such a specialty. I'll just answer the questions a reader would presumably ask me next: Yes, I have been the target of violence (raped at gunpoint and sexually abused as a child). And yes, it would appear that I am still trying to understand the nature of evil. A friend of mine, a psychologist, says that one definition of mental health is when you are able to recognize your *mishigas* (craziness) and use it in a creative or productive way. That is what I tell myself to diminish embarrassment regarding the underlying motivations for my life's work, and for this strange expertise I've honed.

On very rare occasions I've sat with a person I was pretty sure was a psychopath. For example, I spent two afternoons with an imprisoned man who told me he loved to kill people, that he got pleasure from it, that he was disappointed when he got involved in torture as a mercenary for the Croatian military during the war, that it wasn't as pleasurable for him as killing. He didn't like Muslims. He was also a neo-Nazi who didn't like non-Aryans. He also told me that he tortured animals as a child. I got the sense that he feared he might be a psychopath, and he wanted to put all his symptoms out on the table for both of us to consider.

It took me months to recover from those two afternoons. I went straight from the second interview to a sauna near my hotel. I had an irresistible urge to scrub my body, as if scouring the flesh would cleanse whatever his hatred had sullied in me—my soul or my spirit or my heart. I also spent a lot of time sniffing the oil of roses or jasmine, in an effort to get an imaginary scent out of my brain.

He seemed to harbor a wish to contaminate me, to project whatever had damaged him into me. I was not allowed to bring any water or food into the prison, and focusing so intensely on his painful story made it hard for me to keep up my energy. On the second day of our meetings, he brought two meat sandwiches that he had put together for us to eat. I didn't want to be seen scrutinizing those sandwiches, but of course I did inspect them out of the corner of my eye. And I realized that he had taken a bite out of the meat in the sandwich closest to me. I declined to eat that sandwich, but I still felt stained by his apparent intention. When you're sitting with someone like that, the hair sticks up on the back of your neck.

Another time, I met with a jihadi leader who I sensed had become cynical about his holy war and had become financially and spiritually corrupt. He was prepared to offer up the lives of young men for the "jihad" while sitting in his own mansion, with his second wife. With both of these men, I had the feeling I was witnessing evil—the evil that was done to them, as well as the evil they had done to others.

My experience has taught me that the body seems to "know"

it's in the presence of something horribly wrong, even if my annoyingly argumentative mind is coming up with counterarguments and caveats.

When I sat with the man who said he liked to kill people, I had the sensation that he could see inside my body, as if I had no skin; and the only reason he wasn't physically harming me was that he had decided to be polite.

I didn't have that sort of feeling with Karadžić.

I didn't feel that prickle on the back of my neck. Nonetheless, I did notice myself dissociating my fear when I sat with Karadžić. I sometimes had the feeling that the souls of those eight thousand murdered men from Srebrenica were hovering around the corner, just out of sight, perhaps in another one of the prison's rooms. I would swat this nonthought away, telling myself I don't believe in floating souls.

—

In an independent Bosnia, suddenly "his" people—the Bosnian Serbs—would be outnumbered by an ethnic group, some of whose ancestors had provided recruits to the Nazis. How many of us, in the same situation that Karadžić faced, would have done the same? I hope very few, but I'm also not sure of that.

The problem with national leadership is that you're so often making decisions—not between good and bad—but between bad and worse. In the world I think about, in the world of war and peace, these sorts of decisions—between bad and worse and worse even than that—are routine.

Leaders don't necessarily know that they're going to be seduced by evil.

You can't predict when that seduction is going to come, how it will be camouflaged, or how you're going to respond when fear comes to you, when you're afraid.

When evil comes knocking, it may well ask you to protect

your own people. It will take advantage of our biologically formed tribal nature.

If I threaten your child, you will rush to her or his defense, even if it means killing me. The truth is, I wouldn't respect you if you didn't. But what happens if you believe I'm threatening your tribe? The people who share your ethnicity, or sexual preference; the people with white skin, or brown skin, or blue eyes? The people who speak your language, or follow your religion, or share your history? What if you and your people share a history of victimization by the same tribe threatening you now? In a multi-ethnic society, do "your" people have more of a moral claim for protection than others?

If you're elected to represent and protect a group of people, is it morally acceptable to refuse to do so because you don't like the idea of civil war, or you don't want to divide your country into Us and Them? (Of course, this is the problem with identity politics—you might be forced to make decisions like this.)

What if you're not entirely certain how to proceed? In that case, there might be dual temptations: to exaggerate (or minimize) the threat in your own mind and communications with your followers in order to justify your decision to act (or not act).

This, I believe, could well be the trap that Karadžić fell into—the feeling he had to protect his own people, and the recognition that exaggerating the threat would make action more justifiable.

If you choose to protect your people, despite the risk of civil war, you will likely turn to history for support. The terrible things those people did to Us. Our historical rights to that land. The Bible says. The land they stole. Our graves. God promised us. They martyred us. A narcissist will likely be seduced by the desire to be known for a historic role in defending his people, and he will be tempted to go further.

A leader lucky enough to come to power in a time of peace and plenty may never confront these seductions.

You want to be good. You want to be a great leader.

If you're unlucky, your history will include a story about victimization. It may really be true that They committed a genocide against Us. But does that give us the right to massacre them in turn?

—

Here is what I believe happened with Karadžić. So many people I talked with said they never saw signs of his nationalism. After all, they said, he joined the Green Party first; he seemed to crave political power more than he was drawn to a nationalist narrative. But I believe that he *was* a nationalist, that his nationalism was bred in the bone via the stories he heard as a child—about his Chetnik father and about the Turks. And that once Bosnia tried to secede, he took it as a personal insult. That innate nationalism, bred in the bone, emerged as a war cry.

Meanwhile, Karadžić exaggerated the threat posed to ethnic Serbs: For example, Karadžić said that Izetbegović was an Islamist and a polygynist. (He *was* an Islamist. He often tried to hide his Islamist views, even from his own people. He presented differing views to different people. But it is not clear that he was a polygynist.)[1] Karadžić said that Izetbegović intended to create a state based on sharia law and had a plan to impose a tax on Christians. (This was not true. Even if Izetbegović's hard-right circle might have fantasized about modeling Bosnia on Pakistan, Bosnia's largely secular Muslims would have opposed a state based on religious law.) Karadžić also said that jihadis were pouring into Bosnia. (This was an exaggeration.)

—

The situation changed dramatically—both militarily and politically—after the Srebrenica genocide. Was Karadžić the architect of that genocide? He was, in the sense that he was the president of the Bosnian Serb entity within Bosnia, and the commander in chief of the Bosnian Serb Army. The ICTY concluded that he did not plan the genocide, but was fully informed within a few days of the start. He deliberately spread fear in a way that made the mass murder of civilians nearly inevitable. While he boasted to the Bosnian Serb Assembly that he, and not the head of his army, General Mladić, had approved of the "radical" plan, when he realized afterward that he was vulnerable to indictment for war crimes charges, he backtracked, claiming that he hadn't even been informed of what was going on while the attack was under way.

The biggest secret he hoped to keep from his Bosnian Serb supporters was that he had lost control of General Mladić and the armed forces. But his claim, to me and to others, that he knew nothing at the time appears to be equally false. Could he have stopped the genocide? He could have tried. I'm not sure that such efforts would have been successful, given the extent of animosity between himself and Mladić at that point. Additionally, Milošević and Karadžić had been rivals since early in the war. By mid-1995, Milošević had more influence on Mladić than Karadžić did, and a far stronger hand vis-à-vis defense policy.[2] But at least Karadžić could have tried to stop the massacre, and there is no evidence that he did.

Does Karadžić have a personality disorder? His supervisor, Dr. Cerić, seemed to think so, when he referred to Karadžić's grandiosity, his habitual dishonesty, and his apparent lack of a sense of guilt.

—

I have to make a confession. I had been harboring a secret, megalomaniacal dream—that I was going to get him to apologize.

"Is there anything you regret?" I asked him.

He looks at me blankly.

"Is there anything you would do differently, if you could go back to 1992 and start again?"

"No," he said, firmly. "I had to protect my people. Until July 11, 1990, I was looking for someone else to lead the SDS party. I had to act properly. . . . In my family we strive to be 'golden men.'"

Was he deliberately misconstruing my intentions with this question, or did he really not understand me?

"If you were advising other national leaders about how to avoid an ethnic war that resulted in atrocities, what would you say?" I ask.

I couldn't have done anything differently, he said. He repeated the claim that he had to protect his people.

"Right now, your audience is Bosnian Serbs. What if you saw yourself as the Dalai Lama, and you were speaking to the whole world on behalf of all of humanity, about how to avoid a genocide?"

"You cannot be philanthropic or a humanist in general," he said. "You have to be this way toward those closest to you. You start from the guy standing next to you. You show *him* compassion first.

"I would do nothing differently," he repeated.

——

During my last trip to visit Karadžić, I had dinner with two attorneys involved in war crimes trials. One of them had spent a lot of time with war criminals in the Cambodia Tribunal. It's strange, she said, but when you spend that much time with someone, you become fond of them, even though you know they've done terrible things. "Do you know what will it be like when you say good-bye to Karadžić?" she asked. "Are you going to kiss him good-bye?"

As I tried to type the word "kiss," it came out as "kill." I guess my fingers and brain aren't fully collaborating at the moment. The attorney told me that she had experienced this kind of intimacy with "her" war criminals in Cambodia. It's confusing, she said, but normal. I told her that I didn't think that it would be possible for me to kiss Karadžić, but I wasn't sure how I'd feel in the moment of saying good-bye. I promised I'd let her know.

As I have already said, when you're with him one-on-one, Karadžić is not repulsive. He's a likable man. Magnetic. Charming. And there was a kind of intimacy established between us, even if I still couldn't look into his eyes. How often do adults sit across from one another and speak to each other for four hours straight, for several days in a row? We do this as teenagers, when we're trying to create our own personae, separate from our parents. We do this when we're trying to get to know a new lover, simultaneously getting to know ourselves by seeing how we're reflected back. But this wasn't a normal exchange. Karadžić and I didn't discuss me per se; we discussed only him. Nevertheless, I did learn something about myself. There were times when I fell into wanting to tame him. Get him to apologize sincerely and publicly for the genocidal crimes he oversaw. But even if he had, I don't think I could have kissed him good-bye.

This puts me in mind of a conversation I had with a detective at my university. It was around the same time as my discussion with the attorneys about the kiss. I told the detective about my long conversation with Karadžić. (I had met the detective long before, in connection with some work we did together after 9/11.) The detective told me a chilling tale.

Immediately after World War II, just before the Nuremberg trials, a group of American medical societies promoted the idea of studying the Nazi war criminals. The purpose was twofold: to ensure that the criminals were fit for trial, and to try to understand their motivations. The American psychiatrist who had evaluated Hermann Goering before the Nuremberg trials was captivated by his beguiling client, the detective told me. The psychiatrist, Dr. Douglas Kelley, viewed Goering as intelligent and highly cultured, and even came to believe he had a lot in common with Goering. Dr. Kelley had administered the Rorschach tests that he interpreted as showing that the Nuremberg Nazis were psycho-logically "normal." At the same time, Dr. Kelley did not see the leaders he evaluated as evil in a banal sense (which would suggest that they were not ideologically committed to the Nazi cause, but just good bureaucrats following orders).

They saw the Nazi regime and their own part in it as special.[3] "No, the Nazi leaders were not spectacular types, not personalities such as appear only once in a century," he wrote. "They simply had three quite unremarkable characteristics in common—and the opportunity to seize power. These three characteristics were: overweening ambition, low ethical standards, and a strongly de-veloped nationalism which justified anything done in the name of Germandom."[4] His conclusion frightened him deeply about his own country. About the United States he wrote:

> As far as the leaders go, the Hitlers and the Goerings, the Goebbels and all the rest of them were not special types. . . . There are countless hundreds of similar ones, thwarted, discouraged, determined to do great deeds, roaming the streets of any American city at this very mo-ment. . . . Have we no ultranationalists among us who would approve any policy, however evil, so long as it could be said to be of advantage to America?[5]

His observation that the Nazi leaders he evaluated were not uniquely monstrous, coupled with his fondness for Goering, was so confusing to Dr. Kelley that he would later commit suicide, us-ing the same poison (cyanide) that Goering himself used to avoid his sentence—death by hanging.[6] Perhaps the detective was warn-ing me of the psychological distress I might feel were I to allow myself to be mesmerized by an educated, charming war criminal.

—

In the end, I come down on the side of Dr. Douglas Kelley. Karadžić is not a "demonic psychopath," in the words that American psychologist Gustave Gilbert used to describe the Nuremberg Nazis, in opposition to Kelley.[7] He was a nationalist who came to power at a particularly dangerous moment, as such nationalists often do—when there is rapid societal change, identity uncertainty, and demographic shifts that threaten a powerful group's dominance. Aggressive, egocentric, and narcissistic leaders, who lack a conscience, are not rare, Kelley warned us. They can be found anywhere: "behind big desks deciding big affairs as businessmen, politicians, and racketeers," he wrote.[8]

I did not kiss Karadžić.

NOTES

1. Izetbegović was married four times. The *New York Times* obituary for him noted that the newspaper *Slobodna Bosna* published a piece congratulating him on his fourth marriage, and said that his third marriage was conducted "under Shariah, the Islamic code of law." David Binder, "Alija Izetbegovic, Muslim Who Led Bosnia, Dies at 78," *New York Times*, October 20, 2003, https://www.nytimes.com/2003/10/20/world/alija-izetbegovic-muslim-who-led-bosnia-dies-at-78.html.T.

2. According to declassified U.S. intelligence assessments, there was a political rivalry between Karadžić and Milošević and between Karadžić and Mladić. The tension between Karadžić and Mladić began in 1993, due to Mladić's "brazen refusal to obey Karadzic's orders," which arguably made him the "de facto Bosnian Serb leader." DCI Interagency Balkan Task Force, "Intelligence Report: Milosevic, Karadzic, Mladic: Serbs More United," (September 5, 1995, Approved for Release October 1, 2013), https://www.cia.gov/library/readingroom/docs/1995-09-05B.pdf. The political rivalry between Milošević and Karadžić was

highlighted in a 1994 CIA report. See Central Intelligence Agency, "Memorandum: Mladic Running True to Form" (September 6, 1995, Approved for Release October 1, 2013), https://www.cia.gov/library /readingroom/docs/1995-09-06.pdf. See also DCI Interagency Balkan Task Force, "Intelligence Report: The Belgrade-Pale Relationship," (June 23, 1995, Approved for Release October 1, 2013), https://www .cia.gov/library/readingroom/docs/1995-06-23A.pdf. These reports also make clear that Milošević had a lot more influence on Mladić than Karadžić did.

3. Jack El-Hai, *The Nazi and the Psychiatrist* (New York: PublicAffairs, 2013), p. 157. The interpretation of the Rorschach tests remains contested. Douglas Kelley, a brilliant psychiatrist and polymath, was an internationally recognized expert on Rorschach tests. He administered the tests together with Gustave Gilbert, a psychologist who was fluent in German but knew little about the test. According to psychiatrist Joel Dimsdale, the two men drew very different conclusions, which may be an artifact of their different backgrounds. Gilbert concluded that the men were "demonic psychopaths," while Kelley saw the Nazis as "morally flawed individuals influenced by the society they lived in." Kelley was deeply concerned that persons with personalities similar to the Nazi leaders could be found behind big desks anywhere, and that under the right conditions, a Nazi-like political party could emerge anywhere in the world. Dimsdale explains that in many ways the dispute between these two clinicians demonstrates some of the limitations with the test and the impact of tester bias on the results. He notes that Rorschach expert Dr. Molly Harrower did an experiment with the Nuremberg Rorschachs demonstrating that experts could not distinguish between the Nazi war criminals and Unitarian ministers, military officers, civil rights leaders, and others. Joel E. Dimsdale, "Use of Rorschach Tests at the Nuremberg War Crimes Trial: A Forgotten Chapter in History of Medicine," *Journal of Psychosomatic Research*, Vol. 78, No. 6 (2015), p. 517.

4. Douglas M. Kelley, *22 Cells in Nuremberg: A Psychiatrist Examines the Nazi Criminals* (New York: Greenberg, 1947), pp. 237–240.

5. Douglas M. Kelley, *22 Cells in Nuremberg: A Psychiatrist Examines the Nazi Criminals* (New York: Greenberg, 1947), pp. 237–240.

6. Jack El-Hai, *The Nazi and the Psychiatrist* (New York: PublicAffairs, 2013).

7. For an assessment of people who have psychopathic traits but are not violent psychopaths, see Ronald Schouten and James Silver, *Almost a Psychopath: Do I (or Does Someone I Know) Have a Problem with Manipulation and Lack of Empathy?* (Center City, MN: Hazelden, 2012).

8. Douglas M. Kelley, *22 Cells in Nuremberg: A Psychiatrist Examines the Nazi Criminals* (New York: Greenberg, 1947), p. 238.

Acknowledgments

During the initial stages of the project, when it seemed it might be impossible, I benefited greatly from the enthusiasm of colleagues at Harvard's FXB Center for Health and Human Rights and the Hoover Institution Law and National Security Group. In particular, I would like to thank Jacqueline Bhabha, Jack Goldsmith, Jennifer Leaning, and Ben Wittes. I also thank Roger Peterson, Ed Shapiro, Scott Strauss, and Ben Valentino for their early support.

I thank my agent, Martha Kaplan, for believing in this project, even when it sounded improbable, and for her patience. I thank Dan Halpern, my editor at Ecco, for asking difficult questions and continuing to argue back, especially about the title, which he wrote. Thank you also to Gabriella Doob, associate editor. Molly McCloskey also helped with editing.

I am grateful to the many students who helped with the preliminary research, including George Gomes, Kelly Grant, Marina Lažetić, Justin O'Shea, Ibrahim Rashid, Jaclyn Roache, Sarah Schulte, and Klevis Xharda. Nicholas Ngo and Marina Lažetić read over the page proofs and galleys. Neiha Lasharie spent over a year with me, summarizing sources with great care, triple-checking citations, and organizing nearly every aspect of my life so that I could focus on the writing. During that period, both my family and my students came to cherish her quick wit and optimistic outlook.

I received helpful comments at the Seminar on Violence and

Peacemaking at John Jay College, and at the "Brains That Pull the Triggers" conference held at the Paris Institute for Advanced Studies in 2017. I also greatly benefited from residencies at the MacDowell Colony, Yaddo, and the Virginia Center for the Creative Arts. I thank the members of our faculty writing group: Julie Klinger, Noora Lori, and Kaija Schilde. I wrote some of the most difficult passages while sitting with them.

I am deeply grateful to Adil Najam, dean of the Pardee School of Global Studies, for granting me a leave so that I could complete the writing. I thank Ken Froot and Jeffrey McCormick for generously offering me the use of their summer homes. And I thank Howard Gardner and Honor Moore for their friendship and support.

Mladen Mrdalj translated many documents for me and was an intrepid researcher. Unless otherwise indicated, any documents listed in Serbian or Bosnian were translated by Mladen. He also traveled with me to Montenegro. Marco Petrović accompanied me and translated interviews of persons convicted by the ICTY and transferred to European prisons. I am deeply grateful to both of them.

I am grateful to the International Criminal Tribunal for the former Yugoslavia (ICTY) Registry for allowing me to carry out this project. I thank, especially, John Hocking, former registrar. I relied extensively on the treasure trove of documents collected by the ICTY, which are available to researchers at www.icr.icty.org. Several ICTY personnel or former personnel provided advice and direction regarding where to find documents and what to look for in them. I thank in particular Andrea Cayley, Stefanie Frease, Dorothea Hanson, and Nevenka Tromp. I also thank Peter Robinson, Radovan Karadžić's defense attorney. I am so grateful to you, Peter, for believing that I would do my very best to be accurate and fair even if it required a few years' worth of extra digging.

A number of colleagues read parts of the manuscript or even the entire book—among them, Gordon Bardos, Edina Bećirević, Steven Burg, Robert Donia, Peter Galbraith, Lejla Huskic, Indira

Novic, Ron Schouten, and Olivera Simić. I would like to thank especially my dear friend Barbara Pizer, with whom I read every word out loud, multiple times; and Vladimir Petrović, for his careful read and great advice.

I would like to thank Radovan Karadžić for his willingness to speak with me. Anything attributed to him that is not cited was something he said to me during one of our twelve conversations, which took place in the UN Detention Unit at Scheveningen Prison in The Hague between October 8, 2014, and November 11, 2016. As mentioned in the text, the prison did not allow me to record our conversations. I took notes as best I could, but this method of recording is obviously imperfect. Karadžić's spoken English is excellent. Nonetheless, in my rendition of his spoken words, I made corrections, such as adding articles ("the" or "a") that are used in English but not in Slavic languages. (I include a letter he sent me in Appendix C. Readers should note that his spoken English is significantly stronger than his written English.)

My former student Ted Flinter surprised me, some years ago, by telling me that he met success in part due to a job I helped him find. I was astonished and moved when he announced that he wanted to support my research. I am so appreciative of your kindness and generosity, Ted, without which this book would not be possible. Thank you, also, Arthur Applbaum, for putting up with my queries about ethics. I also thank Robert Dorfman for his support.

A large number of former U.S. government and military personnel were very giving of their time. Some of them spent many hours with me, in some cases over several days. I am grateful for their assistance.

In July 2015, a conference called "International Decision Making in the Age of Genocide" gathered together former government and military personnel from Bosnia, the United Nations, Western Europe, North America, and Asia. All had been involved, in some capacity, in the war in Bosnia, most of them trying to stop it. The goal of the conference was to examine the failure of the international community to prevent the Srebrenica genocide, the largest massacre in Europe since World War II. I am grateful to Michael Dobbs, who organized the conference, for arranging for me to observe the proceedings, and also to the many participants who were willing to answer my questions. The conference was sponsored by the U.S. Holocaust Memorial Museum and The Hague Institute for Global Justice, in cooperation with the National Security Archive at George Washington University. A large cache of documents was declassified for the conference. Those documents are now available at a website maintained by the National Security Archive: https://nsarchive.gwu.edu/project/genocide-documentation-project.

My final and most important acknowledgment is that I am American, neither Bosnian Muslim nor Serb. I cannot speak for either side in the tragic war. I represented the facts as I understood them. I regret if any of my inevitable errors trigger pain. Both Serbs and Muslims have long lists of grievances, some quite recent, others going back centuries. But to my mind, it is never acceptable to target civilians, either in acts of terrorism or in war crimes.

EPIGRAPH SOURCES

First quote: Conversation between Dobrica Ćosić and Radovan Karadžić, International Criminal Tribunal for the former Yugoslavia, *Prosecutor v. Momčilo Krajišnik*, Case No. IT-00-39, Exhibit P64A.185.1. Accessed: http://icr.icty.org/LegalRef/CMS-DocStore/Public/English/Exhibit/NotIndexable/IT-00-39/ACE22151R0000149907.tif.

Second quote: As translated on Stormfront, De Groene Amsterdammer, Vol. 121, No. 33, August 13, 1997. Accessed: https://www.stormfront.org/forum/t54165/.

Appendix A

Victims of the War in Bosnia and Herzegovina, 1992–95. Minimum War-Related Death Ratios by Ethnicity.[1]

TABLE 1. ESTIMATION OF CASUALTIES

Category/Ethnicity	Muslim	Serb	Croat	Other	Total
Total Population 1991	1,896,009	1,361,814	758,585	352,106	4,368,514
Killed/Disappeared	57,992	19,398	7,543	4,253	89,186
Percentage	3.1%	1.4%	1.0%	1.2%	2.0%

TABLE 2. CIVILIAN VERSUS MILITARY CASUALTIES BY ETHNIC GROUP

Military Status	Muslim	Serb	Croat	Other	Total
Civilians	21,807	6,370	1,426	1,648	31,253
Militaries	36,185	13,028	6,117	2,605	57,933
Total	57,992	19,398	7,543	4,253	89,186

TABLE 3. THE PERCENTAGE OF CIVILIAN AND MILITARY DEATHS BY ETHNIC GROUP

Military Status	Muslim	Serb	Croat	Other	Total
Civilians	69.78%	20.38%	4.56%	5.27%	100%
Militaries	62.46%	22.49%	10.56%	4.50%	100%

The CIA maintained that 90 percent of the atrocities were committed by the Serbs.[2] But Susan Woodward and others pointed out that in coming up with this figure, the CIA was looking only at areas where Serbs took over territory held by Muslims or Croats, not the areas where Muslims or Croats had forced Serbs out.[3]

NOTES

1. These three tables are adapted from Jan Zwierzchowski and Ewa Tabeau, "War in Bosnia and Herzegovina: Census-Based Multiple System Estimation of Casualties' Undercount," unpublished conference paper (Berlin: February 1, 2010). Accessed: https://pdfs .semanticscholar.org/5b8c/480e42c4c50976fdd51ec90ae4becb5a0060 .pdf?_ga=2.65605998.1199665776.1564424188-1242823170.1564424188.

   Table 1 is reproduced, with minor grammatical corrections, from figure 2 in the cited paper (page 15). The authors note that the ethnicity of 13,654 unmatched records is estimated here based on the ethnic makeup of the 75,532 records matched with the 1991 census.

   The data presented in table 2 and table 3 are based on figures from table 6b (page 18).

2. See the CIA's history of the war, DCI Interagency Balkan Task Force, *Bosnia: Serb Ethnic Cleansing* (Washington, DC: Central Intelligence Agency, 1994), https://www.cia.gov/library/readingroom/docs/1994 -12- 01a.pdf; Roger Cohen, "C.I.A. Report on Bosnia Blames Serbs for 90% of the War Crimes," *New York Times*, March 9, 1995, https:// www.nytimes. com/1995/03/09/world/cia-report-on-bosnia-blames- serbs-for-90-of-the- war-crimes.html.

3. Susan Woodword, interview in *Yugoslavia: The Avoidable War*, dir. George Bogdanich, documentary (1999), 1:48–1:49. A former CIA official who was working on the Balkans at that time confirmed Susan Woodward's assessment. Interview with former CIA operative, February 21, 2019, and March 1, 2019.

Appendix B

TABLE 11.1.

Overview of Major Estimates of Death Toll in Bosnia-Herzegovina, 1992–1995

Victim Categories	Bassiouni (1995)	Kenney (1995)	IPH (1996a)	IPH (1996b)	Prašo (1996)	Bošnjović and Smajkić (1997)	Žerjavić (1998)	Bošnjović (1999)	Tabeau and Bijak (2005)	Tokača (2007)	Obermeyer et al. (2008)	Zwierzchowski and Tabeau (2010)
Killed and disappeared	200,000	42,500	156,824	278,800	329,000	258,000	220,000	252,200	102,622	97,207	176,000	104,732
Muslims	NA	NA	NA	140,800	218,000	138,800	160,000	153,000	69,874	64,036	NA	68,101
Croats	NA	NA	NA	28,400	21,000	19,600	30,000	31,000	8,554	7,788	NA	8,858
Serbs	NA	NA	NA	97,300	83,000	89,300	25,000	72,000	19,211	24,905	NA	22,779
Others	NA	NA	NA	12,300	7,000	10,300	5,000	14,000	4,983	478	NA	4,995
Total number of victims	200,000	42,500	156,824	278,800	329,000	258,000	220,000	270,000	102,622	97,207	176,000	104,732

Notes: NA = not available.

(1) All estimates cover the period from April 1992 to December 1995.

(2) All estimates *presumably* include both civilians and soldiers.

(3) IPH stands for the Institute for Public Health in Sarajevo.

(4) Kenney's (1995) figure of 42,500 war deaths is an average of the two ends of his original interval.

(5) Bošnjović (1999) reported another 17,800 other excess deaths (included in his ethnic figures) in addition to those killed and disappeared.

(6) "Other excess deaths" should be interpreted as indirect war victims, that is, people who died *mainly* as a result of diseases and severe living conditions during the war.

(7) Tokača (2009) reported ethnic structure is as in his 2007 estimate.

Overview of Major Estimates of Death Toll in Bosnia-Herzegovina, 1992–1995.

Source: Ewa Tabeau and Jan Zwierzchowski, "A Review of Estimation Methods for Victims of the Bosnian War and the Khmer Rouge Regime," in Taylor B. Seybolt, Jay D. Aronson, and Baruch Fischhoff, eds., *Counting Civilian Casualties: An Introduction to Recording and Estimating Nonmilitary Deaths in Conflict* (New York: Oxford University Press, 2013), p. 216.

Appendix C

I will answer to you new questions, and my answers may be a bit wider than you may need. I simply wanted you to be completely and thoroughly informed.

I have to tell you that I had been disappointed when learned that you experienced as if I was manipulating you, which I have read in some media.

It was far from my intention, those who know me well – know that I am always the same. I assume that something from my story and conduct surprised you in your expectations. This made me to think that you had been pretty prejudiced about me, as well as about the Yugoslav crisis and Bosnian conflict, which I have concluded after re-reading our correspondence about the psychological matters, projective identification etc.

Initially I was informed by Peter that you were an extraordinary personality and author, and I never rejected such a person intended to bring about the truth. I always had in mind Rebecca West, an extraordinary British lady, who explored Yugoslavia after the WWI, accompanied by Stanislav Vinaver, a great writer and translator, who was a sort of guide and interpreter to Rebecca. Her book "Black Lamb and Gray Falcon" is an eternal monument both of her and of the Serbian people. Every now and then this book had been re-published in many countries.

Why I was disappointed? Pertaining to my personality and role, I have realized that a stereotype that had been created by media and spin-masters reached you and made an effect on you so much that you weren't able to search for the truth, but only for a data that may corroborate this stereotype. Whatever your book turns to be, it is not going to damage me, because there are already so many books of the type, and it would be "one amongst many". But it is going to damage you as a genuine author, who shouldn't be "another among many". Namely, very soon there is going to be the "whole truth" about our crisis and my role in it, a truth that will prevail.

Pertaining to the crisis and war in Bosnia, I got an impression, particularly from our correspondence about the "projective identification" and other psychology issues – I have realized that you adopted a standpoint according to which the main element that determined the course of events – was a personal history, nature and inclinations of individuals that had a prominent or decisive role in it. There are many authors meditating the same issue, and when I mentioned to you about Nazi Germany and allies, it was not about the Nazi leaders, but about the German people, who would never vote for such a men if there was no a cruel and humiliating "ostracism" and cornering them after the WWI. You will always find such a person, but a circumstances are decisive, not a personal profile of a leader. In democratic societies a president is doing what he has to, not what he wants to do. I have noticed that I was not clear enough about my prediction that Mr. Tramp will become President Tramp. It didn't pertain to him at all, because I didn't know anything about him, but I have been guessing the mood of Americans, and their wish to see some changes.

But, relying on the personal psychology matters in our crisis is completely in vain, losing time and point. The Serbs are very difficult to be led, they are always too critical about their leaders, which you could have seen from the transcripts of the Serb Assembly. There is nobody who could persuade them to fight if they didn't see and feel it necessary, or dissuade them from the same. The processes in the Balkans are so dense and frequent, that all of it is fresh in memories of these peoples, particularly since in between there is the same rhetoric, the same attempts to prevail, or the same interest of a great powers to induce and maintain antagonisms and conflicts, as if the Balkans affaires are never settled down finally. So I was disappointed when learned that Holbrook's wife K. Morton wrote that the Serbs were responsible for the WWI. This is not serious! No country all over the Europe would go into a war for the Serb sake. Nor the Austro-Hungarian Empire would attack Serbia only because of Serbia. All of it was about the exhaustion of the current model of the world, and the biggest empire needed a change and expansion to the Middle East, in order to remain the "biggest". The nowadays powers may repeat the Napoleon, Habsburg and Nazi Germany mistakes, and try to endure being the strongest in a wrong way. Occasionally, this Austro-German expansion had to go over Serbia, because of the geographic conditions, and sometimes it looks like a next somebody's expansionism may do the same. Also, Serbia itself was free and independent, and Austria feared from it as an example to other Slavic nations within the Empire, demanding a better position within the Empire, or a full independence. A myth about "Greater Serbia" was created by Franjo Zach (a Czech) and other non-Serb pan-Slavic patriots, hoping that Serbia could have played a role of a Slavic "Piemonte" (Piedmont – as in Italy) and this only contributed to the Austrian suspicions. But, the main reason was a colonial plan to "Drang nach Osten", and the Entente allies couldn't afford themselves that Austro-Hungary and Germany get stronger than they had already been.

I highly appreciate people that write books, and if they are genuine, they are precious. I regret very much whenever I am not original and authentic, as I regret the same case of others. But I am sure Peter was right about your exceptional capacities. Don't worry about me, there will not be any hard feelings. Whatever it be, your book will not be the worst among many. If you for some reasons can not be objective, thorough and meticulous about me and my role, I wish you be objective about the Serbs on the Balkans, and in the Republic of Srpska and Croatia in particular. There are many sources of appropriate knowledge about it, and particularly accessible and instructive could be the "Simon Wiesenthal Institute". The most painful is the negligence of almost three millions of the Serb victims in the two wars in 20th Century.

I wish you all the best, and don't hesitate to keep in touch. Peter is the best mediator.

Respectfully yours,

Dr. Radovan Karadzic

Radovan Karadžić, personal correspondence with author, December 14, 2018.

Index